MORE OF THE
Deadliest Men
WHO EVER LIVED

D1193647

MORE OF THE
Deadliest Men
WHO EVER LIVED

PAUL KIRCHNER
Paladin Press • Boulder, Colorado

Also by Paul Kirchner:

Bowie Knife Fights, Fighters, and Fighting Techniques
Deadliest Men
Dueling with the Sword and Pistol
Jim Cirillo's Tales from the Stakeout Squad

More of the Deadliest MenWho Ever Lived
by Paul Kirchner

Copyright © 2009 by Paul Kirchner

ISBN 13: 978-1-58160-690-4
Printed in the United States of America

Published by Paladin Press, a division of
Paladin Enterprises, Inc.
Gunbarrel Tech Center
7077 Winchester Circle
Boulder, Colorado 80301 USA, +1.303.443.7250

Direct inquiries and/or orders to the above address.

PALADIN, PALADIN PRESS, and the "horse head" design
are trademarks belonging to Paladin Enterprises and
registered in United States Patent and Trademark Office.

Neither the author nor the publisher assumes
any responsibility for the use or misuse of
information contained in this book.

Visit our website at www.paladin-press.com

Contents

Acknowledgments

In the course of researching this book, I received assistance from a number of people to whom I owe my appreciation. These include Patti Novak, an amateur genealogist who was tremendously helpful in locating old newspaper records, particularly on Adelbert Waldron III. Joe Sledge read through the manuscript, gave me insightful comments, and corrected a number of errors. Ed Cassidy shared copies of articles on snipers he had in his files. Alan Taylor advised me to look into Jonathan Davis, little-known victor in one of the most spectacular gunfights of the Old West. Jim Higginbotham directed me to Cassius Marcellus Clay, emancipationist and one of history's prickliest men. R.J. Miller sent me an article on Joe Harrison, the San Francisco cab driver who was involved in at least five gunfights. Leilani Maguire provided me with articles about her father, Hank Adams, as well as photographs. Jerry Pape provided me with a photograph of his father, famed Chicago police officer Frank Pape. Chuck Mawhinney reviewed what I wrote about him and allowed me to use his personal photographs. R.J. Thomas and Richard Barr agreed to be interviewed about the incident in the Vietnam War for which Thomas earned the Navy Cross. John Charles Johnson spoke with me about his experiences as a tunnel rat. Janelle Cooper reviewed and corrected my profile of her late husband, Jeff. A number of people who knew Bert Waldron agreed to respond to my questions about him, and I am particularly indebted to his ex-wife, Betty. I am also thankful for advice and technical information from Les Bengston, Ben Burroughs, Lance Edwards, Lyman Lyon, Larry Mougeot, Charles Riggs, John Schaefer, and Harry Schneider.

I am in debt to a number of research facilities, including the Sterling Memorial Library at Yale University, the New York Public Library, the National Personnel Records Division, the San Diego Sheriff's Museum, the Federal Bureau of Investigation's Records Management Division, and the National Archives. I was particularly impressed by the assistance provided to me by archivists of the Marine Corps. They clearly take pride in their institutional history and are confident that anything that is written about the Corps can only add to its luster.

Dedicated to my daughter Toni, always good company.

Introduction

What is a hero? Today, the term is applied to the POW, the superstar athlete, the political activist who presses an agenda, and the handicapped person who overcomes obstacles. Virtually everyone who has accomplished something noteworthy or borne up under misfortune is a hero. As is typical in our age, we are taking a term that is by definition exclusive and democratizing it.

We must know we're kidding ourselves. For most of human history, a hero was one thing and one thing only: a warrior of such strength, skill, courage, and ferocity that he could turn the tide of battle.

This book is a collection of profiles of such superlative warriors, whom I call *More of the Deadliest Men Who Ever Lived*. In my earlier collection, published in 2001, I acknowledged that a compendium of this sort is infinitely debatable and forever incomplete. I can only consider a tiny minority of warriors—those about whom we have a record—and, within that group, those whose record is sufficiently detailed and interesting to make for a good read. This sequel includes warriors I did not know of at that time, or was unable to find enough information on to include. In no way do I consider them second best to those in the first volume.

Each of them dominated a violent environment and triumphed against overwhelming odds. They fought for blood, not sport, with the weapons of individual combat: fist, knife, sword, bow, pistol, rifle, and machine gun. I included the widest variety of warriors that I could find, from Western lawmen to big-city cops, from crusaders to fighter pilots, from a boy shepherd in Judea to two women ranchers in Kenya. Most of them fought for something beyond survival—a cause, a code, a creed, or a country—while others fought solely in defense of their lives, a worthy enough purpose in itself. Some of them are well known, though I hope I have added something to their stories; others are not so well known, though they deserve to be, and these are the stories I take the most satisfaction in presenting.

In the film *The 13th Warrior*, the Viking leader, Buliwyf, is fascinated that the Arab who accompanies his group can write, or "make pictures of words," as he puts it. Buliwyf says, "A man might be thought wealthy if someone were to draw the story of his deeds, that they may be remembered."

It seems to me that the least we owe the hero is that we remember him. Without remembrance, without honor, we cannot expect to have such men when we need them. Without an awareness of what has been done, we do not realize what can be done, nor are we inspired to do that which should be done.

Hank Adams
(1907–1978)

"You were so cool we used to say you sweat icicles."

—Robert F. Paine

In the autumn of 1942, while America was in the midst of the brutal struggle for control of the Solomon Islands, a picture was splashed across its front pages, showing a lanky Marine sitting on the stump of a palm tree, gazing into the distance, his .45-caliber Reising submachine gun at the ready. The caption read, "Capt. Henry J. Adams Jr., former undersheriff of San Diego, Calif., one of the many 'one-man armies' in the Solomons, recently killed 15 Jap soldiers in an engagement on Tulagi Island."

Lee Echols, an old shooting buddy of "Hank" Adams, said that when he saw the photo "my first thought was 'That's for me!' and I immediately sent in an application for an officer's commission in the U.S. Marines."

3

The photo of Hank Adams that appeared in newspapers all across America in October 1942, under the headline "Executioner of the Japs." (Credit: Army Signal Corps.)

No doubt that picture inspired hundreds of men to report to their nearest recruiting station. It captured a fantasy self-image that lurks in the back of most men's minds, that of the hero who cuts down all enemies, yet emerges unscathed. Adams' classmate from Stanford University Robert F. Paine, then the managing editor of the *Memphis Commercial Appeal*, wrote him the following open letter:

> Doggone it, Hank, I sure had a real thrill when the picture of you sitting there on a stump on Guadalcanal with that mean-looking sawed-off submachine gun in your hands came into my office.
>
> I knew you were over there and figured it wouldn't be long before something like this picture would come along—with the story about you knocking off 15 Japs all by yourself in our first crack at 'em. You're just the kind of guy who could do it.
>
> If I were any Jap on that island, the Marine I would fear most would be Capt. Henry J. Adams, Jr.
>
> When we were classmates at Stanford University you were the coolest, toughest, shootingest son of a gun who ever shot the zoot suit off a gnat at 20 paces, firing from the hip. In a poker game you would raise the pot, draw four cards, and send us out to write dad for more money.
>
> The name "Hank" never fit a man like it did you. You were better than 6 feet 3 inches, your gangling frame was strung with muscles like strings on a bull fiddle and your head was covered with a mop of yellow hair.
>
> You were so cool we used to say you sweat

5

icicles. Probably that's why you turned out to be such a helluva rifle and pistol shot and went on to win more national and international medals than you could drag home in an M-3 tank. You even coached the Marine Corps' rifle team for national competition.

Remember while you were the undersheriff in our home town, San Diego County, Calif., you made all the Chamber of Commerce, Rotary Club, and whatnot luncheons, shooting cigarettes out of guys' mouths with a pistol? And how the local sporting goods store never sold an expensive rifle without having you shoot it to set the sights? If you didn't get 100 bull's-eyes out of 100, they'd send the gun back to the factory to be worked over. You just didn't miss.

I remembered those things when your picture came.

Things look pretty bad over there right now, according to our press dispatches. You are outnumbered and you don't know where or when they will blast at you next. But if there are half a dozen other American Marines there half as cool and as deadly with a gun as you are, you'll handle them, all right. You'll handle the Japs in the Solomons, you'll handle them back in the Philippines again later on, and the day you march into Tokyo, you'll probably be the guy who shoots the buttons off Hirohito's pants as he dives in his hole.[1]

Henry Jackson Adams Jr. was born in Fostoria, Ohio, on April 29, 1907, into a well-to-do family. On his 12th birthday he was given a single-shot rifle and practiced with it constantly.

Hank Adams as a boy. (Courtesy of Leilani Maguire.)

He received formal marksmanship training in summer classes at Culver Military Academy in Culver, Indiana. In 1927, he enrolled at Stanford University, but he was forced to take off the spring semester after suffering a bout of pneumonia, recuperating at a ranch his family owned in central California. His father bought him a new rifle to help him pass the time, and Hank roamed the countryside shooting at tin cans or, more often, at targets set up on a makeshift range.

To learn more about shooting, he joined the National Rifle Association and studied the results of major competitions published in its magazine, *American Rifleman*. He checked the scores against his own and to his surprise discovered that he was doing better than many of the best shots in the country. He competed at Camp Perry in 1928 as a member of the Ohio civilian rifle team, scoring 394 out of a possible 400 points.

While at Stanford, Adams captained and coached the rifle team in 1928, 1929, and 1930. In 1930, he was featured in the *American Rifleman* after a triumphant performance at Camp Perry, where he won the Peters Trophy, given to the individ-

ual long-range small-bore champion; the Clarke Trophy, given
to the highest-scoring civilian in the President's Match; and,
with a teammate, the Hercules Trophy, given to the top long-
range small-bore team.

Adams' father lost most of his fortune when the
Depression hit, and Hank Jr. had to work his way through his
final year at Stanford. After graduation he found employment
as a policeman in El Centro, California, and later as deputy
sheriff in San Diego.

He was a top-ranked competitive shooter through the
1930s, consistently placing among the top three in national
pistol competition, using a .38-caliber Colt Officers Model
Match and a Colt 1911 .45 accurized by famed Los Angeles
gunsmith J.D. "Buck" Buchanan. In 1935, Adams was named
the National All-Around Rifle and Pistol Champion at Camp
Perry, beating out 3,800 competitors. He was featured in a
series of advertisements for Western ammunition, sitting
beside a table piled with trophies. Dressed in a conservative
suit and with his wire-rimmed glasses, he looked more like a
young professor than a shooter. In his competitive career, he
won more than 100 trophies and 800 medals. That same year,
he accepted a commission in the Marine Corps Reserve, which
was offered to him on the basis of his shooting skills.

Lee Echols made friends with Adams in 1935, hoping the
champion could teach him to shoot. Adams asked him if he
had done any pistol shooting, and Echols admitted that he had
not. "Good," said Adams. "You won't have a lot of bad habits
to unlearn."

Echols went on to break four pistol records and win the
1941 National Pistol Championship at Camp Perry, as well as
numerous other championships. He and Adams took to hus-

---

*Hank Adams (left) at Camp Perry in 1930 with his brother, Johnny, also a
national shooting champion. (Courtesy of Leilani Maguire.)*

tling strangers into shooting matches, winning "the shirts, pants, and anything that is loose" off them. As Echols remarked, "There are a few guys in the world that can beat us, but we know all of them."[2]

In April 1940, the Federal Bureau of Investigation (FBI) accepted Adams' application for a position as a special agent, despite the fact that he was neither a lawyer nor an accountant, normally a prerequisite. His interviewer noted that he "would be a very valuable asset to the Division because of his expertness with firearms." He was stationed in Newark, New Jersey, where "he captured more bank robbers than any other agent in the area."[3] Adams remained with the FBI until August 1941, when he went to work as an undersheriff in San Diego.

On April 1, 1942, Adams was called up for active duty. Lt. Col. Merritt Edson, himself one of the top marksmen the Marine Corps would ever produce, was handpicking the officers he wanted for the 1st Marine Raider Battalion, an elite commando-type unit, and he wanted Adams. Edson made him his intelligence officer, though his combat duties were more along the lines of scout-sniper.

At the beginning of May, the raiders arrived at their base on Samoa. There they adjusted to the tropical climate and trained hard. One private described 18-hour days of "Rubber Boating, Judo, Bayonet Fighting, Stalking, Demolition, First Aid, Mountain Climbing, and Communication work."[4] Adams taught the men combat shooting.

On May 3, the Japanese invaded Tulagi, which had been the center of British colonial administration in the Solomons, and stationed 350 troops there.

On August 7, the Raiders set about recapturing Tulagi. As Adams' patrol made its way inland, it came under fire from Japanese troops who were holed up in a pillbox and firing through ports. From a distance of more than 250 yards, Adams put bullets through the pillbox's firing slits, killing three snipers and silencing the guns. He earned a commendation for

Adams (center) putting on a shooting demonstration when he was with the FBI. (Courtesy of Leilani Maguire.)

his actions that night: "Lieutenant Adams was in command of a battalion observation post which was attacked from three sides by a numerically superior Japanese force. Throughout this engagement the coolness and inspiring leadership of Lieutenant Adams resulted in the repulse of the attack and assisted materially in the eventual destruction of the enemy."[5]

The following day, Adams performed the action that was celebrated in newspapers across America. Echols saw Adams as a man singled out by Destiny, who "put her hand on his shoulder and looked him smack in the blue eye. She said, 'Hank, here's what I've got in mind for you. You are going to be the man to show what years and years of competitive shooting means to a nation.'"

Echols wrote, "Destiny turned him loose and he and his eight Marines charged 30 Japanese soldiers, killing 13 of them in the charge and so confusing the remaining 17 that they took sanctuary in a native hut. Then, while his boys held the rear of the shack, Hank crawled around to the front, raised up from behind a coconut stump with his short-barreled gun, and quickly gave them all what they had come to sell.

"A grim and deadly Hank Adams killed 15 of them before they hardly knew he was among them, and I'll bet when he gets back home he'll grin and admit that if he hadn't gotten the Buck Fever so bad, he'd have killed those other two."[6]

One of the Japanese troops managed to get off a shot at Adams but missed.

The following day, Adams accounted for another 11 of the enemy in sniping operations, and more in the days to come. "One part of the island was quite clear of jungle and with visibility up to 500 yards in some places. I shot Jap soldiers out of trees, in foxholes and pillboxes with the aid of a telescope," he told an interviewer.[7]

In early September 1942, while on patrol 20 miles southeast of Guadalcanal's Henderson Field, Adams killed three Japanese troops at a distance of 300 yards as they ran for shelter.

About his scout-snipers, General Edson told an interviewer, "These were made up of expert riflemen, expert scouts, working in carefully trained teams. They were armed with Marine sniper rifles: Springfields, with telescopic sights. Those scopes might surprise you. Lots of them were long, target-type, eight-power instruments, with wide fields. Some were hunting scopes. In either case they were damned effective! Those boys didn't waste a lot of ammunition; they held and squeezed. When they fired, Jap rifles stopped cracking. That's better even than scoring a V on the range. But scoring V's on the range is the way to learn to do it!"[8]

In letters to his parents, Adams made little mention of combat. In one, he wrote, "We're awfully busy over here, and it's terrifically hot—in more ways than one. . . The mosquitoes are so big they fairly raise the nets off our beds. . . . Right now

while I write white ants are crawling all over the typewriter. . . .
We're camped on a swift-moving stream and go swimming once
in a while. Of course we have to be pretty careful, because the
streams are full of alligators."

His father told a reporter, "You would think Hank was on
a camping trip."[9]

Robert Cromie, a correspondent for the *Chicago Tribune*,
accompanied Adams on patrol on Guadalcanal in early
November. Adams was manning an observation post, spotting
artillery strikes through a pair of captured Japanese binoculars
and phoning in corrections until he was ordered to move forward with the advance. When sniper fire slowed the advance,
Cromie wrote, "Capt. Adams—who got nine snipers in a single
morning on Tulagi by lying motionless on a height and sweeping the countryside with his field glasses—put some grass in
his helmet strap to break the outline and crawled with his rifle
into the bushes. Jap machine guns and rifles still fired from
somewhere nearby, and the captain was hopeful of spotting
their positions."[10]

On New Britain, Adams and his 30-man patrol, "by actual
count, disposed of 190 Nips and captured 67 others without a
loss to themselves."[11]

Adams scored an intelligence coup during one campaign,
warning his commander to expect a counterattack the following day. When it came, the Marines were ready. Afterward, his
CO asked Adams how he had known about it. Adams told him
it was Emperor Hirohito's birthday and he assumed the
Japanese troops would want to make a good show. The CO
asked Adams how he happened to remember that April 29
was Hirohito's birthday. Easily, explained Adams: it was his
own birthday as well.

In September 1944 Adams participated in the invasion of
Peleliu, a coral island the size of Iwo Jima. He considered it
the toughest of all his campaigns. "This is one of the unsung
battles of the war," he said. "The First Division fought for a

month and a half with no reserves, against 11,000 Japs, all but 500 of whom were dead when the army's 81st Division finally moved in. There wasn't a place on the island the Japs couldn't cover with artillery fire."[12]

During a 30-day leave in December 1944, Adams accepted a free vacation at a Las Vegas hotel along with Echols. The two didn't know they would be roped into giving a pistol-shooting demonstration to sell war bonds. Adams was famous for such performances, in which he would split playing cards edgewise; shoot over his shoulder, aiming by the reflection of his sights in a facet of his diamond ring; simultaneously break two clay pigeons spaced 6-feet apart, firing a gun in each hand; and, in one second, fire five shots from the hip into a group that could be covered with a calling card. He would also do stunts that would cause apoplexy among shooters today; in this performance, it was agreed that Echols would shoot pieces of chalk out of Adams' ears from a distance of 25 feet.[13] This added an element of suspense to the exhibition, as Echols hadn't had a chance to practice any pistol shooting since the beginning of the war and Adams was suffering from malarial shakes. "I could see he wasn't adjusting too well," wrote Echols, afterward, "but he threw his shoulders back and his jaw out, with the thought that for a man who had waded ashore on four or five bloody beaches, this would be a hell of a time to show the white feather."[14]

Fortunately, Echols was "dead on." The two men sold $80,000 worth of war bonds that night.

There have long been rumors that Adams killed a considerable number of Japanese with the Smith & Wesson .357 Magnum he brought with him. Pistol champion Charles Askins mentioned it in *The Pistol Shooter's Book*, as did Adams' fellow Marine Jeff Cooper in private correspondence with this author. In the *American Rifleman*, Warrant Officer C.A. Brown, USMCR, wrote, "The stories that are told about 'Hank' and that Magnum in the Solomons will have to wait for future publication, but I'll assure you that they will warm the hearts of all pistol lovers!"[15]

We will have to take Brown's word for it, as to the best of my knowledge those stories never appeared in print.

In April 1945, while scouting beyond the lines of the 96th Army Division on Okinawa, Adams was badly wounded in the right arm by shell fragments. Ironically, they were from American antiaircraft shells—the Japanese still had not laid a glove on him. He was hospitalized for five weeks, and while there he received a personal note from J. Edgar Hoover, who wrote, "I hope that this has not endangered your shooting arm in any way, for your accomplishments have become legendary."

After he recovered, Adams was sent home, having spent three years and three months overseas. He had earned a Purple Heart, two Bronze Stars, two Presidential Unit Citations, and an Admiral's Commendation. He was recommended for the Air Medal, for having made 75 observation flights in slow-moving Piper Cubs over enemy-held islands, charting patrol routes. He fought at Tulagi, Guadalcanal, New Guinea, New Britain, Peleliu, and Okinawa. The horrific nature of the fighting was vividly portrayed in E.B. Sledge's memoir *With the Old Breed, at Peleliu and Okinawa*. Sledge was seared by his experiences in two island campaigns; Adams participated in *six*. Though Adams' friends envied the hero status he earned in the Pacific, it clearly took a toll on him. Photographs of him before the war show a sunny, devil-may-care fellow; it's a very different man that looks out from pictures taken four years later.

Adams returned to his position as undersheriff of San Diego. He told the local paper that he was gratified to hear that there had been no persecution of Japanese in San Diego County. "I had a lot of Japanese-Americans under my supervision in the Pacific," he said. "They deserve a lot of credit."

He married and had four children, two sons and two

daughters, in addition to a daughter from a previous marriage. In 1953 he ran unsuccessfully for sheriff, and then reentered the Marine Corps and served as provost marshal of the Marine base in San Diego, retiring in 1957 with the rank of colonel.

Echols, who would be in a position to know, wrote, "Hank killed over 200 Japs."[16] That's an extraordinary number when you consider that the most highly decorated soldier in World War II, Audie Murphy, is estimated to have killed 243 Germans, and that includes those on whom he called in artillery. Adams was profiled in *Leatherneck* magazine, but otherwise got only brief mention in a few books and newspaper articles. Perhaps he was regarded as just another Marine doing his job—a job he happened to do very, very well.

Hank Adams was a warrior of superlative skill who found himself in an environment where that skill could be used to maximum effect. I take satisfaction in placing him first in this book as a representative of all those warriors who performed superbly in battle, yet have been largely forgotten, their stories only sketchily recorded, their memory fading out with those who knew them.

Adams died in 1978 in Arlington, Virginia.

NOTES

1. R.F. Paine Jr., "Old Classmate Lauds Shooting of Capt. Adams," *Ogden Standard-Examiner*, November 8, 1942, p. 15-A.
2. James Atlee Phillips, "Hank Adams Changes Beats," *Leatherneck*, October 1946, p. 29–33.
3. From a tribute by Hon. Paul H. Douglas read into the *Congressional Record*, May 21, 1954.
4. *Edson's Raiders*, p. 63.
5. Adams was given a brevet promotion to captain on August 11, with rank from August 7.
6. Lee E. Echols, "Buck Fever," *American Rifleman*, March 1943, p. 25. Col. Charles Askins believed Adams used his .357 magnum as well as his Reising in this engagement, which makes sense considering that the Reising's magazine held only 20 rounds. Askins wrote, "Hank Adams . . .

killed 14 [sic] Japs as they ran out of a shack. Hank was using a .357 Magnum and a tommy gun. Just how many were bagged with each gun, I do not know, but the toll is a most respectable one." See Col. Charles Askins, *The Pistol Shooter's Book* (New York: Collier, 1962), pp. 279–280.

7. "Adams Returns from 18 Months in South Pacific," *San Diego Union*, October 28, 1943, loose clipping.

8. Interview with Brig. Gen. Merritt Edson, USMC, "U.S. Rifleman M-1944," *American Rifleman*, March 1944, p. 11.

9. "'Awfully Busy' in Solomons: 'Hank' Adams Tells Family of Marines' 'Camping Trip,'" *San Diego Union*, undated clipping.

10. Robert Cromie, "Tribune Writer Dodges Bullets on Guadalcanal," *Chicago Daily Tribune*, November 20, 1942, pp. 1, 6.

11. Ken Bojens, "Off the Main Line," *San Diego Union*, May 31, 1947, loose clipping.

12. "Adams Returns as Sheriff's Aid," *San Diego Union*, July 14, 1945, loose clipping.

13. Adams had a trick of rimming the chalk with his thumbnail so even if it were hit at its far end it would break off right next to his head.

14. Lee Echols, "Dodging Bullets for Wilbur Clark's War Effort," *Nevadan*, December 4, 1983, p. 6L.

15. C.A. Brown, "Teaching the Marines to Shoot," *American Rifleman*, May 1944, p. 11.

16. Lee Echols, "Only Yesterday," *American Rifleman*, August 1946, p. 21.

Chevalier Bayard (Pierre Terrail) (1473–1532)

Sans peur et sans reproche.
(Without fear and without
fault.)

—*A phrase coined to*
describe Bayard

There are some people who so epitomize a trait that their name becomes synonymous with it. We know what it means to call someone a Casanova, an Einstein, or a Quisling, and back when traditional heroes were still celebrated, a literate person would have known what it meant to be a "Bayard": it meant to approach the standard of chivalry set by the French knight, the Chevalier Bayard.

The notion of chivalry seems quaint to the modern mind. Among other things, its code demands that a knight fear God and maintain the Christian religion; serve his king faithfully and valorously; protect the weak and defenseless; refrain from the wanton giving of offense; live for honor and glory, despising pecuniary reward; fight for the general welfare of all; shun unfairness, meanness, and deceit; respect the honor of women; and refuse no challenge from an equal. Examples of the chivalrous ideal include Godfrey of Bouillon, Louis IX, William Marshall, El Cid, the Black Prince (Edward), and Bertrand du Guesclin. These men lived during chivalry's golden age, roughly A.D. 1100–1300, and the accounts of their lives have the hazy quality of legend. Bayard lived almost two centuries later, and consequently we have far more detail about his life, thanks largely to a biography written in 1527 by Jacques de Mailles, who used the pen name *Le loyal serviteur*—the Loyal Servant.

Bayard was born Pierre de Terrail in 1473 at the Castle Bayard in Dauphiny, France. His family had a long and distinguished military pedigree, and Pierre was eager to uphold the tradition. At 14, he left home to begin his knightly education with the Duke of Savoy, and surpassed all the other pages at riding, wrestling, leaping, fencing, and other knightly exercises. He accompanied the duke to the court of Charles VIII, where the king saw him riding in a procession. Impressed with his horsemanship, the king took Bayard into his service, placing him in the care of Lord Ligny for further training. He was only 17 when he received the rank of gentleman.

Bayard went on to distinguish himself in numerous tournaments, but real combat was the true test. The Italian Wars, which occupied France for the first half of the 16th century, provided many opportunities for a knight to prove himself. This series of wars was fought between the major powers of Western Europe, in frequently shifting alliances, for control of the Duchy of Milan and the Kingdom of Naples. They began in 1494, when Charles VIII decided to enforce his rather tenuous claim on Naples. Lord Ligny was given command of the expedition, and he took along Bayard. After the French conquered and sacked Naples, an alliance comprising Venice, Milan, the Papal States, Spain, England, and the Holy Roman Empire was formed to oppose them.

On July 6, 1495, the two sides fought near Fornova. At

Chevalier Bayard. (Credit: Author's collection.)

one point in the battle the Italians made a strong effort to capture the king, and Bayard was among those who rallied to his side and drove them off, knocking several horsemen from their saddles. Although the French were forced to retreat, Bayard had fought valiantly; he had had two horses killed under him and had captured an enemy battle standard. In camp that evening he was presented to Charles VIII, who ordered him to kneel and knighted him on the spot. There could be no more auspicious beginning to a knight's career.

Two and a half years later, Charles VIII died and was succeeded by his cousin, who took the name Louis XII.

In 1499, Louis XII seized Milan, but the following year, Ludovic Sforza, who had previously ruled it, drove the French out. Bayard, who was garrisoned in the area, got news that one of Sforza's captains was in a nearby town with 300 horsemen, and he persuaded his fellow officers to join him on a raid. After a furious fight of about an hour, they routed Sforza's men and pursued them toward Milan. As they neared the walls of the city, Sforza's men turned to fight. Rather than engage in combat so close to the enemy camp, the French officers turned and rode off—all but Bayard. Fired up with battle fever, he pursued the enemy through the city gates and didn't stop until he reached the square in front of Sforza's palace, where he was surrounded by soldiers. Swinging his blade right and left, Bayard fended them off as they tried to pull him from his saddle, creating such uproar that Sforza came out to see what was happening. Sforza commanded that Bayard be brought to him, and Bayard, seeing the futility of further resistance, acquiesced.

It was with more amusement than anger that Sforza asked the young knight what had possessed him to ride into the center of Milan by himself.

Bayard forthrightly replied, "I had no idea I was alone. I thought my companions were behind me, but they are wiser than I and more used to the ways of war, or else they would have undoubtedly been made prisoners as well as myself. In the meantime, in my disgrace, I thank heaven that I have fallen into such good hands as yourself."

Sforza, impressed by Bayard's spirit, told him, "Set your mind at rest, it is my intention to set you free."

Bayard soon rejoined his astonished comrades, who had given him up for lost.

Some time later, bored with the lack of activity, Bayard set out one morning with 50 men to see if they could stir up something. At the same time, a comparable Spanish force under the command of Don Alonzo de Soto Mayor set out from a nearby town with the same intention.

When they saw each other, the two groups charged. The battle went on for about a half hour, with the Spaniards getting the worst of it. Seven of them were killed and the same number captured. The rest fled, Alonzo among them. Pursuing him, Bayard called on him to surrender or be slain ignominiously from behind. Alonzo turned, and after a brief but furious fight, was forced to surrender to the Frenchman.

Bayard took Alonzo back to the castle where the French

troops were garrisoned and set his ransom at 1,000 ducats. Bayard treated his prisoner with respect, allowing him freedom of movement after he gave his word not to go outside the walls. However, Alonzo soon found captivity tiresome and bribed a guard to help him escape. When Bayard visited his room and found him gone, he sent a dozen men to recapture him. After they brought him back, Bayard reprimanded him for breaking his word and had him locked in a tower, but otherwise continued to treat him well. After 15 days his ransom was paid, and he was set free.

Upon returning to the Spanish camp, Alonzo complained of his treatment. When news of this reached Bayard, he was outraged at this slur on his hospitality. He sent Alonzo a challenge, and it was accepted.

Bayard was ill on the day of the duel, but nevertheless appeared at the place of combat, armed and mounted on a splendid charger, and accompanied by 200 knights. He had expected to fight on horseback, but Alonzo, seeing that he was not well, sought to take advantage of that by declaring that they would fight on foot. Brantôme writes, "Bayard's seconds wanted him to raise an objection on the ground of his illness, but the Chevalier would not hear of such a thing. In these little matters he was ever ready to oblige anyone, and fight them just as they pleased."

The weapons selected were a spear and a dagger, with the combatants wearing *gorgets*, or neck armor, and helmets with visors.

Brantôme's account continues:

> Both combatants having entered the lists as aforesaid, each knelt down to pray; but Bayard laid himself down flat "to kiss the earth," and on rising made the sign of the Cross, and then advanced towards his enemy as confidently, so says the story, as if he had entered some palace

hall to dance with fair ladies. Don Alonzo, on his side, was no whit less at his ease, and marching straight up to his enemy, asked of him, "Sir Bayard, what would you of me?"

To which Bayard replied, "To defend my honour," and without another word they met and dealt each other fierce thrusts. Alonzo was slightly wounded on the face and several blows were exchanged without any further result. Bayard then noticing his adversary had a trick of delivering a blow and then parrying,[1] so that he could not be hurt, bethought him of a counter device, and when the Spaniard raised his arm to deliver his thrust the Chevalier raised his too but delayed the stroke, and when that of the enemy had missed him, made such a deadly thrust that the lance—for all the stoutness of the gorget—went four good inches into the man's throat, so that he could not get it out again. Don Alonzo, feeling that he was wounded to death, closed with his antagonist who wrestled with him, and in the struggle both fell to earth one on the other.

But M. de Bayard, with great promptness, drew his dagger and held it to the Spaniard's nostrils, crying, "Surrender, Señor Alonzo, or you are a dead man."

The observation, however, fell on deaf ears, for the man was dead already.

Then [Alonzo's] second, de Quignonnes, came up and said, "Seigneur Bayard, he is dead. You have conquered."

Which was in fact the case, for he never moved again. And no one was more distressed than the victor himself, who "would have given a hundred thousand crowns, if he had had them" to have conquered the man alive. Nevertheless, he knelt and thanked the Almighty for the mercy vouchsafed to him, and kissed the earth three times.[2]

A few days later, the Spanish knights, panting for vengeance, proposed to meet an equal number of French knights in combat. Bayard, of course, accepted. It would be 13 against 13. Rules were agreed on: the combat would be fought in a ring; any man unhorsed or forced across the boundary became a prisoner; and the battle would not be over until all combatants of one side had been defeated. The Spanish used an effective but unchivalrous tactic— they attacked the French horses. When the horses were killed, the knights who were dismounted were taken prisoner. It was not long before only Bayard and Lord d'Orose were left to carry on the contest. Each time the Spanish concentrated their efforts against one of the Frenchmen, he retired behind the slain horses, which provided an effective bulwark. The battle went on for four hours, and Bayard and d'Orose were still in their saddles when darkness fell. The fight was called a draw. The two knights had held off six times their number.

Near the end of the campaign, French and Spanish troops were camped on opposite banks of the river Garigliano, which marks the border between the Italian regions of Lazio and Campania. The French held the bridge, but there was a ford farther down the river.

Early one morning, the French awoke to see Spanish horsemen approaching the ford, each with a foot soldier mounted behind him. As they entered the river, the French cavalry that was guarding the bridge hurried to meet them. They had fallen for a ruse. Bayard was still putting on his armor when he saw 200 Spanish horsemen making for the bridge. Sending a man for assistance, he rode to the bridge alone.

The Loyal Servant describes what followed:

Bayard, crossing the bridge, upon the extremity of which the Spaniards were about to pass, chose his position with some regard to the difficulty which he should probably have in maintaining it. Putting his lance in rest, he charged the head of the advancing column at the very threshold, tumbling two of them headlong into the river, from whence they never emerged, and two more upon the banks, at the very first thrust of his weapon. This brought upon him a host; but their very numbers, impeding their progress in the narrow gorge which he defended, contributed somewhat to his security. Never were charges more desperate or more successful than those that he made that day. Great was the surprise of the Spaniards to behold one man thus furiously darting upon their squadrons. At first they regarded him as one delivered up and devoted to destruction; but not so when they sunk beneath his assault, and were hurled, by his adroit exercise of horse and lance, by threes and fours, headlong into the stream. Astounded, almost appalled at first, they recoiled from before him; but soon recovering, they gave him enough to do. With his back to the railing of the bridge, so that they might not assail him from behind, he confounded them by the rapidity, the dexterity and the force of his movements. As many as might do so assailed him at the same moment. These he was not only to encounter and resist as well as he was able, but he was to do this and keep his position at the same time, so that none of them might contrive to get between him and the bridge. This was no easy performance. But Bayard was not only a brave and skilful warrior—skilful beyond his time—but he was one of those wondrous horsemen whose power of managing the steed is a mystery—such as the Arab of the desert possesses, but such as ordinary riders cannot understand. With an eye that seemed to look out from every part of his body at the same time, and a hand and weapon that seconded admirably every movement of his eye, he beheld, and foiled his assailants, crowding in on every side. The powerful, but docile and well-trained animal that bore his weight, seemed imbued with his own spirit; and the two wrought together so admirably and so successfully, that the Spaniards were persuaded of a miracle. . . . They could make no impression on our chevalier—could advance no footstep; and, looking upon him as a fiend, rather than a mortal, were compelled to admire the skill and courage which promised still to baffle their best attempts.[3]

The French cavalry arrived in time to relieve Bayard before he could be overwhelmed by numbers. The story of Bayard's defense of the bridge spread far and wide, and is commemorated in his insignia: a porcupine, with the motto, *Vires agminia unus kabet*—"One alone is equal to an army."

In 1507, there was a revolt in Genoa, and Louis XII sent an army to crush it. Strategically located on a hilltop overlooking the city was a fortress, well manned and armed with cannon. Asked how he thought the French could take it, Bayard said he would reconnoiter the situation. With 120 picked men,

Bayard climbed the most difficult approach to the fortress and, instead of reconnoitering, he surprised and overwhelmed the garrison of 300 Genoese, bringing the revolt to an end.

On May 14, 1509, at the Battle of Agnadello, Bayard fought the Venetians. Leading a part of the rear guard through a swamp, he flanked the troops of Lord d'Alviano and routed them. In a three-hour battle the Venetian cavalry collapsed and fled; d'Alviano was captured, and some 4,000 of his men were killed. This was a great victory for the French in what was one of the most significant battles of the Italian Wars.

During the long siege of Padua, which began in September 1509, Bayard distinguished himself during the fighting at the outer barriers. As the account reads:

> The barriers were thus won at noonday, by hard fighting, hand to hand. The deeds of every warrior could be seen, and this wonderfully stimulated the courage of the ambitious soldier. But the palm was borne away from all by Bayard. He led the assault, and was the first everywhere in the front of danger. If his reputation was great before, this close and constant struggle, before the barriers of Padua, contributed greatly to increase it.[4]

One night during the siege, Bayard led 150 knights out of the French camp. They made their way behind enemy lines and hid themselves. The following morning, they swept up behind an enemy force twice their number, and in a furious fight killed 20, set 100 to flight, and took 180 prisoners—a number exceeding the size of their own force. This exploit dealt the enemy a double blow, as each prisoner was worth a hefty ransom.

The Venetians took the city of Brescia from France, and in January 1512, 12,000 French troops were sent to retake it, under the command of Gaston de Foix, the Duke de Nemours. Bayard led a company, many of them gentlemen who had been commanders themselves but preferred the honor of serving under Bayard to leading troops of their own. On February 18, as they assaulted the ramparts on foot, their battle cry was not only "France, France!" but "Bayard, Bayard!"

Bayard was the first to leap across the rampart, and in doing so he received a thrust from a pike. The head penetrated deeply into his thigh, and the wooden shaft broke off. When the head was pulled from the wound, it unleashed a torrent of blood. He called to a companion, "The town is gained, on with your people! As for me, I can go no farther. I am slain."

Two archers rushed to Bayard and carried him from the field, binding his wound with strips torn from their shirts. Word quickly spread throughout the army that he had fallen. As the Loyal Servant says, "Warriors much better love to avenge than mourn the death of a comrade," and so it was. After a terrible battle, Brescia was taken, with more than 20,000 killed on both sides. There followed five days of rape, pillage, and massacre, from which the once prosperous city never fully recovered.

Meanwhile, Bayard had been put to bed in one of the city's mansions, where a lady lived with her two teenaged daughters, the father being away. The lady welcomed him into the house, granting that it was his by the spoils of war, adding, "I only ask you one favor, which is that you will preserve the lives and honor of myself and my two daughters."

This, Bayard swore he would do. He ordered the two archers who had carried him from the field to guard the door, assuring them he would make up for what they would lose in plunder. It was five or six weeks before Bayard had recovered sufficiently to get back on a horse, by which time the daughters were treating him like a favorite uncle. So grateful was the lady that she gave him 2,500 gold ducats, which would surely have been plundered without his protection. In true chivalrous

Bayard wounded at the siege of Brescia. (Credit: Author's collection.)

fashion, Bayard gave 1,000 ducats to each of the daughters for their dowry and asked the lady to distribute the remaining 500 among the poor. Each of the daughters gave him something she had made: one, an armlet of gold and silver thread; the other, an embroidered satin purse. These were the only spoils he took from Brescia.

Bayard rode toward Ravenna, where the Duke de Nemours was advancing on the Spanish army. The battle would take place on Easter morning: April 12, 1512.

As Bayard, the duke, and a small company of knights looked over the battlefield, they saw a similar company of Spanish knights with their general, Don Pedro de Paes, doing the same. Bayard noticed that both parties were in range of enemy arquebuses, the heavy, matchlock weapons that he despised; "for while skill and courage were required to wield a spear or sword, any skulking wretch could pull a trigger from behind a stone." Bayard saluted the Spanish knights and said, "My lords, you are walking about, as we are, waiting for the beginning of battle; I pray you not to allow arquebuses to be fired from your side, and I promise you none shall be fired from ours."

Don Pedro readily agreed, and asked Bayard who he was. Once informed, Don Pedro responded, "Lord Bayard, although your arrival in the French camp may not be a subject of rejoicing to us—in fact, quite the contrary, we consider it as good as a reinforcement of 2,000 men for them—still I am no less glad to see you; and if it please God that peace shall be established between our nations, I will prove to you the esteem I feel for you, and the wish I have to be numbered among your friends."

(A demonstration that in the age of chivalry, honor accrued not only to the one who displayed the most courage, but the most courtesy.)

Don Pedro then asked who the lord was who was so magnificently accoutered, and to whom the men showed such great respect. Bayard answered, "He is our general, the Duke of Nemours, the brother of your queen."

At that the Spanish approached the duke, paid him homage, and told him that, but for their obligations to their king, they would gladly be his servants.

The niceties having been properly observed, the carnage commenced shortly. The French opened with a cannon barrage that killed 300 horsemen in the vanguard. The French infantry marched on the Spanish trenches, and 2,000 were killed by the combined fire of 20 cannon and 200 heavy arquebuses. The hand-to-hand fighting lasted more than an hour and a half.

At one point, Bayard, seeing the duke covered in blood, asked him if he was wounded.

"No," said the duke, "but I have wounded others."

France carried the day and the defeat of the Spanish was total, but the exultation of victory was dampened by the news that the duke had been killed. Accompanied by only 15 men, he had rushed to strengthen a weak point in the line and had been overwhelmed.

The following year, the Swiss invaded Milan and drove the French out. Louis XII mounted an attack in response but suffered a humiliating defeat at the Battle of Novara. Louis died in 1515 and was succeeded by Francis I. Francis was only 20 years old but had some military experience, having spent two years fighting on the frontiers. Determined to recapture Milan, he began secretly assembling troops on the border. With one of the largest armies France had ever fielded, equipped with great numbers of cannon, he achieved the element of surprise by taking an unexpected route over the Alps.

Francis was camped at Marignanao on the afternoon of September 15 when the Swiss attacked. The battle was fought until darkness fell and then recommenced when the moon rose. In the thick of it, the king's leather coat was pierced by a pike, which stopped just short of penetrating his chest.

The Swiss concentrated their attack against the French artillery, and Bayard was in the forefront of the defense. He

had a horse killed under him at the beginning of the action
and was now mounted on another. As he hewed his way
through surrounding pikemen, their points tore away his
horse's bridle. Terrified and out of control, his horse ran
through the Swiss ranks and would have carried Bayard into
their midst had it not been stopped by grapevines growing
between posts. In the dim light Bayard slipped from his horse,
took off his helmet and leg armor, and, leaving them behind,
crept quietly back to his own lines. There, the first man he
encountered was the Duke of Lorraine, who was astonished to
see the great chevalier on foot and unarmed. Lorraine gave
him a horse, and Bayard quickly returned to the battle.

As the Loyal Servant wrote:

> Terribly earnest was the fight—without
> cessation or positive result—till the going down
> of the moon, a little after midnight, left the
> combatants in utter darkness; and, knowing
> not where to strike, the parties, with a ferocity
> still unassuaged, but with limbs enfeebled and
> exhausted, threw themselves down upon the
> field, even where the fight had found them, to
> snatch a little rest, if not repose, until the dawn
> of another day should arouse them once more
> to their toils of blood.[5]

At noon of the following day, still fighting as they retreated,
the Swiss left some 10–12,000 of their men on the field.

King Francis had a chapel erected, and that night he held
a victory ceremony. He started out by announcing, "Before
bestowing the honor of knighthood on those who have distinguished themselves in battle, I must myself receive that honor
from one who is a knight; for which reason, Bayard my
friend, I wish to be knighted by your hand this day, because
he who has fought on foot and on horseback better than all

others is reputed the most worthy knight. It is thus with you, who have fought in many battles against many nations, and always valiantly."[6]

Bayard modestly protested, but, upon Francis' insistence, the knight *sans peur and sans reproche* drew his battered sword, laid it on his king's shoulder, and performed the ceremony. Bayard would fight more battles, but, with this, his glory had already reached a pinnacle from which it could ascend no higher.

On the morning of April 30, 1524, Bayard was with a French force that had been forced to retreat before the Spanish. The French suffered losses from enemy arquebusiers who were hidden on either side of the road and fired missiles of lead and stone, while the Spanish cavalry followed close behind the column and occasionally launched sallies. Working the rear guard, Bayard repeatedly charged the enemy, unhorsing knights and driving the others back. He was returning from one of these forays when he was struck by a stone bullet that fractured his spine in two places. As he tottered in his saddle, he raised his sword, kissed its cruciform hilt, and repeated a verse of Psalm 51: "Have mercy on me, O God, according to thy steadfast love; according to thy abundant mercy blot out my transgressions."

He was quickly helped from his horse. His men would have carried him with the retreating army, but he felt he could not survive travel and asked only to be placed against a tree, facing the enemy. "I am mortally hurt. I know it, and I would not, in my last moments, turn my back upon the enemy for the first time in my life."

Bayard bid farewell to his friends, urging them to leave before they were captured by the approaching Spanish. But, writes the Loyal Servant, "The tidings of his mortal injuries had already reached them, and produced a profound sensation of grief among their ranks. The foe whom they most feared, honored by their very fears, and whom they so particularly desired to capture or to slay, now that he could do them hurt no longer, remained before their eyes only as the impersonation of all nobleness, and of the most admirable perfection in arms and chivalry."

The first of his enemies to approach Bayard was the Spanish general, the Marquis of Pescara. He said, "Would to God, most gentle Lord of Bayard, that by shedding my own blood, short of death, or by abstinence and prayer, I could save your precious life, and keep you as my prisoner. Then should you see how highly do I honor your exalted character and prowess, for since my first lessons in arms have I never seen or heard mention of any knight who can match with you in all admirable qualities."[7]

The marquis had his own bed brought up and Bayard was lifted into it, and then the marquis' tent was set up over him. A guard was posted outside, and a priest sent in to whom Bayard could make his confession. He died at sunset. He was 48 years old.

French knights were permitted to retrieve his body, which was interred in a church near Grenoble.

NOTES

1. The translator notes that the phrase *couvrait le visage* (covering his face) could mean either parrying or closing his visor.
2. *Duelling Stories of the Sixteenth Century*, pp. 53–5.
3. *Life of the Chevalier Bayard*, pp. 123–4.
4. *Life of the Chevalier Bayard*, p. 151.
5. *Life of the Chevalier Bayard*, p. 352.
6. *Story of the Chevalier Bayard*, p. 222.
7. *Life of the Chevalier Bayard*, p. 392.

Tsukahara Bokuden (1488–1571)

In 1467, with the outbreak of the Onin War in Kyoto, Japan was thrown into what is called the Warring States period, as *daimyos*, or local warlords, fought for a century to expand or defend their domains. This was the great age of the samurai. The Japanese sword had reached technical perfection, schools of swordsmanship flourished, and daimyos vied with each other for the services of skilled swordsmen.

Tsukahara Bokuden was born in 1488 in Kashima, Ibaraki Prefecture.[1] Bokuden's father was a priest at Kashima's shrine dedicated to Takemikazuchi, one of the patron deities of the martial arts, and he relentlessly trained his young son in the *Kashima-ko* style of fencing. Bokuden's rapid progress and intuitive responses to unfamiliar situations amazed his father, who saw in him a fencing prodigy.

Tsukahara Tosanokami Yasumoto, a relative of the Kashima daimyo, adopted Bokuden at age 14, after his own son had died. Yasumoto, himself a renowned fencer of the Shinto school, recognized Bokuden's talent and trained him personally.

At age 17, Bokuden set out on his *musha shugyo*, or warrior's pilgrimage, in which the swordsman tested his skills against recognized masters trained in different styles. While traveling through Kyoto in May 1510, he issued a

Statue of Tsukahara Bokuden in Kashima City, Japan. (Copyright 1994 Diane Skoss/Koryu Books.)

challenge to Ochiai Torazaemon, a renowned swordsman, who at age 40 was considered to be at his peak. Ochiai was so confident in victory that he announced the time and location of the duel so that a crowd would gather to watch.

Held on the grounds of Kiyomizu Temple, the duel was fought with real swords. Ochiai, who stood 6-feet tall, towered over the short but powerfully built Bokuden. Ochiai assumed the middle attack stance, his sword perpendicular to his chest. Bokuden took his position, then slid his right foot back, and lowered his sword until it was perpendicular to his hip, leaving his chest unprotected. This unusual stance drew a gasp from the onlookers, who wondered whether he was a fool or a madman. But when the signal was given to start the duel, it was over almost immediately, with Ochiai flat on his back and Bokuden standing over him, the tip of his sword at Ochiai's shoulder. Clearly, if Bokuden had chosen, he could have killed the famed swordsman on the spot. Instead, he turned and walked away.

Within hours, news of the match had spread throughout the capital. Gamo Sadahide, lord of Hino in Omi Province, invited Bokuden to visit, and when they dined he entreated Bokuden to serve him as fencing instructor. Not yet ready to interrupt his pilgrimage, the swordsman politely declined.

The following morning, as Bokuden departed the castle, he sensed something amiss as he walked through the entrance hall. Though he carried his sheathed sword in his left hand, his right hand went for the hilt of his short sword as a sword-wielding assailant leaped at him from behind a screen. Bokuden's short sword slashed through the assailant's side, mortally wounding him. The assailant was none other than Ochiai, who had been a samurai in Lord Gamo's service. Disgraced by his defeat in the duel, he had sought revenge.

Gamo's men were astonished that Bokuden had been able to defend himself against the surprise attack. They asked him how he thought to use his short sword, which was tucked in his belt, rather than his long sword, which was in his hand. He shrugged and answered, "I was attacked suddenly. There was but a short distance separating us, and little time to react. Because I could not have successfully countered with the long sword, I drew my short sword."

That he could make this decision in a split-second added greatly to his reputation.

Ochiai was but one of a number of opponents Bokuden defeated during his *musha shugyo*. Upon his return home, his adoptive father offered him the hand of his daughter in marriage. Bokuden married, but he never settled down. He regularly left home for long periods to fight in battles, to train with different masters, or to meditate in seclusion.

He studied at the dojo of the master swordsman Kamiizumi Isenokami, in Minowa, Kozuke Province. A group of *yamabushi*, ascetics who trained in the martial arts, lived on nearby Mt. Haguro. While Bokuden was away and Isenokami was sick in bed, the *yamabushi* came down to challenge the fencing school. They were led by a monk named Shinamuru Nyudo Enkai, who wielded a *kongozue*, a large club reinforced with steel. After subjecting four high-ranking students to humiliating defeat, Enkai made insulting remarks to Kamiizumi.

When Bokuden found out what had happened, he immediately set out for Mt. Haguro. There he defeated 18 out of Enkai's 80 disciples and slew Enkai himself. In recognition of this feat, he received the *Shinkage Ryu Gokui* (Secrets of New Shadow School) from Kamiizumi.

In another duel, Bokuden fought Kajiwara Nagato, famed for his ability with the *naginata*, a halberd-type weapon with an 18-inch blade attached to a 4-foot handle. Nagato was said to be so fast and precise with his blade that he was able to kill a bird in flight. Nagato had never lost a duel and was so cruel that he would smile as he told opponents the precise order in which he would dismember them: "First your left arm, then your right, and finally I will behead you."

Bokuden's disciples feared that he was overmatched. They asked him how he could defeat a man with a weapon that was nearly 6 feet long, when he had a sword that measured only 3 feet. "Do not be concerned," Bokuden assured them. "The outcome of this duel will be determined solely by the difference in the length of the blades."

Rather than view the *naginata* as a pole arm, Bokuden instead fought as if it were a sword wielded by an opponent who was closer to him than was actually the case. With this approach, in the first clash he sliced at this imaginary swordsman and cut the handle of the *naginata* in half. Nagato was rendered defenseless and, shortly thereafter, headless.

Bokuden is said to have spent 1,000 days praying and meditating at the Kashima shrine to gain enlightenment. During this period he spoke to no one and subsisted solely on a diet of grains. It was during this period that he perfected his style, based on *hitotsu no tachi*, the "single stroke." In 1727, a military tactician, Masaki Masahide, put forth an interpretation of the technique based on surviving documents. He wrote, "A swordsman must first position himself directly opposite his opponent's sword. He can place his sword either aloft before him or at his side; the only essential point is that he must look unprotected, provoking his opponent to a conventional attack. If the opponent's sword is more than one inch away from his body, the swordsman should not parry his attack. When that sword is only half an inch away, however, the swordsman should take one step forward and slay his opponent. The essential factor is the ability to distinguish the narrow margin which separates one inch from half an inch. . . . Since your opponent expects a defensive posture, a dodge at even one inch, your lightning-fast attack takes him completely off guard."[2]

A technique that relies on such a precise judgment of distance and timing could only be employed by a master.

After one noted swordsman challenged Bokuden to a duel, Bokuden sent his disciples to gather information. He learned that his opponent favored a one-handed technique and a left-foot-forward stance. This was unusual, as most swordsmen employed a two-handed grip and stood with their right foot forward. Bokuden wrote to his opponent and accused him of cowardice for employing such an unorthodox style, demanding that he fence more conventionally in their duel. His opponent scoffed at his objections, reminding him that he was free to forfeit if he was afraid to face him. Undeterred, Bokuden followed up with 10 additional letters complaining about the unfairness of his opponent's technique.

By the time the day of the duel arrived, the swordsman was convinced that Bokuden was as good as dead. Instead, he himself was killed almost immediately with a single blow to the head. Bokuden's sole purpose in complaining about his technique was to get him to place too much confidence in it.

In the course of his life, Bokuden went on three warrior pilgrimages, and by the end of the third his fame was so great that he was accompanied by a retinue of more than 80 disciples. He fought more than 100 duels, 13 of them with steel blades.

He also served the lord of Awa Province in 37 battles, where his specialty was singling out and killing enemy commanders. He is said to have taken the heads of 21 noteworthy opponents and killed 212 men in all. In the course of these battles, he suffered only six minor wounds from arrows.[3]

At 50, Bokuden had matured to the point that he no longer felt the need to test himself against others. On one occasion, he was on a ferryboat when another passenger, a samurai, was loudly boasting of his great skill. Bokuden sat silently, his eyes shut as if he were meditating. The samurai, who saw that Bokuden was armed, was infuriated by his indifference. "Hey, you over there!" he shouted. "Don't you like this kind of talk? You don't even know how to wield a sword, do you? What is your school called?"

Bokuden replied, "It is called *Mutekatsu-ryu* [style which wins without a sword]."

"Mutekatsu-ryu?" repeated the samurai, contemptuously. "Don't be ridiculous. How can you defeat an opponent without using a sword?"

"My sword cuts down vanity and pierces vicious thoughts," replied Bokuden calmly.

This drove the samurai into a fury. "Let me see this school you call Mutekatsu-ryu!" he shouted.

"Very well," said Bokuden, and he ordered the ferryman to pole them to a small island that would be suitable for a duel.

The samurai eagerly jumped onto the shore, but Bokuden took his time. After handing his long and short swords to the ferryman, he reached for the ferryman's pole. "My style is *Mutekatsu-ryu* and I have no need for a sword," he said, pushing the ferry away from the shore with a powerful thrust.

Bokuden poled the boat swiftly down the river as the stranded samurai raged helplessly. This incident was reenacted by Bruce Lee in *Enter the Dragon*.

At age 66, Bokuden retired to a small hermitage in his hometown, Kashima. Seeking a successor to carry on the *hitotsu no tachi* technique, he decided to test his three sons to see which of them was the most worthy. He propped a wooden pillow on top of the sliding door to his room so that it would drop on anyone who entered. He then called in his first son. As his first son opened the door, he raised his hand and caught the pillow as it began to drop, then entered the room. His father dismissed him. Bokuden replaced the pillow above the door and summoned his second son. As the second son entered the room, he dodged the falling pillow, and his hand flew to the hilt of his sword. His father nodded and excused him. At last, he called the third son. As the pillow dropped, the third son drew his sword and split it open in midair.

The third son's reflexes were instantaneous, but the first son had anticipated the problem and dealt with it without reaching for his weapon. He had passed the test, and Bokuden initiated him into the secrets of *hitotsu no tachi*.

How can one explain the sixth sense demonstrated by the first son, a quality ascribed to many famous warriors in the East? It may be that he was able to tap into powers that defy explanation. Erich Hartmann, the German pilot who holds the all-time record as an ace, with 352 victories, explained his survival by saying he had "an extremely sensitive back to his neck." Jim Cirillo, of the New York City Stakeout Unit, said that before a confrontation he felt as if someone were tapping him on the shoulder. Mitchell Paige, who earned the Medal of

Honor on Guadalcanal, said he once felt a force pushing back his body an instant before a stream of machine gun fire passed inches in front of him. There are countless such incidents in the literature of war, far too many to easily dismiss.

Bokuden died in 1571 at the age of 83 and is buried on a mountainside in Kashima. Visitors still journey to his grave to burn incense in his honor.

NOTES

1. Bokuden was known as Takamoto when he was a youth, but for clarity I am using the name by which he is best known. Some accounts give his date of birth as 1489 or 1490.
2. *Lives of Master Swordsmen*, pp. 25–26.
3. Numbers given in records from this period are assumed to be unreliable but are included with that proviso.

"Mad Jack" Churchill (1906-1996)

"He survived both the war and subsequent adventures virtually unscathed; achieved, in the main, by facing danger calmly and, indeed, with interest, and not by hiding or blindly running from it."

—Rex King-Clark

In August 1945, most Allied troops were enormously relieved to hear that the atomic bomb had been dropped on Japan and the war was over. However, when British Commando "Mad Jack" Churchill got the news, he observed, ruefully, "If it hadn't been for those damned Yanks we could have kept the war going for another ten years."

Churchill saw life as a series of adventures, with war being one of the best adventures available. He took part in four major Commando operations and was awarded the Military Cross and two Distinguished Service Orders, but that is not the reason he is included in this collection. He is included because it wouldn't be right to leave out a man who stormed beaches while playing the bagpipes, who took 42 Germans prisoner at swordpoint, and who may remain the last soldier in a European army to kill an enemy with a longbow.

Born September 16, 1906, into a family of distinguished pedigree, Churchill attended Britain's Sandhurst military academy, receiving his commission in 1926. He served in India and Burma for the next six years. An avid motorcyclist, he decided to ride his Zenith 1,500 miles from Poona to Calcutta. There were no roads through much of Burma, so he followed the railway line. To cross rivers on the railroad bridges, he had to steer the motorcycle by hand along one rail, while carefully stepping from one crosstie to the next; there was nothing between them. The trip was briefly interrupted near Indore, in central India, when he collided with a water buffalo, but after the necessary repairs were made he was able to complete the journey.

It was during this period, while staying with the Cameron Highlanders, that Churchill learned to play the bagpipes. In 1938 he won second place in a military piping championship. He also trained himself as an archer and qualified as a member of the British team at the World Archery Championships in Oslo in 1939. War was brewing when he returned from this event. Between September 1939 and May 1940—the so-called "phony war"—Churchill served in the British Expeditionary Forces with the 2nd Manchesters. Before embarking, he had Purle of London make him an 85-pound bow of Spanish yew and a quantity of broadhead aluminum hunting arrows. The arrows were expensive, and the money came out of Churchill's pocket, as it had been several hundred years since the War Office had taken responsibility for archery supplies.

At the end of 1939, Churchill served a tour with the French army along the Maginot line. As Donald Featherstone put it in *The Bowmen of England*, "Frustrated by the official policy of not provoking the enemy, Captain Churchill decided on a symbolic gesture that he thought would not only give him great satisfaction but might also create a certain alarm, despon-

·KIRCHNER·

"Mad" Jack Churchill.

dency, and bewilderment in the enemy lines."[1] On December 31, while on patrol in no-man's land, he stealthily made his way to about 50 to 80 yards from the German positions and fired three arrows in quick succession. "There was a sudden commotion in the enemy's position, and from the shouting and the confusion it sounded very much as if perhaps one of my broadheads had found a better mark than an inoffensive stag or bushbuck. Anyway, it is pleasant to think so."[2]

On May 27, 1940, Churchill was in command of a mixed force holding the village of L'Epinette against the German advance during the retreat to Dunkirk. From a vantage point in the loft of a small granary, he had a clear view of five Germans sheltering behind a wall some 30 yards away. Quietly summoning two infantrymen, he instructed them to wait until he had fired an arrow at the center man and then shoot the others. After taking careful aim, Churchill loosed a shaft, which struck the German in the left side of his chest, killing him, just as the others fell to rifle fire. Churchill ran to the body in the hope of retrieving his arrow, but it broke as he tried to pull it out. The enemy then opened fire from a nearby position, forcing Churchill to dive for cover and withdraw.

During the retreat from L'Epinette, Churchill continued to fire Parthian shots with his bow. For successfully extricating the remains of his company through the German lines at night, he was awarded the Military Cross.

An old friend of Churchill's, Rex King-Clark, also with the 2nd Manchesters, recalls seeing Churchill a day or two later, on his motorbike. His longbow was tied along the frame, and his arrows were stored in the baskets alongside the rear wheel. Over the headlight was hung a German officer's cap he had taken as a souvenir at L'Epinette. The 4th Infantry Brigade diary covering the period of the Dunkirk evacuation notes, "One of the most reassuring sights on the embarkation was the sight of Captain Churchill passing down the beach with his bows and arrows! His actions in the Saar with his arrows are known to many."[3]

At the end of June 1940 a call went out for volunteers for the newly formed Commando units. Winston Churchill, no relation to Mad Jack, wanted a "butcher and bolt" raiding force to assault, disrupt, and reconnoiter the Germans in the occupied countries. "Jack was probably the first volunteer; this was just his cup of tea," wrote King-Clark.

In training camps in Scotland, Commandos were trained

in survival, land navigation, close quarter combat, silent killing, signaling, demolitions, and amphibious and cliff assaults. They learned to use every type of weapon they would be likely to encounter.

On December 27, 1941, Churchill led two Commando squads (or "troops" in British terminology) of 50 men each in an attack on Maaloy Island, near the mouth of Norway's Nord Fjord, in what was called Operation Archery. If that was any reference to Churchill, it was passé, as he had retired his longbow in favor of a claymore sword. To a general who asked him about the blade, he explained, "In my opinion, sir, any officer who goes into action without his sword is improperly dressed."

Churchill played "The March of the Cameron Men" on his bagpipes as his landing craft approached the shore. He was determined to be the first man into action. He was stowing his bagpipes when his boat touched land and two Commandos pushed past him, but he quickly leapt ashore and ran ahead, his sword in one hand and pistol in the other. The Commandos met only token resistance. However, while Churchill was celebrating their success with a case of Moselle he had found in the German commander's hut, a demolition charge exploded nearby and broke the bottle in his hand, causing a piece of glass to gash his forehead. The wound was painful but not serious, and got him much sympathy when he returned home. Churchill later claimed to King-Clark that it began healing too quickly and had to be touched up with his wife's lipstick to keep the "wounded hero" story going.

It had always been Mad Jack's view that a bold, small force, with the benefit of bluff, could often succeed where a larger, slower-moving force would fail. Whenever possible, he preferred to operate with a few men in whom he had complete confidence.

On September 15, 1943, during the Salerno landings, Churchill was ordered to make a raid into Pigoletti, a village strongly garrisoned by the Germans, with the object of taking prisoners. Churchill and a Corporal Ruffell soon got far ahead of the rest of his troop and entered the village street, Churchill ahead, Ruffell about 20 yards behind. As two German sentries approached him, Churchill brandished his sword and shouted, "*Hände hoch!*" (Hands up!)

They immediately obeyed. Looking around, Churchill saw an 81mm mortar emplacement in the middle of the square, with its crew sleeping around it. Ordering Ruffell to keep the sentries covered with his submachine gun, Churchill woke up the mortar crew and demanded their surrender at swordpoint. There were 10 of them, but, taken by surprise and befuddled with sleep, they raised their hands.

As other Commandos entered the village and took over the guard duty, Churchill looped the slipknot of his revolver's lanyard around one prisoner's neck, stuck his sword against his back, and made the rounds of the sentry posts. As they approached each post in the darkness, the sentry would call out his challenge, the prisoner would give the password, and then Mad Jack would put his sword to the sentry's throat and take him prisoner. Repeating the process, he captured the entire garrison.

With the assistance of two Commandos, he marched his 42 prisoners down to the brigade area in Mercatello, forcing them to carry their own weapons. As he explained to King-Clark, "I always bring my prisoners back with their weapons; it weighs them down. I just took their rifle bolts out and put them in a sack, which one of the prisoners carried. The prisoners also carried the mortar and all the bombs they could carry and also pulled a farm cart with five wounded in it."

Churchill was recommended for a Victoria Cross for his capture of the German troops, but it was downgraded to a Distinguished Service Order. The nature of the achievement may have been too individualistic for official recognition. It was, Churchill conceded, "a bit Errol Flynnish."

In January 1944, No. 2 Commando was given the task of reducing the pressure on Marshall Tito's Partisan forces by tying up elements of the German 118th Mountain Division in Yugoslavia. From the Commando base on the island of Vis, Churchill launched an attack on the German garrison on the nearby island of Hvar on January 26. Commando veteran Bob Bishop wrote, "After thoroughly shooting up the place, we returned to Vis with prisoners, who appreciated greatly that their captors were British and not Partisans. Not being one who would change a winning system, Colonel Jack twice returned to Hvar and twice repeated the process within five days."

Churchill also authorized raiding parties on passing German ships—in effect, piracy. These raids were popular with the men because the vessels were well provisioned with food.

A major operation to draw pressure from the Partisans was launched in June. On the night of June 3, 1944, Churchill led No. 43 Commando and 2,000 Partisans in an attack on the German-held island of Brac, off Yugoslavia. After fierce fighting to take a fortified hilltop, Churchill found himself isolated with a small party of Marines, three of whom were wounded, two seriously. He sent off two Marines to bring up reinforcements and told his radioman to take up a more sheltered position farther down the hill and try to call in artillery support.

Churchill gave an account of what followed. Note that he does not draw attention to his own active defense of the position, though he must have played the leading role.

> This reduced my post to 6, including Col. Manners, Captain Wakefield, and a wounded Marine.
>
> Enemy fire was now heavy, and a counterattack seemed imminent. I was distressed to find that everyone was armed with revolvers, except myself, who had an American carbine. Colonel Manners was firing his revolver, as were some of the men. A mortar-bomb fell

among us and killed Captain Wakefield and 2
Marines and wounded another. Soon Col.
Manners was hit again, this time through the
right shoulder. While I was trying to remove
his equipment and small pack, a Marine—I
think Mne Wood of the Intelligence section—
suddenly joined me, and asked, "Can I help
you, Sir?" While helping me to remove the
Colonel's equipment, he was shot through the
head. About 20-30 enemy advanced toward us,
but were stopped by rapid fire [presumably
Churchill's], and took cover perhaps 75 yds
away. Some men on our flanks began to withdraw, but we shouted to them to stay. A small
post to our left rear was holding well and firing, and called back. I believe Lt Beadle of Y
Troop was commanding it.

I rolled over onto my back, and played
"Will ye no' come back again", on the pipes, to
indicate that we still held the hilltop, and hoping to attract [D Troop] 43.[4] Soon afterwards
we heard shots, and D Troop 43 under Capt
Blake put in a timely appearance nearby. Our
position was growing precarious.

The revolver ammunition was finished, but
I still had one magazine (15 rounds) for the
carbine. The enemy now appeared to have got
round our right flank. The small arms fire was
very severe, and the dead and wounded in my
post were continually being hit. Col Manners
was the only one still conscious.

Finally there was a flurry of grenades and a
fragment cut a furrow in my helmet, slightly
cutting my scalp, and stunning me. This must
have preceded the assault, as on coming to, I

found Germans prodding us, apparently to discover who was alive.[5]

Churchill was taken prisoner. The Germans were quite
excited, under the misapprehension that he was related to the
British prime minister. His sword and pipes were confiscated
and later put on display in the War Museum in Vienna. He
was taken to Berlin and imprisoned in the Sachsenhause concentration camp. Along with an RAF squadron leader, Jimmy
James, he determined to escape. They tunneled their way
under the outer wall of the camp, and on September 23 they
emerged in the gutter of the road outside. They set off to follow the railway line toward the Baltic coast. Unfortunately, as
they approached the coastal town of Rostock in heavy morning mist, they nearly stumbled onto a work party, which
chased them. Reaching a tall wire fence, they scaled it. Beyond
that was another fence, which they scaled as well, only to find
that they had broken into a prison camp.

Along with a group of other prisoners, Churchill was
moved to Niederdorf in Austria. Planning to escape at the first
opportunity, he gathered some survival supplies and kept them
on his person at all times: a rusty tin can, some matches, and
some onions. On the night of April 20, 1945, he at last got his
chance when the floodlights failed while he was with an outside work party. He walked away, alone. For the next week, he
survived by stealing vegetables from gardens and boiling them
into soup in his tin can. After eight days, he made it through
the Brenner Pass into Italy. He spotted an armored column on
a road far below him and was able to make out the white stars
that indicated they were American. Despite a badly sprained
ankle, he rushed down the hillside and managed to stop the
last vehicle, a tank. Dirty, disheveled, and out of breath, he
looked like a scarecrow and could hardly talk. "But I still managed a credible Sandhurst salute, which may have done the
trick," he said.

As Churchill rode off on an American tank, he regretted that he did not have his bagpipes with him to mark the splendor of the moment. To his great frustration, the war in Europe soon ended. "However, there are still the Nips, aren't there?" he asked his friends, hopefully. He got himself to Bombay, arriving just days after the atomic bombs had been dropped on Hiroshima and Nagasaki.

The Yanks had spoiled everything.

Churchill earned his parachute wings at age 40, in 1946. He transferred from the Manchesters to the Seaforth Highlanders, and in 1948 he was appointed second in command of the Highland Light Infantry, then in Jerusalem.

On April 13, 1948, a month before the British Mandate expired, a convoy of Jewish doctors, nurses, and patients, which was trying to make its way to the Hadassah Hospital, drove into an Arab ambush and was pinned down. The road had been mined, and snipers were firing on the vehicles.

Hoping to bring the Jews out safely, Churchill headed for the scene in an armored personnel carrier, accompanied by two armored cars. Parking the vehicles where their machine guns could cover the houses in which the Arab gunmen lurked, Churchill walked 30 yards toward the convoy to try to convince the Jews to come with him. Having come directly from a parade, Mad Jack was resplendent in glengarry, tunic, kilt, Sam Browne belt, sporran, and red-and-white-checkered knee socks. As he walked he swung his blackthorn walking stick and grinned broadly in every direction. "People are less likely to shoot you if you smile at them," he observed.

The Jews were counting on being rescued by the Haganah (the Jewish army), and Churchill was unable to persuade them to come with him. In the end, 75 of them were killed and 25 wounded.

In 1953, posted as an instructor at the School of Land/Air Warfare in Australia, Churchill took up surfing and became a passionate devotee of the sport. He returned to England with a

16-foot surfboard, which he towed on a trailer behind his Vincent "Black Widow" motorcycle. There wasn't much surf available locally, but it occurred to Churchill that the tidal bore on the River Severn offered possibilities. The inrushing tide is funneled through an ever-narrowing channel and can reach a height of 6 feet and a speed of about 10 miles per hour. It is not technically a wave, but rather the front end of a single slab of water thundering up from the sea. On July 21, 1955, Churchill became the first man to surf a tidal bore, making a run of a mile and a half.

Churchill's last job was with the Ministry of Defence in Whitehall. On his train ride home, he would sometimes astonish his fellow passengers by opening the window, hurling out his briefcase, and then calmly leaving the train at the next stop. They thought him quite mad, having no way of knowing that he had flung the briefcase into his own back garden.

"Mad Jack" Churchill died at his home on March 8, 1996, aged 89.

NOTES

1. *Bowmen of England*, p. 189.
2. Col. Jack Churchill, "Taking the Bow and Arrow Seriously," *Strand Magazine* (December 1945), p. 22.
3. *Bowmen of England,* p. 191.
4. In the German report of the action, Churchill's piping was described as "the doleful sound of an unknown musical instrument."
5. *The Commandos 1940–1946*, p. 348.

CASSIUS MARCELLUS CLAY (1810–1903)

> *"When society fails to protect us, we are authorized by the laws of God and nature to defend ourselves; based upon the right, 'the pistol and Bowie knife' are to us as sacred as the gown and the pulpit."*
>
> —Cassius Marcellus Clay

Cassius Marcellus Clay was born on October 19, 1810, at White Hall, the family plantation in Madison County, Kentucky. His father had a penchant for classical names, and Clay's middle name, which means "martial," could not have been more appropriate. In his final years, looking back on nine decades, Clay observed that every one of them had involved a good deal of fighting.

One of the first fights he described in his memoirs was with a playmate named George, a slave who was quite a bit bigger and stronger than he. After the two had had a disagreement, George suggested that Clay would not dare fight him if he didn't have his parents backing him up. Clay accepted the challenge.

George was evidently my overmatch in size and strength, so I thought of stratagem. I selected the ground. The grey limestone, fine for building, lies near the surface. Here was a steep descent toward the Kentucky River, and the stone being taken out in horizontal layers, left a nice level bench, now covered with moss and dry leaves. So I took my place near the declension, leaving space for George to take his stand on the level land, with my face toward the ravine. Striking George the first blow, I sent him staggering down the hill; and then advancing to the very edge of the plat, I was taller than he, and had all the advantages, as he had to labor up the hill when struck, and I had time to blow. Of course, I was triumphant, and George asked for quarters, and admitted himself beaten.[1]

In 1829, Clay enrolled at Transylvania University, in Lexington, Kentucky. He had political ambitions and knew that he would need a good education to fulfill them. In 1831, he transferred to the junior class at Yale. His sojourn in New England brought about a marked change in Clay's outlook. Comparing its prosperity to the poverty of his home state, he concluded that the South's slave-based economy depressed the value of labor and promoted agriculture over industrial development. He was convinced that slavery must be ended but considered himself an emancipationist rather than an abolitionist as he felt the process should be handled slowly.

After graduating from Yale, Clay returned to Transylvania University to study law. While there, he courted Mary Jane Warfield, and their marriage was set for February 26, 1833. A few days before the wedding, a rival for Miss Warfield's hand, Dr. John P. Declary of Louisville, wrote her mother a letter describing Clay as an unsuitable match. After being shown the

Cassius Marcellus Clay. (Credit: Kentucky Historical Society.)

letter, Clay traveled to Louisville, stopping first at a cooper's shop, where he "got a good tough hickory cane about as big around as your finger." He then walked streets until he ran into Declary. Demanding an explanation and receiving none, Clay proceeded to give Declary a caning. After a few unsuccessful efforts to arrange a duel, Clay returned home, where he got word that Declary had announced he would horsewhip him the next time they met.

As Clay told an interviewer:

> I went to Louisville to give him a chance. I went into the dining room of his hotel and leaned against a pillar to wait for him. As I stood there I heard someone behind me rise. I turned and saw Declary. He was as pale as death, and I saw the coward in his eye. He walked out of the room and did not return. A man who acted like that could not, in those days, be respected in Kentucky, and Declary committed suicide the next morning by cutting his arteries.

"Curious, isn't it," mused Clay, "that a man will have the bravery to commit suicide and still not have enough physical courage to fight?"[2]

In 1835, Clay was elected to the state legislature as a Whig representative from Madison County. Politics was rough in those days, physically as well as verbally, and he described a conflict he had with another representative, James C. Sprigg, in early 1838. The two had exchanged angry words in the House, and Clay expected a challenge. He wrote:

> Sprigg was a dear lover of the State beverage—"old Bourbon"—which, as elsewhere, here was apt to loosen the tongue. So, on one occasion, he revealed to me, confidentially, how

he had always been triumphant in personal encounters. He approached his antagonist, when a fight was inevitable, in a mild and conciliatory manner, dealt him a sharp blow, and followed that up with unrelenting severity till he was whipped. "Thus," said he, "size and strength amount to nothing against mind!" Sprigg had no doubt forgotten that he had ever revealed to me his system of tactics.

So, when the House adjourned, as we both boarded at the same hotel, and the weather was cool, I found Sprigg sitting on the far side of the fire-grate, and several members of the Legislature present in the same room. As soon as Sprigg, who was evidently awaiting my arrival, saw me, he advanced past all these gentlemen toward me, with a pleasant look, without speaking. I remembered his methods; and when he got within reach, without a word on either side, I gave him a severe blow in the face, and brought him staggering to the floor. As fast as he would rise—for I played with him as a cat with a mouse—I repeated my blows; allowing him always to rise, as I felt myself greatly an overmatch for him, and would not strike him when down. When the bystanders saw the unequal fight, and felt that Sprigg, who was a notorious bully, was fully punished, one of them caught him by the coattail . . . and tearing his coat to the very collar, pulled him away; and thus ended the set-to. The upshot was that Sprigg, the aggressor, was severely punished— eyes blacked, nose bleeding, and coat torn; whilst I stood smiling, without a scratch.

Sprigg laid by for several days; and all

> thought now, at least, a duel was inevitable. After a while he ventured out, with his eyes marked with wide, black rings. Approaching me, smiling, with outstretched hand to show peace, he said: "Clay, old fellow, here's my hand. I taught you my tactics, and you have beaten your master at his own game." Of course, I accepted his hand, and we remained good friends.[3]

Clay centered his political career on his emancipationist views, which put him in a peculiar position, as he had inherited his family plantation with the restriction that he could not sell it. Thus, he campaigned against slavery as a member of the slave-owning aristocracy. (Clay would not free his slaves until 1844.)[4] Though Clay would never give up his political aspirations, he could not win an election after 1840, as there was such fear of abolitionism in the South that the issue could not be calmly discussed.

In 1841, Clay fought a duel with a political opponent, Robert Wickliffe Jr., who had accused him of being a tool of the Yankees. The two met on May 13 and exchanged shots three times at 10 paces without effect. Clay demanded another exchange, but as three exchanges were all that were approved by the code, the seconds refused. "We left the ground enemies, as we came," wrote Clay.

His opponents tried to intimidate him into silence, but Clay continued to speak his mind, carrying a pistol and a bowie knife to back up his words. "I knew full well that the least show of the 'white feather' was not only political but physical death," he wrote.

Clay was active in the 1843 campaign, speaking on behalf of Whig candidate Garret Davis, who opposed Democrat Robert Wickliffe Jr. During his speeches, Wickcliffe would read a handbill denouncing Davis, and Clay would interrupt him to declare that the accusations were untrue and had been proven so. To silence Clay, Wickliffe and his cronies brought in Samuel M. Brown, whom Clay described as "a political bully." It was said of Brown that he had had "forty fights, and never lost a battle."

On the afternoon of August 1, Clay attended a Wickliffe rally at Russell's Cave in Fayette County. He had left his pistol at home and was armed only with a bowie knife, which he carried under the left side of his jacket.

Clay wrote:

> When Mr. Wickliffe repeated the usual *role* [list], I interrupted him again, as before, saying: "That hand-bill has been proven untrue." At the moment, Brown gave me the "damned lie," and struck me simultaneously with his umbrella. I knew the man, and that it meant a death-struggle. I at once drew my Bowie-knife; but, before I could strike, I was seized from behind, and borne by force about fifteen feet from Brown, who, being now armed with a Colt's revolver, cried: "Clear the way, and let me kill the damned rascal."
>
> The way was speedily cleared, and I stood isolated from the crowd. Now, as Brown had his pistol bearing upon me, I had either to run or advance. So, turning my left side toward him, with my left arm covering it, so as to protect it to that extent, I advanced rapidly on him, knife in hand. Seeing I was coming, he knew very well that nothing but a fatal and sudden shot could save him. So he held his fire; and, taking deliberate aim, just as I was in arm's reach, he fired at my heart.[5]

To an interviewer, Clay described what followed:

> I felt the ball strike me in the breast, and I
> thought it had gone through me, and I deter-
> mined to kill him if I could before I died. I
> came down upon his head with a tremendous
> blow of the bowie knife, but did not split open
> the skull. I struck him again and again, and
> stunned him so that he was not able to fire.
> With one cut of the knife I sliced his nose right
> in two, so that it separated in the middle and
> came out as flat as a pancake. With another
> blow I cut off his ear so that it hung by a shred,
> and with a third I put out his eye. The conspir-
> ators now seized me, and I was struck with
> hickory sticks and chairs, some of the blows of
> which I still feel.[6]

Fearing that Clay would break loose from their grip, the conspirators threw Brown over a stone wall in order to protect him. This fence, which enclosed the yard near the steep descent to the cave and spring, was about 2 feet high on the upper side, but 7 or 8 on the lower side. This fall put Brown completely out of the fight.[7]

Clay's friends took him to a nearby house to see what damage the bullet had done. "It struck me just over the heart," recalled Clay years later, "and I would have been killed but for one thing. The scabbard of my bowie knife was tipped with silver, and in jerking the knife I pulled this scabbard up so that it was just over my heart. Brown's bullet struck the scab-bard and imbedded itself in the silver, and we found the ball there. There was a red spot just over my heart, and the whole thing seemed almost providential."[8]

To his outrage, Clay was indicted and tried for mayhem, while Brown was not charged with attempted murder.

However, during Clay's trial, Brown testified that he had been put up to the shooting by Wickliffe and his cronies, three of whom helped subdue Clay at the scene. Clay's distant relative Henry Clay, the great politician and orator, successfully defended him.

After his acquittal, Clay wrote Brown thanking him for his evidence and offering his friendship. "He refused, however, to bury the hatchet, and when I remembered his condition I did not wonder at it. The doctors had patched him up pretty well, but he was a horrible-looking object, and I expected that he would insist upon a duel with me, or would attack me and have his revenge. I met him several times afterward, however, and he never touched me. I have no doubt that he stayed in Lexington intending to kill me, but that the probability is that he had not the moral courage to attack me."[9]

The Whig champion may have won his fight, but Wickcliffe defeated Davis in the election, convincing Clay that he needed to work harder to persuade the public of the soundness of his views. To this end, he founded an antislavery newspaper, the *True American*, in 1845. He leased a brick building for its office and fortified it against attack. The outside doors and window shutters were lined with sheet iron. The front door was fitted with a heavy chain that permitted only a narrow opening, and inside, facing it, he set up two brass 4-pounder cannon loaded with shot and nails. He hired a platoon of supporters to back him up and stockpiled firearms and pikes. In the event these defenses were breached, he could escape his office through a hatch in the roof, and he kept a keg of gunpowder near his desk to blow up the premises if necessary.

Clay declared war on slavery in his first issue, and subsequent issues included vituperative attacks on his political foes as well as veiled threats of insurrection, pillage, and rape. His firebrand journalism damaged his reputation among Kentuckians so badly that when the Mexican War broke out in 1846, Clay regarded it as a welcome opportunity to redeem himself. He volunteered and funded the Kentucky Volunteer Cavalry Regiment.

In January 1847, he and a force of 72 men went on a scouting expedition to probe enemy strength. The third day out, their camp was surrounded by a Mexican cavalry force that outnumbered them 40 to one and forced them to surrender. The following day, one of the Americans bolted through the Mexican lines and escaped. Seeing this as precursor to a mass uprising, the Mexican commander ordered his men to kill the prisoners with their lances. As they advanced, Clay told his men to lie down and make no show of resistance. Standing alone, he bared his breast and shouted, "Don't kill the men—they are innocent! I alone am responsible." This theatrical gesture prevented a massacre.

Clay and his men were marched to Mexico City and held for eight months. When Clay was finally repatriated, he found himself a hero and capitalized on it with a return to politics. Having lost faith that the Whigs would carry out his programs, he supported the new Emancipation Party. One of its candidates was a friend, Rev. Robert J. Breckinridge. Concerned for the reverend's safety, Clay went to his home to give him a weapon he had designed and had had constructed.

As Breckinridge recalled:

> He then produced the wickedest-looking blade that anybody in the Bluegrass had ever seen or heard of—with a seven-inch blade, two inches in width at the hilt—and proceeded enthusiastically to demonstrate its wonderful simplicity of construction and efficiency of operation.
>
> Strapped securely but loosely under the left arm, it hung from its scabbard of coin silver— unlike all other knives—*handle down*, the blade

held in place by a spring at the hilt. A grasp of
the handle would trip the spring and release
the long, curved, razor-sharp, double-edged
blade at "belly level!" No assailant would ever
be looking for a weapon drawn from that position. With the utmost economy of motion, all
the Doctor had to do as the foe advanced upon
him, [Clay] explained, was to "point the instrument at his navel and *thrust* vigorously"![10]

Years later, when showing the weapon to his youngest
son, the reverend confessed that he always felt sinful
wearing it while campaigning. As he recalled, "Every time
I gestured heavenward, that infernal knife thumped
against my ribs!"

During the campaign of 1848, Clay continued to preach
the emancipationist doctrine despite threats of violence. A
town near Lexington posted placards threatening antislavery
spokesmen with death, but Clay appeared at a meeting there
with a carpetbag under his arm. According to a widely told
story, he took his place on the speakers' platform and declared,
"For those who support the laws of our country, I have an
argument from this," and placed a copy of the Constitution on
the table beside him.

"For those who believe in the Bible," he went on, "I have
an argument from this," placing a Bible on the table.

"And for those who believe in neither the laws of God nor
of man"—looking directly at the most threatening element in
the crowd—"I have this argument," and he pulled out two
long-barreled pistols, laid them on the table, laid his bowie
knife across them, and proceeded to give his speech, uninter-
rupted. (In his memoirs, Clay scoffed at the notion that he
would have laid his weapons on a table, where an enemy
might have seized them—he kept them on his person or in the
carpetbag at his feet.)

On June 15, 1849, Clay was debating Democratic candidate Squire Turner when violence erupted. As he wrote:

> The next meeting was at Foxtown, my immediate neighborhood. That lulled my suspicions, and I expected no assault there, at least. So, though I always went armed, and had pistols in my hand-sack, I had only a Bowie knife when I spoke. Turner opened the debate, as usual, but became extremely violent. With great animation, he depicted the evils of agitation of the slavery question, and was more earnest than usual. In response, I was equally in earnest; and when interrupted by a young lawyer, named Runion, I denounced him as "Turner's tool," and defied him. As soon as I stepped down from the table on which I stood, Cyrus Turner, the lawyer's son, came up to me, gave me the lie, and struck me. I had already been told, calmly, by one of my neighbors, who was now among the conspirators, that if I did not quit the discussion of the subject I would be killed. So knowing, as in Brown's case, what this meant, I at once drew my knife. I was immediately surrounded by about twenty of the conspirators, my arms seized, and my knife wrested from me. Thinking it might be a friendly intervention to prevent bloodshed, I made but little resistance. But I found that the loss of my knife but subjected me to renewed attack. I was struck with sticks, and finally stabbed in the right side, just above the lower rib—the knife entering my lungs, and cutting apart my breastbone, which has not united to this day. Seeing I was to be murdered, I seized my Bowie knife; and, catch-

ing it by the handle and the blade, cutting two of my fingers to the bone, I wrested it from my opponent, and held it firmly for use.

The blood now gushed violently from my side; and I felt the utmost indignation. I flourished my knife, clearing the crowd nearest me; and looked out for Turner, determining to kill him. The way was opened, and I advanced upon him, and thrust the knife into his abdomen, which meant death. At this time my eldest son, Warfield, being about fourteen years old, had procured a pistol, and handed it to me. It was too late. I was feeble from loss of blood; and, crying out that "I died in the defense of the liberties of the people," I was borne to my bed in the hotel by my friends. Turner was also taken into another room.[11]

Clay attributed his survival to the fact that his enemies assumed he was mortally wounded. His recovery was no doubt helped by his orders that his wound not be probed or medicine administered, "relying on my vigor of constitution, and somewhat upon my destiny." In the mid-19th century, one was as likely to die from a doctor's care as from one's injuries.

Clay wrote to Cyrus Turner. "I regretted the necessity of having given him such a wound (which I knew to be fatal), and proposed a reconciliation. This he accepted, and returned me a friendly answer of forgiveness. He died, and I lived," Clay wrote.

Turner was widely mourned as a martyr, while Clay was denounced as a "damned nigger agitator." Though he had won the battle, the savage affray brought disgrace on the emancipationist cause.

Clay was influential in the founding of the Republican Party in 1856 and hoped to be its candidate for president. He was disappointed that year and again in 1860, when Lincoln ran successfully, but he went to Washington and lobbied for a cabinet post.

With the outbreak of war in April 1861, Clay quickly formed a volunteer brigade to defend the nation's capital, then in danger of being cut off from the North. In a diary entry for April 22, 1861, Lincoln's secretary John Hay wrote, "It was dramatic to see Cassius Clay come into the President's reception room today. He wore, with a sublimely unconscious air, three pistols and an Arkansas toothpick."[12]

Clay finally got an appointment as ambassador to Russia. While there, his pugnacious manner occasionally provoked challenges from the aristocrats with whom he socialized. As the challenged party, Clay retained the choice of weapons, and he invariably specified the bowie knife, to which the Russian elite was not partial. One man tried to get around the procedural point by provoking Clay into issuing the challenge. Clay was eating dinner in a café when the Russian came up to him, slapped him on the cheek with his glove, and stepped back to receive his response. Unconstrained by European norms, Clay jumped up and punched him in the nose, sending him crashing over the table behind him, and then resumed his dinner.

Clay returned to America in 1869. A legend persists that around this time he wrote a pamphlet entitled *The Technique of Bowie Knife Fighting*, which contained the following advice:

> The first move you should make upon your adversary is to obtain a headlock with your left arm, and then drive very viciously in back of their left clavicle, thus severing the jugular. But you frequently run into an agile adversary who thwarts this maneuver. Under no circumstances must you then shift to the chest walls as I used to do before I became experienced. There is too much danger of hit-

ting a rib. The thing for you to do if you are
thwarted, in what is the finest early tactical
maneuver, then you should shift and drive to
the hilt with great force on a line with the
navel. It has been my experience that this pro-
duces great shock and that it almost invariably
puts an end to the encounter.[13]

The quote, from a speech given by William Townsend to
the Chicago Civil War Roundtable in 1952, has been repeated
in a number of news articles and biographies. However,
Townsend offered no source for it, and in his 1969 biography
of Clay he omits the story entirely. Though it would be a fasci-
nating document, there is no evidence that Clay wrote any
such manual.

Clay broke with the Republicans and campaigned for the
Democratic presidential candidate in 1876. It was as violent a
campaign as those that preceded the Civil War, and there was
particular antipathy against Clay. Shots were fired at one of
his sons and two companions, and one of the latter was killed.
Three of Clay's foremen were murdered in succession, as well
as some of their relatives.

After his candidate was defeated, Clay returned to his
fortress-like mansion, White Hall, where, increasingly, he lived
under siege. He was divorced, Mary Jane having objected to
his much-publicized indiscretions in Russia. The product of
one of these indiscretions, a boy named Launey, lived with
Clay at White Hall along with a few trusted black servants.

In 1877, after noticing that 10-year-old Launey was growing sick, Clay intercepted a letter that indicated that his cook,
Sarah White, and her husband were poisoning the boy. Clay
immediately ordered them off his property. White's son Perry,
whom Clay described as "a general loafer [who] rode a fine
horse and saddle, went well-dressed, and carried a pistol
always," let it be known that he intended to kill "Cash" Clay.

On September 30, while he was out riding, Clay encountered Perry near his stable. Clay instantly dismounted and advanced on him, pistol in hand, ordering him to kneel and put his hands up. As Clay demanded to know what he was doing there, Perry reached for his pistol. Clay fired twice, striking him in the neck and heart. Perry died on the spot.

In 1894, the still-robust Clay attracted national attention when he married a 15-year-old servant, Dora Richardson. His heirs, believing that he had gone mad, attempted to prevent the wedding and later to declare him legally incompetent. Dora left him after three years and married a local ne'er-do-well, Riley Brock.

Clay was concerned that Brock and his gang would break into White Hall and rob it, and they apparently attempted to do so on a night in January 1900, when the sound of a window being forced awakened Clay. Arming himself with a pistol and bowie knife, he confronted the intruders. Details of this incident are lacking, but when the authorities arrived they found one man on the floor of the library, killed by a pistol shot, and another behind the springhouse outside, dead of a knife wound in the abdomen. If Brock had been among the intruders, he had managed to escape.

Clay became increasingly wary. He was completely alienated from his children, and those few visitors who ventured onto his property were held at gunpoint until they explained their business. He slept with two revolvers and a Winchester rifle beside his bed. He still had the pair of brass cannons from his newspaper office, and he kept them in his entryway, loaded with nuts, bolts, nails, and pieces of chain.

On April 5, 1901, the 90-year-old Clay was involved in an incident that made page one of the *New York Times* under the headline "Gen. Clay Routs a Posse." When local authorities attempted to serve papers on him, Clay barricaded himself inside his house and drove them off with shotgun and rifle fire, all the while shouting, "The vendetta! The vendetta!" Clay was nearly blind, and his shots went wild. The sheriff decided that discretion would advise returning at some future date.

In the summer of 1903, Clay took ill. Two doctors were summoned from Lexington, but when they arrived, Clay's servant, Joe Perkins, told them that Clay would not see them. "He is seated on the side of his bed with two revolvers lying by him and a Winchester rifle in his hands, and says he will not permit any man to enter the door," said Perkins.

Clay died on July 22. That night a severe thunderstorm struck Madison County. Lightning destroyed the statue of Henry Clay in Lexington, and the wind blew the steeples off all the churches in Richmond and the roofs of all the buildings of the White Hall estate except the main house.

It was as if the old fighter could not depart without raising one last ruckus.

NOTES

1. *Life of Cassius Marcellus Clay*, pp. 29–30.
2. "His Life a Stormy One," p. 10.
3. *Cassius Marcellus Clay*, pp. 78–79.
4. The boxer Cassius Marcellus Clay Jr., who was named after his father, claimed to be descended from slaves owned by the Clay family, but whether by the original Cassius Marcellus Clay is not known. The boxer was originally fond of the name. "Don't you think it's a beautiful name?" he used to ask interviewers. "Say it out loud: Cassius Marcellus Clay." However, when he joined the Nation of Islam in 1964 he renounced it as a slave name and became Muhammad Ali.
5. *Cassius Marcellus Clay*, pp. 83–85.
6. "His Life a Stormy One."
7. According to some accounts of the fight, it was Clay who threw Brown over the wall.
8. "His Life a Stormy One," p. 10.
9. Ibid.

10. William H. Townsend, *Lincoln and the Bluegrass* (Lexington, KY: University of Kentucky Press, 1955), p. 163.

11. *Cassius Marcellus Clay*, pp. 185–86.

12. John Hay, *Lincoln and the Civil War in the Diaries and Letters of John Hay* (New York: Da Capo Press, 1988), p. 8. "Arkansas toothpick" was a slang term for the bowie knife.

13. Keven McQueen, *Cassius M. Clay: Freedom's Champion* (Turner Publishing, 2001), p. 98.

Jeff Cooper
(1920–2006)

A critic once described him as "a bon vivant and recreational killer," a characterization that delighted him. It is perhaps the most succinct description possible of this many-faceted man, a Marine Corps officer and World War II veteran, big-game hunter, evangelist of the Colt 1911 .45, originator of the modern pistol technique, founder and first president of the International Practical Shooting Confederation (IPSC), founder of Gunsite, author of more than 500 magazine articles and 20 books, and member of the National Rifle Association's board of directors and its executive council.

Jeff Cooper was born on May 10, 1920, to a comfortably well-off family in Los Angeles. His father had wanted to name him Jefferson Davis, but his mother preferred

Jeff Cooper on his Honda trike at Gunsite in 1986. (Credit: Author's collection.)

John Dean; his father acquiesced but persisted in calling him Jeff, and that is the name that stuck. As a boy, his experiences were varied and stimulating: he summered on Santa Catalina, traveled to Europe several times, and camped in the Rockies. He was introduced to shooting at age 6 and bought his first .22, a Remington model 34, at age 13. (He still owned and regularly shot that rifle at the time of his death in 2006.) In high school he joined the

ROTC, partly because it ensured him a free supply of ammunition for practice.

Cooper attended Stanford University, where he continued with the ROTC. His training included firing the Colt 1911 .45 from the back of a horse, a course in which he qualified expert. He also competed for a prize offered to the cadet who maintained a B average or better, who was a commissioned officer equivalent, and who shot the highest score with a pistol on the army course. Cooper won that prize, a Colt 1911A1. He fenced on the varsity team, choosing the saber rather than the foil or épée, as he considered saber technique to be the most like actual fighting. During summers he made a series of hunting trips, taking 14 prime trophies; two of these, the bighorn sheep and Canadian moose, were national first prizes. While at Stanford he also met and courted Jane Ellen "Janelle" Marks, a woman very much his match.

Upon graduation in the spring of 1941, Cooper entered the Marine Corps Basic School, a one-year program that would earn him a commission. Cooper's family had no tradition in the Marines and he had more friends in the Army, but the glamour of the Marine Corps dress uniform was too hard to resist. With the attack on Pearl Harbor, the Marine Corps announced that his class would be considered graduated in January 1942. Cooper put in for Fleet Marine Force, as he wanted to lead a rifle company. To his disappointment, he was assigned to Seagoing and ordered to report to the naval yard at Vallejo. While in California he seized the opportunity to elope with Janelle—secretly, as it was against regulations for a junior officer to marry.

Cooper was assigned as part of the 100-man Marine detachment on the USS *Pennsylvania*. The World War I–vintage battleship was sister to the ill-fated *Arizona*, but it had been in dry dock at Pearl Harbor and thus survived the raid.

When Cooper went to war he took with him the .45 automatic he had been awarded at Stanford. He also brought a .45-

caliber Colt Peacemaker with a 5 1/2-inch barrel, having been persuaded by the writing of Charles Askins that the Colt single-action revolver was the handgun of choice for a warrior. Askins claimed that its stock design helped the shooter instinctively point at his target, making it superior to the automatic for nighttime use. Cooper also brought along a box of 50 cartridges, which turned out to be more than enough—"You don't shoot much in a war," he later observed. He was not authorized to carry the revolver, but there were no regulations barring it and no one seemed to object.

Onboard ship, Cooper was assigned to gunnery watch. The *Pennsylvania* was dubbed "the shootin'est ship of the war" for its many shore bombardments—it is calculated to have lobbed more than 11,000,000 pounds of steel at enemy positions. After these bombardments, Cooper was sometimes sent ashore as part of a three-man squad that would assess the results and bring back whatever intelligence it could gather. Of these three, one would be a radioman, one would take photographs, and one would act as a sentry. On these forays, which might last three or four hours, Cooper always wore his sidearm and sometimes carried a rifle as well.

In later years, the many fans of Cooper's articles and books often wondered whether—to put it bluntly—he had ever killed anybody. It was a subject he never addressed. The only oblique reference to it was in *Cooper on Handguns* when he wrote, on the topic of stopping power: "In the three cases in which I was personally able to observe the effect of my own shot, my adversary was flung violently backward twice, but fell toward me in the other instance."[1] When she was writing his biography, his daughter Lindy felt that she had to answer this question. Subsequently, this author had the occasion to discuss the subject with him further.

It was on Kwajalein, in February 1944, during one of the reconnaissance patrols, that Cooper had his first face-to-face lethal confrontation. Hearing a man approach, his patrol had

taken cover. A Japanese soldier appeared, trotting toward
them, carrying a Type 97 automatic rifle. He was completely
unaware of their presence. Jeff was carrying a Garand rifle,
but his revolver was in his hand. He aimed and fired one-
handed, hitting the Japanese soldier in the center of his chest.
The soldier fell to the ground without uttering a sound. One
leg kicked around a little, and then he was still. Cooper and
his men moved out of the area and continued with their
patrol. The incident did not strike him as particularly significant, and no notice was taken of it.

In the course of several such patrols, Cooper changed his
mind about the Colt revolver. For one thing, while Askins
claimed that it pointed better in the dark, Cooper noted that it
was next to impossible to *load* it in the dark, especially in a
hurry. Also, while its first shot could be delivered quickly,
follow-ups were problematic. Finally, it got dirty too fast in the
sandy conditions of the islands. Cooper had come to favor the
Colt automatic. Onboard ship he carried it in Condition
Three—chamber empty, hammer down, and a loaded magazine seated—but while on patrol he transitioned to Condition
One—a round in the chamber, hammer cocked, safety on.

On Saipan, in June 1944, Cooper was two or three hours
into a patrol when he had his second lethal confrontation.
Looking to meet up with another Marine patrol, he had
crawled up on the broken trunk of a palm tree to get a better
view, his pistol in his right hand. Nearby, on the side of a hill,
below and to his right, he saw a group of Japanese soldiers.
One of the soldiers noticed him and turned toward him, raising his rifle; the move was awkward, as he had to turn uphill.
Cooper aimed his .45 and fired one-handed. The soldier spas-
modically threw his rifle into the air as he fell to the ground.
Cooper immediately dropped from the tree and moved off with
his men, as it was not their mission to engage in firefights
with the enemy.

After the war, the Coopers settled in at Quantico, where

he was an instructor in military intelligence and military history at the Command and Staff School. Cooper began to make use of the FBI shooting range on the base, as he was intrigued by the FBI's combat-style training. The revolver was still standard issue for FBI agents, and Cooper found that his .45 automatic gave him a distinct advantage over them. They considered that unfair, an objection that struck him as amusing.

At that time Cooper was practicing the then-standard point-shooting technique, in which the pistol is drawn and fired from chest level, without the use of the sights. He developed considerable skill and was able to consistently place his shots within a 2-inch circle at 7 yards. Some years later, during an exhibition, he performed a quick draw and actually split a bullet on the edge of an ax, breaking clay pigeons on either side of it. This was intended to be a trick shot, as the clay pigeons would be broken by the lead splatter wherever the bullet hit the steel backplate, but Cooper's reflexes were so well tuned that he made the shot for real. However, he never claimed he could repeat it, and as he often said, "The measure of marksmanship is what the shooter can do on demand."

With the demobilization after the war, Cooper saw little future for himself in the Marine Corps and resigned his commission as a lieutenant colonel. With the outbreak of the Korean War he attempted to return to active duty, but there was no call for officers of his rank and specialty. However, the CIA had use for his services. He was tasked with stirring up trouble along China's southern border to force it to divert troops from Korea. While on this assignment in Thailand in 1951, Cooper had his third lethal confrontation. He was traveling in Thailand's northernmost province, Chiang Rai, in a Land Rover that was being driven by a member of the constabulary. On his belt was holstered the same 1911A1 he had carried in World War II. Though there was no reason to expect trouble, a man suddenly stood up in a ditch at the side of the road and fired at the car with a submachine gun. Three bullets

struck the car, one passing through the door right in front of
Cooper. Cooper shouted, "Stop!" and the driver hit the brakes
so hard that they skidded to a halt crosswise in the road. The
would-be assassin had emptied the magazine of his 9mm Sten
and was attempting to insert another when Cooper shot him
in the chest, once, one-handed and using his sights. The range
was about 25 yards. As the gunman dropped, Cooper and his
driver took cover in the ditches on either side of the road.

It had been rash for Cooper to engage the gunman rather
than keep driving, as he had no idea whether the gunman was
acting alone, but the attack had made him angry and he had
reacted accordingly. He and his driver waited 20 minutes or so
to be sure that the gunman was dead and that the action had
concluded. Finally Cooper took a look down the road and saw
the gunman's foot sticking up where he had fallen. The two
men inspected the body, and Cooper retrieved the gun while
his driver searched the man's pockets for papers.

Cooper never did get any explanation of what had moti-
vated the attack. He theorized that the local opium traders
assumed his mission threatened their activities and decided to
take him out. He came out of the experience with renewed
conviction that the big-bore pistol is an effective stopper when
a shot is well placed, and also that fully automatic fire from a
handheld weapon is largely a waste of ammunition. "You are
outgunned only if you miss," as he put it.

In 1956, a civilian once more, Cooper moved Janelle and
their three daughters to Big Bear Lake, in California's San
Bernardino Mountains. In August 1957, for the area's annual
"Old Miners' Days" festivities, he organized a "Leatherslap"
fast-draw competition to be held at the Snow Summit ski
resort. About 125 people competed for a prize of 500 silver
dollars. Local competitors decided to get together for a match
each month, calling themselves the Big Bear Gunslingers.
Cooper set the rules for the competitions, allowing maximum
room for experimentation while keeping things as practical as

possible. He required shooters to wear serviceable, safe holsters and use a full-duty defensive weapon with full-charge ammunition. They had to start with their weapons loaded, holstered, and safe, their hands clear. They competed man against man. The target represented a man or the vital zone of a man, and meaningless scoring gradations were not used. Scoring was based on speed and hits to the vital zone. The shooting scenarios were changed regularly, so no one could game the course. Most shooting was at short range and high speed, but longer ranges were also included. Since in skilled hands the pistol provides an edge of one man over many, the sustained use of the weapon was emphasized, and reloading time was included in the shooter's score. These competitions became Cooper's laboratory. With his analytical bent, he studied which techniques proved most effective and incorporated them into what became the Modern Technique of the Pistol.

Its essential elements are as follows:

- *The Weaver Stance.* Named for Big Bear Gunslinger Jack Weaver, this is a two-handed hold in which you push out with your shooting hand while pulling back with your support hand, creating isometric tension.
- *The Presentation.* A swift, fluid, and consistent presentation of the pistol from the holster to a ready or firing position.
- *The Flash Sight Picture.* With practice the shooter will master the "flash sight picture," an almost subliminal confirmation of sight alignment. Cooper stressed the use of the sights even in close-range shooting situations.
- *The Compressed Surprise Break.* The key to trigger control is the "surprise break," in which you apply gradual pressure to the trigger so that you do not determine when the hammer will fall. With training, you can compress this effect into a fraction of a second.
- *The Big-Bore Automatic Pistol.* The pistol should hit the hardest blow you can control, with a caliber of .40 or larger

considered adequate. Cooper recommended the single-action automatic, specifically the 1911 pattern .45.

Cooper was the overall Champion of the Big Bear Gunslingers in 1959, 1960, and 1961. His daughter Lindy remembers an example of his shooting ability during the annual Leatherslap in 1965. He had set up several crowd-pleasing exhibitions, including one in which competitors would take turns shooting at an ordinary pink balloon anchored at a distance of 164 yards. The idea was that tension would build as the shooters tried, failed, and kept taking turns until eventually someone hit it. Cooper was first up. He shot at the balloon and hit it: Game over. Lindy heard a small boy ask his father how the man had done that. The father explained that there must be a marksman hidden in the woods who had shot the balloon with a .22 rifle.

By 1963 so many practical shooting clubs had sprung up in Southern California that a parent organization was necessary to guide, oversee, and encourage competition among the clubs. Thus the Southwest Pistol League was born, which in 1976 would lead to IPSC, of which Cooper was the founder and first president. Cooper gave it the motto DVC, standing for *Diligentia* (Accuracy), *Vis* (Power), and *Celeritas* (Speed), the holy trinity of combat shooting. Each was of equal importance. As he wrote, "To serve its purpose, a handgun must deliver its bullet with precision, it must deliver it with decisive force, and it must deliver it quickly."[2]

Cooper began writing for *Guns & Ammo* in 1958, an association that would continue for nearly half a century. At the time, gun magazines focused primarily on target shooting, hunting, and collecting, so some considered Cooper's stress on the combat use of the handgun radical. Nevertheless, his bracing, authoritative style attracted a strong following, and with his obvious command of the subject he quickly established himself as the preeminent authority on the handgun.

Cooper relentlessly promoted the Colt .45 automatic, to the

point that he admitted some might think he had an obsession with it. He felt that its inventor, firearms genius John Moses Browning, had achieved a kind of perfection in its design. It was simple, rugged, and easily maintained; its cartridge offered the optimum balance of power and controllability; its single-action trigger was good and could be made very good; its safety and magazine release were in exactly the right place (for the right-hander); and its 8-round capacity was sufficient. He dismissed such popular calibers as the 9mm and .38 Special as unreliable fight-stoppers. Of smaller calibers he was contemptuous. Regarding the .25 auto, he once advised, "Carry it if it comforts you, but never load it. If you load it, you may shoot it. If you shoot it, you may hit somebody. If you hit somebody, he may become very angry with you and do you violence."[3]

During the 1960s and 1970s, Cooper regularly traveled to the world's hot spots as a firearms consultant and trainer. In 1969, while giving a private class in Guatemala, then in the throes of revolution, a student asked him when they would know they had passed the course. He responded, "At such time as you are really convinced, when menaced by an armed attacker, that he is in greater danger from you than you are from him, you will have passed the course."

Within a week Cooper had an opportunity to apply this test to himself. As he and a student named Pedro left the club at which the class was being given, a car pulled into the drive and stopped about 10 feet from them. There were two men in the backseat and a driver in front. All stared directly at Cooper. Pedro told him, "Watch it. This is the FAR," using the acronym for the *Fuerzas Armadas Rebeldes*, the Rebel Armed Forces.

Cooper stood ready, his .38 Super Colt on his hip.[4] He was confident he could get at least two of the men before they could bring their guns into play and Pedro could handle the other. The driver asked a few idle questions and then drove off, his wheels kicking up gravel from the driveway.

Cooper asked Pedro if they should call the police. Pedro told him that that might be counterproductive, as the policeman who answered the phone might very well be a rebel sympathizer himself.

A few days later, as Cooper was being driven from the club, he saw a man, evidently a lookout, duck up a side street. A moment later a large American sedan pulled out and began tailing Cooper's car. It contained six men. There followed a slow-motion car chase through the streets of the town as Cooper's driver made random turns. Cooper went to Condition Red, his pistol in hand. This was the way assassinations had been set up for years in Guatemala: a car would pull alongside its target, on the left, so that two passengers could empty submachine guns into it. Cooper instructed his driver not to let them pass and rolled down his windows to allow himself freedom of movement. When his car was forced to stop in traffic, he closely watched the other vehicle, which remained two or three car lengths behind them. He had decided that if its doors opened, he would hit the pavement first and do as he had trained himself: focus on the front sight, aim at the center of mass, and make every break a surprise break. Cooper's driver finally managed to lose the tail, but as Cooper later put it, "Throughout, it was very clear that, while I was in trouble, my assailants were in much worse trouble. A perfect case of 'I see what I mean!'"

To Cooper, this was the most successful sort of "lethal confrontation"—one in which the shooter's alertness and confidence prevent the confrontation from taking place at all.

In 1975, Jeff and Janelle sold their Big Bear house and moved to an undeveloped 160-acre piece of land in the high desert near Paulden, Arizona. They named it Gunsite Ranch; it would be home not only to the Coopers, but to the American Pistol Institute (API) as well.

The Coopers built their home in the Southwestern style, with a red-tiled roof, walls that resemble adobe, and a spacious, sunny balcony looking out over rolling hills sparsely

The Sconce, the Coopers' home at Gunsite. (Credit: Author's collection.)

covered in scrub trees and prickly pear cactus. He dubbed it the Sconce, a word that means a small fort, and it was designed along architectural principles Cooper had picked up in his travels to Rhodesia and Latin America, where home invasions were a serious threat.

It is set into a hillside so that there are no windows at ground level. The tiled roof is fireproof and the walls, built of filled concrete block, provide cover from small arms fire. To approach the front door, you must stand in a recessed entryway, exposing your back to a firing slit in the wall behind you; in fact, there is no point on the outside of the house that is not covered by a projecting bastion with firing ports. Cooper's study is a small room atop the roof that commands a view in all directions. From inside the house the study is accessible only by a spiral staircase—very hard to rush. The hallway to the bedrooms is closed off at night with a wrought iron gate that, while keeping an intruder out, would not prevent him being seen and shot at. No fortification can provide security in itself, but Cooper designed the Sconce so that those attempting to break in could not do so without alerting him and without placing themselves at a severe tactical disadvantage. In the event of a break-in, Cooper said that he would call the police, but only so they could write their report and help clean up the mess.

The API opened for classes in 1976. Cooper described its mission as teaching "close range, interpersonal crisis management." In his years of training shooters worldwide, he had developed a teaching method by which a high level of competence could be imparted to the average student within a week. Although there were training facilities elsewhere, Gunsite was the first to offer instruction not only to police and military personnel, but also to private citizens who could present documentation of good character. Gunsite later introduced courses in the rifle, carbine, and shotgun. Today, covering 2,000 acres, it is considered the premier firearms training facility in the world.

At Gunsite, students as well as staff and instructors go armed at all times. This was only natural to Cooper, as he expected that after students complete their training, they will remain armed for the rest of their lives. If they didn't, they had missed the point. As to safety, students were drilled in the "Four Rules" that Cooper formulated. These are as follows:

1. All firearms are always loaded.
2. Never let the muzzle cover anything you are not willing to destroy.
3. Keep your finger off the trigger until your sights are on the target.
4. Be sure of your target.

With the strict observance of these rules, no accident is possible, and Gunsite was always a remarkably safe operation.

To those who might still be anxious, Cooper would observe that "safety is nice, but it is not first. Life is first and life is not safe." A gun, by design, is not "safe." It could not serve its purpose if it were. Cooper liked to tell the story of a man who walked up to a Texas Ranger who had a cocked-and-locked .45 automatic in his holster. The man asked, "Is that loaded?"

"Yup," said the ranger.

"Isn't that dangerous?" asked the man.

"You damn betcha," replied the ranger.

Students at Gunsite were taught safety, proper gun-handling, marksmanship, and tactics, and heard a lecture from Cooper on the combat mindset. With examples drawn from his personal experience and cases he had studied, he impressed on students that we live in a dangerous world and we must take responsibility for our own defense. It is futile to expect the police to be there when trouble arises. According to Cooper, the average person goes through life in what he termed Condition White: relaxed, unaware, and unprepared. If attacked, his first thought will be, "Oh my god, I can't believe this is happening!" The armed citizen should strive to remain in Condition Yellow. Yellow is a state of relaxed awareness in which you continually use your eyes and ears to take in information and are attentive to your surroundings. In Yellow, you see no specific threat, but you are prepared to do something if necessary. If confronted by violence, your reaction will be, "I thought this might happen some day." The next level is Condition Orange: someone or something is not quite right and has gotten your attention. You are identifying a potential threat and shifting your primary focus to it. The next level is Condition Red: fight mode. In Condition Red you have decided that you will use lethal force if certain triggers are tripped, such as a weapon being drawn. Might you be frightened? Possibly. Turn that fear to anger, Cooper said. You should be outraged that someone would *dare* to threaten you.

Cooper considered self-defense not so much a matter of personal choice as a positive social duty. He outlined his philosophy in *Principles of Personal Defense*:

> Violent crime is feasible only if its victims are cowards. A victim who fights back makes the whole business impractical. It is true that a victim who fights back may suffer for it, but one who does not almost certainly *will* suffer for it. And, suffer or not, the one who fights back retains his dignity and self respect.

Cooper did not want to hear any bleating from Gunsite graduates. As he put it, "Tell us not what the mugger did to you. Tell us what you did to the mugger."

In addition to instruction, Gunsite offered students a unique experience. Cooper gave it a style, from its ubiquitous raven totem to rules specifying violations such as "ostentatious ugliness" and "conspicuous stupidity in a public place," with punishment for a first offense listed as "muttered abjuration." Classes might have a 50-50 ratio of private citizens and professionals, giving doctors and businessmen a chance to train alongside Navy SEALs and members of SWAT teams. Most of those who attended Gunsite were familiar with Cooper through his writing and looked forward with some trepidation to meeting "the gunner's guru."

One visitor to the school described the class awaiting Cooper's appearance on Monday morning as "hushed and tense as novitiates waiting for the pope in the Sistine Chapel."[5] Cooper never failed to live up to expectations. He was 6 foot 2, barrel-chested, with tight-cropped hair, and the pale blue eyes of the gunfighter. A holstered .45 and an extra magazine were on his belt. His presence was commanding and his manner formal. This was a man who expected excellence and did not suffer fools. An old friend, Elden Carl, once said of him, "Rest assured that beneath that gruff exterior there beats a heart of stone."

Students instinctively addressed him as "Colonel." In relaxed moments, he was happy to discuss history, philosophy, politics, high-performance automobiles, technical matters concerning firearms, and hunting and military experiences, but he had an impatience with small talk that many people found brusque.

As classes were conducted on the various ranges, Cooper would travel between them on his three-wheeled ATV. The term "tricyclophobia" was coined for the students' nervousness upon hearing his approach. No one wanted to screw up in front of the Colonel, to receive the "Guru's glare."

The week's training ended on Saturday morning with the final shoot-off and the awarding of certificates: "Marksman" for the many, "Expert" for a select few. Expert was a somewhat subjective category based on a combination of skill, tactical judgment, and mind-set, awarded only to those whom the instructors felt they would be comfortable going into battle with. Every graduate was now a "Raven" and welcomed into what Cooper called the Gunsite family. All were invited to visit with the Coopers at their home. Janelle served brownies and lemonade in the Sconce's high-ceilinged living room, with its massive fireplace and walls decorated with hunting trophies, several of them from Jeff's hunting trips to Africa. Jeff received visitors in his basement armory, a fair-sized room secured with a bank-vault door. Here some of his personal weapons and memorabilia were on display.

Jeff Cooper died at the Sconce on September 25, 2006, after a long illness. Surviving him are Janelle, their three daughters, five grandchildren, and five great grandchildren. Surviving him also are the thousands of people he trained to take control of their environment, many of whom would not have survived otherwise.

NOTE: Jeff Cooper is the only subject in this collection whom I can describe as a personal friend. Our relationship started in the mid-1980s, when I wrote him a fan letter and received a thoughtful reply. After I sent him examples of my artwork, he invited me to design some logos for Gunsite and later to illustrate his books. We did seven books together, and as partial payment I took courses with him. We also met socially on numerous occasions and maintained a regular correspondence over a twenty-year period. He was one of the few larger-than-life people I have known. I was continually struck by his wide-ranging intellectual curiosity; his often profound insights; his absolute commitment to the truth as he saw it; his enormous energy and enthusiasm; and the positive role he played in so many people's lives, teaching them not only how to shoot, but how to approach life.

NOTES

1. *Cooper on Handguns*, p. 48.
2. *Cooper on Handguns*, p. 102.
3. *Cooper on Handguns*, p. 33.
4. The .45 ACP caliber is restricted to military use in certain Latin American countries.
5. *Shooting to Kill*, p. 70.

David
(11th Century B.C.)

Prophet, poet, warrior, and king, David is one of the most complex and compelling figures in the Bible. Throughout his life, he showed that he could be as resourceful and ruthless as was necessary, and never more so than when he went *mano a mano* with Goliath.

David was born in Bethlehem in about 1037 B.C., the youngest of eight sons of Jesse, a small landowner. He was an Israelite, a hill people who were in almost constant warfare with the Philistines, who inhabited the more fertile plains. Technologically more advanced than the Israelites, the Philistines had chariots, and swords and spears of iron, while the Israelites could only make weapons of bronze.

In about 1047 B.C., the Israelites united under their first

king, Saul, and he established
a standing army. As the
story of David begins, the
Israelite army is facing the
Philistine army across the
Valley of Elah, halfway
between the Judean hill
country and two major
Philistine towns,
Ashdod and Gath.
Young David had three
brothers in the army, and
his father took him from
his sheep-tending duty to
deliver supplies to them.

The Israelites were
camped on a rocky hill-
side, which was favor-
able for defense and
inaccessible to the
enemy's chariots. To pro-
voke them into leaving
their position, a Philistine
champion, Goliath of
Gath, would stand in the
dry riverbed between
the two armies and chal-
lenge one of the
Israelites to meet
him in single
combat. This
type of battle was
common between
ancient armies
and is mentioned

Sculpture of David by Bernini. (Credit: Author's collection.)

94

a number of times in the Bible—such champions were called "men of the space between" in Hebrew.

Goliath is usually described as a giant standing 6 cubits and a span, or 9 1/2 feet tall. However, this is apparently a transcription error: the Dead Sea Scroll fragment for this verse reads *4* cubits and a span, a far more believable 6 1/2 feet.

Scripture describes him in this fashion:

> He had a helmet of bronze on his head, and he was armed with a coat of mail, and the weight of the coat was 5,000 shekels of bronze [125 pounds]. And he had greaves of bronze upon his legs, and a javelin of bronze slung between his shoulders. And the shaft of his spear was like a weaver's beam, and his spear's head weighed 600 shekels of iron [15 pounds]; and his shield-bearer went before him.[1]
>
> He stood and shouted to the ranks of Israel, "Why have you come out to draw up for battle? Am I not a Philistine, and are you not servants of Saul? Choose a man for yourselves, and let him come down to me. If he is able to fight with me and kill me, then we will be your servants; but if I prevail against him and kill him, then you shall be our servants and serve us." And the Philistine said, "I defy the ranks of Israel this day; give me a man, that we may fight together." When Saul and all Israel heard these words of the Philistine, they were dismayed and greatly afraid.

Shortly after David arrived, Goliath strode out between the lines and bellowed his challenge, as he had every morning and evening for 40 days. Dismayed that no one would take him up on it, David declared that he would do so himself.

When word of this got to King Saul, he sent for David and told him, "You are not able to go against this Philistine to fight with him; for you are but a boy, and he has been a man of war from his youth."

David responded that as a shepherd he had killed lions and bears, adding, "the Lord who delivered me from the paw of the lion and from the paw of the bear, will deliver me from the hand of this Philistine."

Saul equipped David with armor, including a bronze helmet and a sword, but David found the accoutrements too heavy, saying, "I cannot go with these; for I am not used to them." Instead he armed himself only with his staff and his sling, and chose five smooth stones from a creek bed, which he put in his shepherd's bag.

David approached Goliath, his staff in one hand and his sling in the other. Goliath, accompanied by his shield bearer, looked on the youth with disdain, asking, "Am I a dog, that you come to me with a stick?" And cursing David, he said, "Come to me, and I will give your flesh to the birds of the air and to the beasts of the field."

David responded, "You come to me with a sword and with a spear and with a javelin; but I come to you in the name of the Lord of hosts, the God of the armies of Israel, whom you have defied."

To quote the biblical account,

> When the Philistine arose and came and
> drew near to meet David, David ran quickly
> toward the battle line to meet the Philistine.
> And David put his hand in his bag and took
> out a stone, and slung it, and struck the
> Philistine on his forehead; the stone sank into
> his forehead, and he fell on his face to the
> ground. So David prevailed over the Philistine
> with a sling and with a stone, and struck the

Philistine, and killed him; there was no sword
in the hand of David. Then David ran and
stood over the Philistine, and took his sword
and drew it out of its sheath, and killed him,
and cut off his head with it.

When the Philistines saw that their champion was dead, they fled. And the men of Israel
and Judah rose with a shout and pursued the
Philistines as far as Gath and the gates of Ekron,
so that the wounded Philistines fell on the way
from Sha-ara'im as far as Gath and Ekron.[2]

David became a soldier and soon was promoted to "captain
of a thousand," and after that was made a member of Saul's
inner circle. As a commander, David enjoyed great success in
battle, so much so that Saul began to view him as a threat.
When David returned to the castle-fortress in Gibeah from a
victorious battle, women sang, "Saul has slain his thousands,
and David has slain his tens of thousands."[3]

Saul's daughter Michal fell in love with David, and as her
bride price Saul demanded the foreskins of a hundred Philistines.
(At the time it was not unusual to keep count of the slain by
removing body parts, and the genitalia of enemy soldiers were
often mutilated in any case.) Saul hoped that David would be
killed in this enterprise, but not only did David survive, he
brought back twice the number of grisly trophies requested.

Saul's jealousy of David grew until he drove him from his
court. Taking refuge in a cave at Adullam, David gathered an
army of outcasts, some 400 to 600 men. He protected the local
population from raids by desert tribes, and at the same time he
raided and plundered those tribes himself.

After the death of Saul, David accepted the throne, becoming the second king of the Israelites. In a series of masterful
campaigns, David consolidated a kingdom extending from the
border of Egypt to the Euphrates River.

The epic story of David covers dozens of pages in the Bible, but let us return to the incident that started it all: the killing of Goliath. Biblical scholar Alexander Maclaren expressed the conventional view when he wrote, "The story is, for all time, the example of the victory of unarmed faith over the world's utmost might. . . . The youthful athlete leaps into the arena, and overcomes, not because of his own strength, but because he trusts in God. . . . The five smooth stones have become the symbol of the insignificant means, in the world's estimate, which God uses in faithful hands to slay the giants of evil."[4]

Did David really plunge into combat virtually unarmed but for his faith? Or did he make certain calculated decisions that, in fact, gave him an advantage? General Moshe Dayan leaned toward the latter view, arguing that David's victory could be viewed not as a miraculous example of divine intervention, but as a triumph of sound tactics. Customarily, single combatants were equally armed, but David chose not to compete with Goliath on his own terms. Goliath's heavy weapons and armor were suited for close combat, but distinctly unsuited for pursuing an unarmored, fleet-footed adversary. David realized that his security lay in his mobility, his ability to stay out of his opponent's reach. Furthermore, he retained an element of surprise: his weapon was concealed until needed. (Goliath remarked on his stick but not his sling.) However strong his faith in God, David gathered not one but *five* stones. He could strike a decisive blow at a distance and, if necessary, rapidly fire additional missiles.

The image of David's vulnerability comes from the fact that he does not use a noble weapon, like a sword or a lance, but a shepherd's simple sidearm, one that can be formed from strips of leather with a few minutes' labor, and its ammunition picked up from the ground. While modern readers may think of a sling as something of a toy, for millennia it was frequently employed in battle, where corps of slingers, along with archers, thinned the enemy ranks as the armies closed for hand-to-hand combat. A stone hurled from a sling could travel 250 yards at a velocity of 120 mph, and the rate of fire of a slinger would probably be comparable to that of an archer, six or more shots a minute.

There are a number of historians who remark on the sling's effectiveness. Roman historian Vegetius wrote, "Often, against soldiers armored with helmets, scale coats and mail shirts, smooth stones shot from a sling or staff sling are more dangerous than arrows, since while leaving the limbs intact they inflict a lethal wound, and the enemy dies from the blow of the stone without the loss of any blood." Up to about 60 yards, potential accuracy was quite good, especially among those who had trained with the weapon from childhood, like David. Livy claimed that Achaean slingers were able to "wound not merely the heads of their enemies but any part of the face at which they might have aimed." The Bible mentions the sling elsewhere, as when it describes the Benjamites (Judges 20:16): "Among all the soldiers there were 700 chosen men who were left-handed, each of whom could sling a stone at a hair and not miss." Alexander the Great suffered a serious head wound from a sling stone, and his vision was impaired for some time afterward.

With these factors in mind, Goliath seems rather like the man who brought a knife to a gunfight.

NOTES

1. The heavy spear mentioned appears to be a lance, which Goliath or his shield bearer carried in addition to the javelin. He also had a sword, which is mentioned later. The Philistines had an advantage over the Israelites in that they had weapons of steel. The arms with which Goliath is accoutered are not characteristic of a Philistine warrior at this time but represent a random assortment of weapons and armor from a later time when the account was written.
2. Biblical scholars have noted glaring inconsistencies in the story of

David. In 1 Samuel 16:18 David is described as first having met Saul when he served as a court musician, and yet later, in verse 17:55, seems to be unknown to Saul at the time of the combat with Goliath. Furthermore, 2 Samuel states that Goliath, "the staff of whose spear was like a weaver's beam," was slain by a man named Elhanan, at a time when Saul was long dead and David was the king of Israel (2 Samuel 21:19). Some have suggested that those who wrote the Bible felt obliged to include all the information they had on certain characters, whether or not the result was contradictory.

3. This is assumed to be an exaggeration. To kill even a few hundred enemies in battle at this time would be unusual.

4. Alexander Maclaren, *Expositions of Holy Scripture* (Grand Rapids, MI: Baker Book House, 1977), p. 236.

Jonathan R. Davis
(1816–1890s?)

*"Possibly the single most
extraordinary feat of self-
defense by an American
civilian in the annals of
frontier history."*
—John Boessenecker

In the annals of Western gunfighting, there are a few cases
in which one man killed three opponents. In 1866, lawman
Steve Venard killed three stage robbers near Nevada City,
California. In 1881, Marshall Dallas Stoudenmire killed three
men in a gunfight in El Paso. In 1887, Sheriff Commodore
Perry Owens killed three men resisting arrest in Holbrook,
Arizona Territory. However, in 1854, the performance of one
man in a little-known gunfight in California dwarfs these others. The gunfight involved 14 participants, 13 of whom died,
11 of those at the hands of one man. The last man standing,
victor in one of the most spectacular affrays of all time, was a
veteran of the Mexican War named Jonathan R. Davis.

Davis was born on August 5, 1816, into a wealthy family

in Fairfield County, South Carolina. In December 1846, when the Palmetto Regiment of the South Carolina Volunteers was organized for the Mexican War, Davis enlisted for a six-month tour. He was promoted to second lieutenant and signed up for a second tour in July 1847. On August 20 of that year he was wounded at the Battle of Churubusco, where the regiment's commander, Pierce M. Butler, was killed leading a charge in the face of devastating fire. Less than a month later, the regiment was in the vanguard of the final assault on Mexico City and was the first to plant its flag on the city walls.

Davis participated in five battles and was discharged at war's end with the honorary rank of captain.

With the defeat of Mexico, the United States took possession of California at the same time that gold was discovered there. Captain Davis made his way to the gold fields in 1849. He made a name for himself in the diggings as a first-class pistol shot and "second to none" in fencing.

Thousands of young, rootless men flooded into the unsettled areas of California, seeking their fortune, and bandits soon followed. It was a land without formal government or law, through which men rarely traveled unarmed. On December 19, 1854, Davis was walking with two other prospectors, Dr. Bolivar A. Sparks of Mississippi and James C. MacDonald of Alabama, up a trail through Rocky Canyon, in the Sierra foothills in the northwest portion of El Dorado County. It was a remote area. Except for a 17-man mining camp at the trailhead a mile distant, there were no inhabitants within 7 miles. The three men were heading 24 miles north to work a claim staked by Sparks. All were armed with revolvers.

A band of robbers had prepared an ambush and were hiding in the brush alongside the trail. The gang comprised two Americans, one Frenchman, five "Sydney ducks" (convicts from Australia), four Mexicans, and two men just arrived from London. They had commenced operations just three days previously and had already robbed and killed six Chinese men and four Americans. As the prospectors reached the ambush point, the bandits sprang out from hiding and began shooting. There was no call for "your money or your life"—the bandits intended to take both. MacDonald was killed before he could draw his pistol. Sparks got off two shots and then collapsed with bullet wounds. Davis, armed with two revolvers, had been the first to respond to the attack. He later described himself as being in "a fever of excitement at the time," but he made his shots count. By the time he had emptied his guns, he had killed or mortally wounded seven of the bandits. A number of carbine and pistol balls passed through his hat and clothes, but he suffered only two minor wounds.

The shooting had attracted the attention of three miners on a nearby hill, John Webster, Isaac Hart, and P.S. Robertson. At the inquest, they described what followed:

> The only four surviving robbers made a charge upon Captain Davis, three with bowie knives and one with a short sword or sabre. Captain Davis stood firmly on his ground until they rushed up abreast within about four steps of him; he then made a spring upon them with a large bowie knife, warding off their blows as fast as they were aimed at him—*gave three of them wounds that soon proved fatal*—and having wounded the other one, (it seemed very slightly,) and disarmed him by throwing his knife in the air in warding off a blow, a generous impulse seemed to force him not to inflict another wound upon him and to spare his life.

Evidently, two of the knife-wielding bandits were not in

full fighting form. As the captain said later, "Two of the four that made the charge upon me were unable to fight on account of their old wounds. They came up with the rest, making war-like demonstrations by raising their knives in a striking posture, and I acted accordingly. I noticed that they handled them with very bad grace, but attributed it altogether to fright or natural awkwardness."

In a letter to the newspaper, Webster wrote, "I never saw so much work of the kind done in so short a time, in all my life before! And as you know, I have shared in some trying scenes on the battlefields, in my time."

The three witnesses hurried toward the scene. Webster, who described Davis as a tall man in a white hat, continued:

> We got within good speaking distance of
> the scene of action, ere the "white hat man"
> saw us; but scarce had he turned his face
> toward us, when, in an instant, he sprang to
> his deceased companion, seized his revolver,
> which was yet loaded, cocked, and leveling it at
> us, ordered us to "halt!" and then told us that
> if we raised one of our guns it would be at our
> "peril!" He then ordered us to advance "ten
> paces." His order was given in so commanding
> a tone that we were, at once, brought into calm
> submission. Having brought us to a "halt," he
> asked who we were, and what our business
> was? We informed him that we were peaceable
> miners, camped nearby. We were out hunting
> game, and that if he would go with us to our
> camp, we would satisfy him that we had given
> a true account of ourselves.
>
> With the remark that we had "the eyes of
> honest men," he told us that he wished a
> Coroner's inquest held over the deceased bod-

ies; that he needed aid in moving them and attending to the wounded; that he would go with us to our camp, but that we should go as his prisoners.

He then ordered us to leave our arms with his wounded companion; that if we were what we represented ourselves to be, he could get aid, and would be under lasting obligations to us; but that, at the first indication of treachery, we should share the same fate of these deceased robbers if he lived long enough to shoot us, though even a hundred guns were being fired at him, at the same time, from other quarters.[1]

At the miners' camp, Davis recognized an acquaintance, which alleviated his suspicions. He urged the men to accompany him to the scene so that they could attend the wounded and check the others for papers. A search of the dead bandits yielded 4 ounces of gold dust, $491 in gold and silver coin, and seven gold and two silver watches, among other valuables. Davis elicited sworn statements from the witnesses, and presented them at the inquest.

The surviving bandit, who had had his nose and forefinger cut off and who had been expected to recover, died the following day.

Sparks succumbed to his wounds on December 26.

The Rocky Canyon gunfight received national attention, including coverage in the *New York Times*. Many doubted the truth of the story, but the sworn testimony of the 17 miners, three of them eyewitnesses, supported it. Davis invited those who still had doubts to visit the robbers' graves with him.

The Miner's Court in Placerville, which reviewed the case, ended its statement with, "In conclusion, we deem it due to state that from all the evidence before us, Captain Davis and his party acted solely in self-defence—were perfectly justifiable in killing these robbers—and that too much praise cannot be bestowed upon them for having so gallantly stopped the wild career of these lawless ruffians."

In a letter written January 6, 1855, Davis said, "I did only what hundreds of others might have done under similar circumstances, and attach no particular credit to myself for it."

After the Rocky Canyon fight, Davis considered himself a marked man in the area. He drifted north to Yreka for a while before settling in San Francisco, where he resided for the rest of his life.

NOTE

1.   "Desperate Fight," p. 1.

Kenelm Digby
(1603–1668)

"His prowess and erudition, his extraordinary personal strength and his gigantic stature, rendered him the wonder and admiration of foreign courts."

—John Henneage Jesse

Born in Gayhurst, Buckinghamshire, England, on July 11, 1603, Sir Kenelm Digby represented the ideal of the Renaissance man, distinguishing himself as a courtier, naval commander, statesman, philosopher, and scientist. Like most gentlemen of his time, he was a well-schooled fencer. Large and powerfully built, he once picked up a chair in which a man was sitting, using only one arm.

In 1641, at a banquet in France, Digby toasted England's King Charles, which provoked a derisive laugh from a French nobleman, Lord Mont le Ros. A little later, Mont le Ros again laughed at the mention of the English king. Digby resented the insult, telling Mont le Ros that "twice [you have] reviled the best king in the world, in the hearing of me, who am his faith-

ful subject, wherefore for satisfaction, I require a single combat of you, where either you shall pay with your life for your
sauciness, or I will sacrifice mine in the behalf of my King."
   Digby (referring to himself in the third person) described
what followed:

> The French Lord being of a resolute spirit,
> condescended to fight, the place was appointed;
> dinner being ended, they both arose from the
> table, and privately went together. Being in a
> field, off they plucked their doublets, and out
> they drew their weapons.
>   Mars would have bashful been to have seen
> himself by noble Digby there excelled, long
> work with the contemptible French Lord he
> would not make, for fear lest any should lie in
> ambush and so he might hazard his own life,
> wherefore in four bouts he run his rapier into
> the French Lord's breast till it came out of his
> throat again, which so soon as he had done,
> away he fled . . .[1]

Digby was involved in several other affairs of honor that
were resolved without bloodshed.
   Digby's most impressive work with the sword was performed not in a duel, but in a street fight in Madrid. He wrote
a detailed account of it a few years afterward.
   On the evening of February 15, 1623, the day he arrived
in Madrid, he dined at the home of his uncle, Lord Bristol,
then England's ambassador to Spain. By the time Digby was
ready to return to his lodgings, the hour was late and the
streets were deserted. However, it was a clear night with a
full moon, so Digby turned down the offer of an escort of
torch-bearing servants in favor of walking with his cousin
(Lord Bristol's son) and an unidentified friend. As they

Kenelm Digby. (Credit: British Library.)

strolled the streets, enjoying the cool serenity, they heard a woman singing on a balcony. Digby's cousin knew her, and the three of them approached to listen. Suddenly, "fifteen men, all armed, as the moon shining upon their bucklers and coats of mail did make evident, rushed out upon him with much violence, and with their drawn swords made so many furious blows and thrusts at him that if his better genius [i.e., his instinct] had not defended him it had been impossible that he could have outlived that minute."

In addition to swords and mail, the attackers had bucklers (small, round shields) with lanterns affixed to the top of them, constructed so that their light shined ahead.

Digby's cousin reacted instantly, drawing his sword and striking the foremost attacker on the head. Rather than kill him, the force of the blow merely caused the attacker to reel back a few steps, as he wore a protective steel cap underneath his hat. At the same time, the blow shattered the cousin's sword, leaving him with only the hilt in his hand. Finding himself disarmed, the cousin decided that his best course was to run to his father's house for assistance. Meanwhile, the unnamed friend, who was defending himself as best he could, also had his sword break, "as though they [both] had conspired to betray their masters in their greatest need."

The friend remained by Digby, warding off blows with what remained of his sword. However, the attacking mob saw that he was effectively disarmed and pressed by him, focusing its attack on Digby, who was blocking that part of the gang that was trying to chase his cousin. The leader of the gang was in this group, and as he fought with Digby, the rest surged up to support him.

Digby had backed into a narrow part of the street in order to keep all his attackers in front of him. Here, however, the overhanging penthouses blocked the light of the moon, and the lanterns attached to his enemies' bucklers dazzled and confused him.

Digby wrote (again describing himself in the third person):

> The number of his enemies and the dispari-
> ty of the weapons might have given him just
> cause to seek the saving of his life rather by the
> swiftness of his legs than by an obstinate
> defence; but he, that did not value it at so high
> a rate as to think it could warrant such an
> action, resolved rather to die in the midst of his
> enemies, than to do any thing that might be
> interpreted to proceed from fear: with which
> resolution he made good the place he stood in,
> and whenever any of them were too bold in
> coming near him, he entertained them with
> such rude welcomes, that they had little
> encouragement to make a second return.[2]

After Digby had remained some time "thus beating down their swords and wounding many of them, and shewing wonderful effects of a settled and not transported valour," the attack began to slacken in its fury. Only then did he have an opportunity to think about his situation, and he realized that there must be some mistake behind this attack by complete strangers. Speaking to them in Spanish, and as courteously as he knew how, he asked what had caused them to attack him when he could not possibly have given offense to any of them, having arrived in Madrid only that day.

He described the response:

> One that seemed to be of the best quality
> among them, by a cassock embroidered with
> gold, which he wore over his jack of mail,
> answered him with much fury in his manner.
> "Villain, thou liest, thou hast done me wrong
> which cannot be satisfied with less than thy

life; and by thy example let the rest of thy las-
civious countrymen learn to shun those gentle-
women where other men have interest, as they
would do houses infected with the plague, or
the thunder that executeth God's vengeance."
These words put all patience out of
[Digby's] breast, so that now he dispensed his
blows rather with fury than art; but his hand
was so exercised in the perfectest rules of true
art, that without his endeavours or taking
notice, it never failed of making exactly regulated motions, which had such force imparted to
them by a just anger, that few of them were
made in vain.[3]

Digby's attackers attempted to flank him, some of them
running down a side street and coming around to attack him
from behind. Digby was made aware of them when he was
struck on the shoulder, "but it seemed that the fearful giver of
it was so apprehensive lest [Digby] should turn about, that his
quaking hand laid it on so softly that it did him no hurt, but
served to warn him of the danger he was in."

With enemies all around him, Digby decided to cut his way
through the thickest of them, "so it might appear that he
wrought his own liberty in spite of their strongest oppositions."

Digby made a quick thrust at the chest of his nearest opponent, putting the whole weight of his body behind it. As the
man's mail vest did not give way, he was knocked back into
those behind him, collapsing them like dominoes. Running at
him, Digby scrambled over him and escaped the encirclement.

Digby then began a retreat toward his uncle's house, "but
in such a manner, that though his feet carried him one way
his face looked another, and his hands sent forwards many
bloody messages of his angry spirit." One of the gang
advanced eagerly and unwarily upon him, and as he lifted up

his sword to make a blow at Digby, Digby avoided it with "a gentle motion of his body" and gave him "a strong reverse upon his head." This was the same assailant upon whose iron cap Digby's cousin had broken his sword, but the iron cap had been lost in the ensuing scuffle. Digby's blade split his head in two, "and his brains flew into his neighbour's face."

Digby turned toward the foe who had been spattered with brains. "Stepping in with his left leg, [Digby] made himself master of his sword, and with his own did run him into the belly under his jack, so that he fell down, witnessing with a deep groan that his life was at her last minute."[4]

As the mortally wounded man cried out, the other gang members recognized his voice as that of their leader. As it was in his quarrel that they fought, they left off attacking Digby and rushed to their leader's side. Without uttering a word, he died on the spot.

Digby, who had suffered only a minor wound to his hand, walked in a leisurely manner toward his uncle's house. He soon encountered a number of armed men hurrying to his rescue. His cousin had found the gate locked when he returned home, and it had taken him some time to rouse the household.

Digby awoke the following day to find himself the talk of Madrid, and news of his fight soon carried back to England. The cause of it was revealed: a Spanish nobleman, who was a rival with Digby's cousin for the gentlewoman who lived near Lord Bristol's house, had forced her to sing in the window where the three men saw her. His intention was to entice Digby's cousin into an ambush.

There were no repercussions, and Digby remained in Spain until September. In addition to the foregoing account, a reference to the event was found appended to Digby's personal horoscope, reading, "Being 19 yeares old, 7 monethes, wth. 4 dayes, he had a wound on the same hand [the right hand] in a verie dangerous fray, being many upon him."[5]

Among the most interesting details in Digby's account is

this: "He dispensed his blows rather with fury than art; but his hand was so exercised in the perfectest rules of true art, that without his endeavours or taking notice, it never failed of making exactly regulated motions." A fencer is at a severe disadvantage when emotion or the pressures of combat cause him to forget his technique, but Digby was so well schooled that muscle memory and programmed responses did their job. As the saying goes, in combat a man does not rise to the occasion, he defaults to his level of training.[6]

NOTES

1. *Private Memoirs*, pp. lix, lx.
2. *Private Memoirs*, pp. 159–60.
3. *Private Memoirs*, pp. 161–62.
4. *Private Memoirs*, p. 164.
5. *Sir Kenelm Digby and His Venetia*, p. 72.
6. Barrett Tillman, *The Sixth Battle* (New York: Bantam Books, 1992), p. 82.

Herman H. Hanneken (1893–1986)

As one of the leaders of a successful revolt, Guillaume Sam became president of Haiti in March 1915, the fifth president of that turbulent nation in five years. He had been in office barely four months when he faced an uprising himself. Events came to a head on July 27, when he executed 167 leading citizens whom he suspected of rebel sympathies. A mob stormed his palace, forcing Sam to take refuge in the French embassy. Outraged citizens followed him inside, dragged him out of a bathroom in which he was hiding, broke his arms so that he couldn't resist, tossed him into the street, and chopped him to pieces with machetes.

During the anarchy that followed, U.S. President Woodrow Wilson sent in the Marines, justifying the incursion under the

Monroe Doctrine. Within a month, order was restored to the capital and a new government installed, but rebel bands continued to operate from the hills. Called bandits by the Americans, but known as *cacos* locally, they harassed the occupiers while supporting themselves by robbing their countrymen.

Herman H. Hanneken. (Credit: United States Marine Corps.)

To combat the cacos, the United States started a native police force called the Gendarmerie d'Haiti, commanded by officers and noncoms of the Marine Corps temporarily detached from their units. Commanding the Gendarmerie in the Grand Rivière District, and holding the brevet rank of captain, was Sgt. Herman Henry Hanneken.

Hanneken was born in St. Louis, Missouri, on June 23, 1893. He was 6 feet tall, lean and muscular, and was described as having the face of a "Viking warrior burning with the ambition to kill."[1] He had pursued a youthful desire to become a priest, then worked as a cowpuncher, and at 21, concerned that he was drifting, enlisted in the Corps. After serving in the Mexican campaign, he was posted to Haiti a year later at the outset of the insurrection. He found himself at home there and quickly picked up the native language, Creole, even mastering the different dialects. His leadership qualities were recognized, and within five years he had risen to sergeant, an unusual accomplishment in the Old Corps.

By early 1919, an army of cacos was operating in the back-country under the command of Charlemagne Massena Péralte. Charlemagne was a member of the Haitian aristocracy and, like many of the nation's elite, had been educated in France. In November 1917, after he had been convicted of attempting to steal a government payroll, he was sentenced to five years at hard labor, working on a road crew. He escaped after eight months and headed for the island's interior, where he gathered a band of cacos that eventually numbered 15,000.

Through the spring and summer of 1919, Charlemagne stepped up his guerrilla activities, looting and burning small towns. Brig. Gen. John H. Russell, commander of the Gendarmerie, ordered Maj. James J. Meade, who was responsible for the northern area of the island, to "get Charlemagne!"

This was a daunting task. It meant finding one Haitian in a nation of several million, and that one Haitian was well protected by bodyguards and enjoyed considerable popular support. Moreover, he was hiding in an unmapped mountainous area and never slept two consecutive nights in the same place.

Meade needed someone who was intelligent, cunning, fearless, and discreet. One who knew the country, was fluent in Creole, and had a good understanding of the people. The man who came to mind was Hanneken. Meade asked him, "Do you think you could get Charlemagne?"

Hanneken answered, "Yes, sir, I believe I could arrange to get him, if I have carte blanche."

His conditions were met, and Hanneken set about developing his plan. He knew there was little he could do on his own:

as the captain of the local Gendarmerie, he was a well-known figure whose movements would undoubtedly be reported to Charlemagne. What he needed was a local who could infiltrate Charlemagne's organization, gain his confidence, and then set him up.

Hanneken arranged a secret meeting with a local business-man, Jean Baptiste Conzé. He told him of the $3,000 reward for the bandit leader, but to his surprise Conzé had his own, non-mercenary, reasons for helping him. Hanneken said, "He knew Charlemagne, knew him well, but thought he was doing wrong to the country, that he had tied up the entire central part of the country . . . and that he should be eliminated so they could have peace. And he was willing to do the job, to go out and organize, and he said he could do it because he knew a lot of men in the district, that he could organize a band quickly."

In agreeing to the task, Conzé understood the chance he was taking. Those who crossed Charlemagne were executed as slowly and painfully as possible.

One thing Conzé requested was a secretary who could write French, as he could not and it would be necessary in order to correspond with Charlemagne. Hanneken assigned one of his Haitian troops, Private Edmond François, to the task. François would pretend to desert and join the cacos. Hanneken also gave Conzé 14 good rifles, 500 rounds of ammunition, and Hanneken's own nickel-plated, pearl-handled, .38-caliber Smith & Wesson revolver for his protection.

A few days later, Conzé left Grand Rivière, telling people he was going to join Charlemagne and fight Hanneken. It was a market day and the town was crowded, ensuring that word would spread far and wide. Conzé set himself up at Fort Capois, an old colonial fort at the top of a high hill, five hours' walk from town. In a short time he had gathered 60 men, whom he was able to feed with money Hanneken advanced him from his own pocket. Like all cacos, Conzé raided small villages and stole from the market women, and soon the locals were demanding that Hanneken do something about him. Hanneken made a couple of raids on Conzé's camp, always warning him in advance, and keeping his men at such a distance that the exchange of fire was ineffectual. Conzé sent messages to Charlemagne saying he wanted to join his army, but Charlemagne was suspicious, as the rumor had been spread that Conzé was acting as Hanneken's agent. Eventually the bandit chief sent a delegation to meet with Conzé, and, fortuitously, it was present for Hanneken's third raid. This time, after the bullets began flying, Hanneken ducked into the bushes and spilled a bottle of government-issued red ink over his arm, which he then wrapped with a bandage. Sounding the retreat, he pulled his men out, leaving Conzé's men to believe they had scored a great victory. "And of course we went back to Grand Rivière, and it happened that it was a market day with a lot of people, mostly women, at the market, and they saw me ride in, lying low on my horse, as though I was very badly hurt," said Hanneken.

For days Hanneken wore his arm in a sling, cursing in pain if it was jostled. No one was told of the ruse, and Hanneken had to fend off offers from the Marine doctor to dress his wound properly. The townspeople mocked him behind his back, and his reputation slipped badly among his fellow Marines.

With this triumph, Conzé at last earned the respect of Charlemagne. He was taken to meet him, and Charlemagne commissioned him "General Jean." Seeing Conzé's fine revolver, Charlemagne badgered him into exchanging it for his own pitted and tarnished model. Conzé consented in the name of goodwill.

Near the end of October, Charlemagne and as many as 5,000 of his cacos moved down to Fort Capois. Up to this point, Conzé had been slipping into Grand Rivière a few nights a week to report to Hanneken and get further infusions of cash, while telling his men that he was getting money from

Capt. Herman H. Hanneken and 2nd Lt. William R. Button in Haiti in 1919.
(Credit: United States Marine Corps.)

political supporters. Charlemagne did not permit this. Conzé kept insisting, and Charlemagne at last relented, sending some of his own men to accompany him. Along the way, Conzé took them to visit a distillery owned by his brother. After Charlemagne's men had gotten drunk and passed out, Conzé made his way alone to report to Hanneken. Hanneken was particularly irked to learn that the caco commander in chief was now the proud possessor of his pistol.

It was time to spring the trap. Hanneken told Conzé to attack Grand Rivière on the night of October 31. Hanneken would notify Colonel Meade so that a reception party of Marines would be awaiting them. Though Charlemagne was extremely wary, Hanneken thought Conzé could persuade him to set up headquarters in a house above Mazaire, 2 miles upriver from town, where he would consider himself safe from the fighting, but close enough to march into the town in the event of victory. While he was there, Hanneken would take a group of men and capture him.

On the afternoon of the 31st, when Conzé was ready to launch his attack, Charlemagne suddenly announced that he would remain at Fort Capois and wait for a messenger to bring him news. Conzé left with his men but sent back a few spies to follow Charlemagne. They saw him relocate his camp four miles away, atop another hill, very high up. Charlemagne didn't know he had been followed, but obviously he was still distrustful of Conzé. Unfortunately, there was no way at this time to get word to Hanneken of this hitch in the plan.

The same day, Hanneken took his subordinate, Lt. William R. Button, into his confidence, telling him that he had "volunteered" him for a "special and highly dangerous mission that night." Relieved to learn that his superior officer was no coward, Button jumped at the opportunity, though he had been suffering from recurring bouts of malarial fever. Hanneken also summoned 14 of the Haitian gendarmes in whom he had the most confidence. He told them that that night they would get Charlemagne, but if any of them didn't want to go, they didn't have to. They all volunteered.

Hanneken and Button rubbed lamp black over their skin, checking each other over to make sure they didn't miss any spots. Then the whole group dressed in dirty clothes like the cacos wore. Hanneken and Button put on sombreros to cover their hair and obscure their faces. The gendarmes carried their issue carbines, with their ammunition in a *macoutte*, or cloth bag. Hanneken carried a Colt model 1911 .45 in his waistband at his side, and a .38 revolver tucked in at the small of his back. Button was entrusted with a Browning Automatic Rifle and a pouchful of loaded 20-round magazines. "I wanted an automatic rifle," said Hanneken. "I knew I didn't have a chance with the carbines and the pistols that I carried. . . . I wanted a Marine that knew how to operate a gun well, and he did."

Hanneken gave an order: "Nobody, none of you people, fire a rifle no matter for what purpose, until I fire the first shot with my .45." As he later explained, "I could not have a shot fired going up to where Charlemagne was, it would spoil the whole show, because it would put them on the alert and they would be watching everything."

The group waited in a coffee grove above the town until the rattle of rifle fire let them know that Conzé's attack was under way. Hanneken and his men headed for Mazaire, where they expected to find Charlemagne. However, before they reached it, they were intercepted by Private François, who told them that the commander was still high in the hills, accompanied by 700 handpicked men.

This was a crushing blow to a plan that had been in the works for four months. Most men would have scrubbed the mission, but Hanneken knew that if he gave up now he would have failed miserably, having done nothing but funded the cacos and allowed them to operate for months undisturbed. It seemed to him that there was still a chance for success.

"Button," he said, "we will be the caco detachment that carries the news of victory to Charlemagne."

Button, who was suffering one of his bouts of fever, said, "Captain, I don't think I can make it."

"All right, but give me the rifle," said Hanneken. "You can go back to Grand Rivière to my quarters."

"I can't do that."

"I'd rather have you do that than fall out on me up in the hills and I'd have to disband the whole plan because I can't leave you alone."

"Captain," said Button, "I won't fall out. I'll go with you. I won't fall out."

"Well, all right then," said Hanneken.

Setting off at around 10 o'clock, the group hiked for two hours until it was stopped by a sentry, who called, "Halt, *qui vous?*"

François gave the proper countersign, "General Jean," and suddenly they were surrounded by a group of about 40 cacos. Hanneken was confident he could handle the dialect well enough if he had to talk, but he knew Button could not. They had several of their men crowd closely around them to discourage anyone from approaching. The cacos were impressed by the new rifles the gendarmes carried, which they said they had captured from the barracks at Grand Rivière. In the middle of the hubbub, Hanneken told François to hurry up the trail ahead of them and report to Charlemagne that Conzé captured Grand Rivière, and that General Bias was waiting at the first outpost to come up with the report. François hesitated, but Hanneken said, "You've got to do it, this is life or death for our crowd."

François hurried up the trail, met with Charlemagne, and about an hour later came down with permission for "General Bias" to proceed. However, François didn't think they could pass through all the security. "Captain, you can't get up there," he insisted. "You've got to go through five outposts, and they'll probably stop you at every one."

"Let's go," said Hanneken.

They were waved through the next two outposts, but at the fourth there was a giant of a man standing guard. He stood by the trail with a pistol in his hand and his back to a tree, and on the other side of the trail there was a steep drop-off, off of which he could actually have pushed any man as they passed by. Hanneken walked by him, mumbling a response to his challenge, but as Button attempted to pass, the giant grabbed his arm. "Where did you get that pretty rifle?" he demanded.

Button had folded his arms over the BAR to cover its protruding magazine, but was unable to conceal its stock and barrel. Hanneken rested his hand on his .45; as he later said, "I'd have killed him, naturally, but the whole show would have been off." One of the trusted gendarmes, Sergeant Compere, intervened, insisting that they had to hurry to see Charlemagne, and the guard released Button.

At the last outpost, they were stopped by four guards who said that only General Bias was to proceed and that his men must remain behind.

François responded angrily, "Why? The general wants his men up, these are his men. What's the matter with you people? They have been fighting down in Grand Rivière, and now they're up here and you mistrust them?"

The guards relented. "Go on," said one of them.

As they approached Charlemagne's camp, François said, "There he is," and then ducked into the bushes. Said Hanneken, "I didn't look back, I didn't care about anything else just so Button was with me. I wanted that rifle near me."

As he neared the clearing, he was glad that he had sent François ahead earlier, as there now was a campfire going in Charlemagne's camp, whereas otherwise it would have been in complete darkness. Hanneken said:

So I kept on going, and when I got up there,

there were two big trees and the trail looked
like it was going between the two trees and I
saw Charlemagne. I had not met him but I had
seen him before, and I knew what he looked
like, and I picked him out right away. There
were about ten men around him; they were his
staff. He looked to me as though he was arranging to go down to Grand Rivière, he was issuing orders about what he wanted done, and
they were talking, and, of course, I kept on
going. Outside of the woman that was kneeling
with a coffee pot over this little fire, which was
making it possible to see, I could see everybody.
. . . I walked up and got between the two trees,
where there was a sentry on each side with a
rifle, and the barrel of the rifle hit my head, it
stopped me . . . and I pulled my head up and I
saw that the two men, although they stopped
me and had me there, were not looking at me.
They were looking over to Charlemagne . . .
they wanted to know whether to let this bum
come up, in other words. Well, by that time, he
was dead. The minute I saw they weren't looking I pulled my gun up and fired one shot at
Charlemagne. I aimed right at his heart.

After his shot, a blow knocked Hanneken to the ground,
possibly from the rifle barrel of one of the sentries (it isn't
clear from his account), causing him to drop his .45. Button
opened fire with his BAR. The woman poured the coffee over
the fire, dousing it immediately. Hanneken pulled his .38 and
got back up, shooting the two sentries while Button fired
bursts at Charlemagne's men. At the same time, the gendarmes were coming up the trail. "I thought I was going to
die right there, by my own men," Hanneken recalled. "They

were shooting from the hip, coming up, and I don't know how it was possible that I wasn't hit, but I yelled loud right away, 'Cease fire!' and everyone heard me, even Button stopped firing. . . . He fired a hundred shots before I yelled out to cease fire."

Hanneken continued:

> So next, I got them up to where I was and I put the men in a circle [prone, facing outward] and I put Button in the center of the circle and I got in the center and of course it was pitch dark, you couldn't see nothing, but they started shooting at us from three different angles, and when they did I had Button fire a blast at them, you know, about ten rounds in that area. . . . Finally, after about half an hour, there was no more firing from the bandits from Charlemagne's outfit. So by this time, I don't know what time it was, it was getting probably toward four o'clock. I told Button, "Look, everything seems quiet now, I'm going to try to crawl up there where I thought Charlemagne was, where I fired the one shot."
>
> So I went up there crawling on my knees, and when I got up there I felt a pair of shoes and a leg and I went up the leg to the holster he had, I pulled my pistol out of his holster, and I knew in the dark that it was my pistol, so I knew it was Charlemagne. I'd done something there which I never reported—I fired two more shots into him, from an angle like this, you know, and the two shots also went through his heart. When the doctors examined him they told me that three bullets went through his heart. I shouldn't have done that [but] I didn't

know whether he was dead. The guy could have
had a knife and could have stabbed me. He
could have been suffering, but I didn't know,
and I was mad, too, that he had my pistol.

Hanneken pulled Charlemagne's body into the center of
his men. While they were still on guard, two Haitians came
out of the jungle and were taken prisoner. Hanneken lit a
match and showed them Charlemagne's corpse. "One of them,
he was on his haunches, he just flew out of there, and that's
what I really wanted, them to go back to tell the others that
Charlemagne was dead."

Getting a door from a shack, the gendarmes tied Charlemagne's body to it so that they could carry it back. They also
brought down the bodies of nine of Charlemagne's top men who
had been killed, nine rifles, three revolvers, seven swords, 200
rounds of ammunition, 15 horses, and a large amount of correspondence that would provide valuable intelligence.

While they were on the trail, they encountered a group of
cacos returning from the attack on Grand Rivière—an attack
that had gone badly, thanks to Colonel Meade's Marines.
Hanneken said, "I was riding a horse, and I was in the lead,
and when they came around a bend in the road they saw us
and they wanted the countersign, so we gave everything. And
then I let them all come up, till I thought we had enough
alongside of us, and then we opened up on them. You never
saw how fast people can disappear."

Hanneken sent a man ahead with a message to Colonel
Meade letting him know that they were coming in, so that
they wouldn't be mistaken for cacos. In the crowded market-
place of the town, his men laid down the door with
Charlemagne on it.

Hanneken and Button tried to slip back to his house unno-
ticed to clean up, but Meade shouted, "Three cheers for
Captain Hanneken!" and the Marines hurrahed in response.

The next day Hanneken took a group of Marines to mop up the cacos still left at Fort Capois. Within days, hundreds of cacos came down to Grand Rivière to surrender. Charlemagne's body was photographed and the prints distributed throughout Haiti as proof of his death; with the popular belief in voodoo, this was felt to be necessary.

The reward money for Charlemagne was divided between Conzé, Private François, and Sergeant Compere. As a Marine, Hanneken received no share of the reward, and in fact had difficulty being reimbursed for the $800 he had spent funding the operation.

The death of Charlemagne broke the back of the uprising in Haiti. The exploit was widely celebrated, and President Wilson described it as one of the "most singularly important acts of heroism in my time." Hanneken and Button were awarded the Medal of Honor, and Hanneken received an officer's commission.

The attention grated on Hanneken, who was a modest, reserved man and something of a loner, more concerned with his next mission than with collecting accolades.

On April 1, 1920, Hanneken killed a second Haitian bandit leader, Osiris Joseph, for which he was awarded the Navy Cross. From what little we know, this was handled very much like the Péralte hit, with Hanneken slipping into Joseph's camp and taking him out. In keeping with General Lejeune's wishes, Hanneken never discussed this mission. Lejeune, who was sensitive to accusations of Marine atrocities in Haiti, declared that he did "not desire any publication which refers to the 'shooting and killing' of bandits to be released."[2]

Button died in 1920 from malaria, but Hanneken went on to a long and brilliant military career. In February 1929, in Nicaragua, he captured Gen. Manuel Maria Jiron Runano, rebel chief and chief of staff to Augusto César Sandino (the leader of the rebellion against the U.S. military in Nicaragua between 1927 and 1933), earning him a second Navy Cross and the nickname "the Bandit Catcher." Again, few details were ever released. In World War II Lieutenant Colonel Hanneken served in the Pacific, commanding the 2nd Battalion of the 7th Marines. He picked up a nickname, "Hard-Headed Hanneken," a play on his initials as well as his nature. He earned the Silver Star at Guadalcanal, the Legion of Merit at Pelelieu, and the Bronze Star at New Britain.

There is little information about his World War II experiences, but Medal of Honor awardee Mitchell Paige had an interesting encounter with him on Guadalcanal when Hanneken visited the front lines. Wanting a closer look at the situation, he told Paige to get a machete and follow him into the jungle, which was very thick in that area. Paige wrote:

> He reminded me of a cat the way he put each foot down and the way he suddenly stopped and stared at one point. I was just wondering where we were going when, without any warning, the colonel had his .45 caliber pistol out and fired one round up into a tree. I stopped in my tracks and a moment later I saw a black clad body falling out of a tree just ahead of us. With his pistol still in his hand, the colonel eased over to the victim and rolled him over into the brush. This was a Japanese sniper in his sniper suit, including the split-toe cloth sandals.
>
> When we returned to my position I couldn't forget the laconic comment Colonel Hanneken exhorted me with. "Don't forget—always keep your eyes in the trees as well as on the deck."[3]

There is also this tantalizing tidbit in a *New York Times* account of the battle for Pelelieu: "During the night the Japanese tried their typical infiltration of American lines. The next morning 20 dead Nipponese were counted around Hanneken's command post."[4] Perhaps it's merely coincidental, but three magazines for a .45 hold 21 rounds. Even Hanneken may have needed more than one shot occasionally.

Hanneken retired from the Marines in 1948 with the rank of brigadier general. He never wrote his memoirs and refused to sanction a movie to be made about the killing of Charlemagne Péralte. However, in 1982 he met with a Marine Corps historian and provided a detailed oral history of the incident, which provides the basis for this account.

Hanneken died on August 23, 1986, in La Jolla, California, at age 93.

NOTES

1. R.R. Keen, "Death by Firelight," *Leatherneck*, February 1991, p. 23.
2. Lt. Col. Jon T. Hoffman, USMCR, *Chesty: The Story of Lieutenant General Lewis B. Puller, USMC* (New York: Random House, 2001), p. 37.
3. Mitchell Paige, *A Marine Named Mitch* (New York: Vantage Press, 1975), pp. 125–6.
4. "Yanks Invade Second Palau Island; Smash Jap Attacks," *Chicago Daily Tribune*, September 18, 1944, p. 1.

John Wesley Hardin (1853–1895)

> *"I swear before God that I never shot a man in my life except in self-defense."*
>
> —John Wesley Hardin

At John Wesley Hardin's birth, the midwife is said to have predicted he would either be a great hero or a monumental villain, and which of those he was is still the subject of some debate. His supporters describe him as a man of honor, a devoted husband and father, and a hero of Reconstruction-era Texas who stood up for Confederate principles against federal oppression. His detractors describe him as a vicious racist and psychopathic killer, who once shot a man for snoring.

There is no question that he was the foremost gunfighter of the Old West, though there is some disagreement about how many men he killed. He had exceptional talent with his pistols, according to men qualified to judge. Texas Ranger Jack Duncan said, "He was the quickest man with a pistol I ever

John Wesley Hardin, probably photographed at the time of his wedding in 1872.
(Credit: Oklahoma State Library, Western History Collection.)

saw, and was a dead shot. He could take one in each hand and
swing them around his forefingers and keep one of them going
off all the time."[1] Ranger James Gillett said that Hardin could
manipulate a pair of pistols "as a sleight-of-hand performer
manipulates a coin . . . the quick draw, the spin, the rolls, pin-
wheeling, border shift—he did them all with magical precision."[2] Another ranger, Napoleon Jennings, wrote that Hardin

was able to shoot with his left hand as well as his right. He added, "He could fire a Winchester repeating rifle so rapidly that a continuous stream of fire came from the muzzle and four or five empty shells from the ejector were in the air at the same time, falling at different heights, to the ground."[3]

A few months before his death, Hardin wrote his autobiography, and it provides the only information we have on most of the events of his life. He describes about 30 separate gunfights in which he killed between 40 and 42 men, depending on how many of those he shot died as a result. Nearly half of these incidents were with the pistol and the rest with shotgun or rifle. Whether the number is exaggerated or understated is anyone's guess, as is Hardin's truthfulness in recounting the details of those fights. He presents himself as an honorable man who had no choice but to defend his life on a great number of occasions. As one journalist wryly put it, "[He] must have been the sort of young man that people just naturally picked on."[4]

Hardin was born in Bonham, Texas, on May 26, 1853, son of a circuit-riding Methodist preacher. He grew up hunting and was a crack shot by the time he was 9, by which time he wanted to run away from home to fight the Yankees. His father gave him a sound thrashing to disabuse him of the notion, but still, as he wrote, he "grew up a rebel," hating the Union and all it stood for.

Texas was never successfully invaded by the North, yet at war's end, it was occupied by federal troops under Reconstruction rule. The Emancipation Proclamation was enforced in June 1865, overturning the racial hierarchy and destroying the state's plantation-based economy. Many former slaves were hired as state policemen by the radical Republican governor, Edmund Davis. These factors had the effect of stirring up anti-government feelings and racial animosity.

Hardin killed his first man at age 15, a freed slave named Mage. Hardin and a cousin had had a wrestling bout with

Mage, which had ended with Mage's nose being bloodied. Mage wanted to continue the fight, but bystanders stepped in and prevented it. Mage threatened to get his gun and kill Hardin. Hardin went to get his as well, but his uncle prevented him from returning to the fight. The following day, Hardin was riding along a road when he encountered Mage on foot, carrying a stout stick. The two argued about the events of the previous day. Hardin tried to ride away, but Mage ran up and grabbed his horse by the bridle, threatening Hardin and striking him with his stick. Hardin pulled a Colt .44 revolver and, as he wrote, "I shot him loose. He kept coming back and every time he would start I would shoot again and again until I shot him down."

By the standards that prevailed at the time, this would be considered a fair fight: there was an existing quarrel between the two men, both were armed (albeit unequally), and both had expressed an intention to kill the other. However, Hardin did not think he would fare well in court. He wrote, "The killing of a Negro meant certain death at the hands of a court backed by Northern bayonets. . . . I became a fugitive, not from justice be it known, but from the injustice and misrule of the people who had subjugated the South."

Six weeks later, he got word that three soldiers were coming to arrest him. Hardin armed himself and set up an ambush at a point where they would have to ford a creek. "I waylaid them, as I had no mercy on men whom I knew only wanted to get my body to torture and kill. It was war to the knife with me, and I brought it on by opening the fight with the double-barreled shotgun and ending it with a cap-and-ball six-shooter."

Local farmers took the soldiers' horses and concealed the bodies.

There followed a steady stream of homicides: Hardin killed one soldier in a squad in a "free and fast fight"; he killed a local, Benjamin Bradley, after an argument following a card game; he shot a circus roustabout who had hit him; and he killed the male half of a couple that set him up for robbery.

In January 1871, Hardin was arrested. While in jail, he was able to buy a loaded revolver from one of the other prisoners. Hearing he was to be transported to Waco, 225 miles away, he tied it under his arm beneath his clothes. The deputies who came to escort him, E.T. Stokes and Jim Smolly (sometimes spelled Smalley), failed to find it in a cursory search. As they set out, the lawmen told the 17-year-old Hardin they would kill him should he attempt to escape, and he acted suitably frightened. "I, of course, talked very humbly, was full of morality and religion and was strictly down on lawlessness of all kinds. I tried to convince them that I was not an outlaw and did not wish to escape anywhere," wrote Hardin.

After a few days on the trail, he was left alone with Smolly, while Stokes went to a farm to requisition fodder. Sitting on a stump, Smolly idly cursed and threatened Hardin. Hardin leaned against his pony and pretended to be crying while he loosened the pistol from under his arm. When it was free, he turned and ordered Smolly to put his hands up. When Smolly went for his pistol, Hardin killed him and escaped on his horse before Stokes returned. An elderly black woman who witnessed the shooting recalled it differently: she said that Hardin shot Smolly in the back, and again in the stomach as Smolly drew his pistol and turned toward him.[5]

In the spring of 1871, Hardin headed a cattle drive to Abilene. He had grown into a man who stood 5 foot 9, weighed about 160 pounds, and had piercing gray eyes tinged with violet. Ranger Jennings wrote that his eyes "had the glitter and very much the expression of a rattlesnake. They were ever moving here and there and were not quiet for a moment. This habit of glancing continually right and left and behind him was caused by the constant outlook he had to maintain against surprise, for he had many bitter enemies who would not have hesitated to kill him from behind, although they dared not face him."[6]

Within days of the start of this trip, he shot a Mexican who drew a knife on him after they quarreled over the rules of a card game; he killed an Indian whom he claimed shot an arrow at him; and he killed another Indian who was trying to cut a steer from his herd.

On May 28, after he had forded the Little Arkansas River, Hardin got into an argument with the driver of a Mexican herd who had allowed his steers to intermingle with Hardin's. According to Hardin, the Mexican, whom he identified only as "Hosea" (José), retrieved a rifle from a wagon and shot at him from about 100 yards. The bullet knocked off Hardin's hat. José tried to get off another shot, but his weapon malfunctioned. He then pulled his revolver and advanced on Hardin, shooting as he walked.

Hardin wrote, "I was riding a fiery gray horse and the pistol I had was an old cap and ball, which I had worn out shooting on the trail. There was so much play between the cylinder and the barrel that it would not burst a cap or fire unless I held the cylinder with one hand and pulled the trigger with the other."

After a few failed attempts to do so, Hardin finally dismounted, let go of his horse, gripped the cylinder, and put a bullet into José's thigh at about 10 paces, which "stunned him a little." Hardin tried to shoot again, but the hammer fell between the firing caps.

At this point the two men grappled. While they fought, six or seven other Mexicans rode up close. Hardin's cousin Jim Clements persuaded the gathering *vaqueros* not to shoot and separated the two men. Hardin's blood was up, but he agreed to return to the camp, as his pistol was useless and Clements' was unloaded.

At camp, Hardin and Clements armed themselves with better revolvers as half a dozen Mexicans began approaching them on horseback. One of the cowboys, Fred Duderstadt, said, "At Hardin's request his companions took no part in the fight, as he considered two Texas cowboys were equal to six Mexicans."[7]

José fired at Hardin from about 75 yards and missed. Hardin wrote, "I concluded to charge him and turn my horse loose at him, firing as I rode. The first ball did the work. I shot him through the heart and he fell over the horn of his saddle, pistol in hand and one in the scabbard, the blood pouring from his mouth."

There were two parties of Mexicans continuing to shoot at them, one from about 75 yards and the other from about 150 yards. "We charged the first party and held our fire until we got close to them. They never weakened but kept shooting at us all the time. When we got right on them and opened up, they turned their horses, but we were in the middle of them, dosing them with lead. . . . A few more bullets quickly and rightly placed silenced the party forever."

As the second party rode at them, firing their weapons, Hardin shot a steer in the nose, starting a stampede. Most of the vaqueros scattered, but there was one who stood his ground and kept using his pistol. "We cross-fired on him and I ended his existence by putting a ball through his temples."

Two more participants pretended to surrender and then pulled pistols and fired at Hardin at short range. Hardin wrote, "I don't know how they missed me. In an instant I fired first at one, then at the other. The first I shot through the heart, and he dropped dead. The second I shot through the lungs and Jim shot him too. He fell off his horse, and I was going to shoot him again when he begged and held up both hands. I could not shoot a man, not even a treacherous Mexican, begging and down. Besides, I knew he would die anyway."[8]

This account was substantially verified by Duderstadt, as well as by accounts published in local newspapers. It is Hardin's best performance as a gunfighter, far outclassing most of his others, which were inglorious affairs he could have avoided by not picking fights or gambling while drunk.

The fight brought Hardin's score up to 20 men. His reputation spread, and by the time he reached Abilene he was the talk of the town. Cowhands debated whether he or the town's famed marshal, Wild Bill Hickok, would win a showdown.

Hardin flouted Abilene's laws against carrying firearms, wearing two Colt Army revolvers at all times. Hickok, who had made a point of being friendly with the young pistolero, overlooked the transgression as long as he could. But when Hardin provoked Hickok by flaunting the weapons in front of him, Hickok ordered him to take them off and told him that he was under arrest. As Hardin took his pistols out of their holsters and offered them butts first, Hickok reached for them. Hardin described what followed:

> I reversed them and whirled them over on him with the muzzles in his face, springing back at the same time. I told him to put his pistol up, which he did. I cursed him for a long haired scoundrel that would shoot a boy with his back to him (as I had been told he had intended to do to me). He said, "Little Arkansaw, you have been wrongly informed."
>
> By this time a big crowd had gathered with pistols and arms. They kept urging me to kill him. Down the street a squad of policemen were coming, but Wild Bill motioned them to go back and at the same time asked me not to let the mob shoot him.
>
> I shouted, "This is my fight and I'll kill the first man that fires a gun."
>
> Bill said: "You are the gamest and quickest boy I ever saw. Let us compromise this matter and I will be your friend. Let us go in here and take a drink, as I want to talk to you and give you some advice."[9]

According to Hardin, the two parted as friends, with Hickok giving him permission to carry his guns.

That incident happened before noon, but the day was far from over. In a restaurant that night, Hardin overheard a man cursing Texans. When Hardin stood up and responded, "I'm a Texan," the man went for his pistol. The two men exchanged shots and missed. As the man ran for the door, Hardin fired a second round that hit him in his mouth and exited behind his left ear. Hardin left the restaurant, jumping over his late assailant, and, encountering a policeman on the sidewalk, pointed his pistol at him and ordered, "Hands up!" The policeman complied. Hardin got on his horse and rode to Cottonwood, 35 miles north, "to await results."

While Hardin lingered in Cottonwood, drinking and gambling, a cowboy there named Billy Coran (sometimes spelled Cohron) was shot in the back by a Mexican vaquero named Bideno, who fled southward. Such was Hardin's reputation as a gunman that some cattlemen urged him to apprehend the killer. They provided him with a warrant and appointed him a deputy.

On June 27, Hardin set out with three other cowboys. They rode hard and in a few days caught up with Bideno at a restaurant in Sumner City, Texas. With his weapon drawn, Hardin entered the restaurant and confronted Bideno, saying, "I am after you to surrender. I do not wish to hurt you, and you will not be hurt while you are in my hands."

According to Hardin, Bideno went for his gun, so he had to shoot him.

A newspaper in the nearby town of Oxford gave a different account of the killing, leaving out the part about the offer of surrender and assurance of good treatment. According to this account, Hardin walked in and without a word shot Bideno. The article says: "The shot took effect in the forehead, passing through the head and the partition, barely missing a lady in the next room. It flattened against the stove. The so-called Mexican was totally unconscious of danger. Though facing the door fairly in which the assassin stood, [he] was struck down while drinking coffee, with the cup to his lips."[10]

The most infamous killing attributed to Hardin occurred on August 6, in Abilene's American Hotel. A newspaper provided this account: "As he went to bed in a small rooming house, the rumbling snores of another guest in an adjoining room disturbed his rest. The outraged Mr. Hardin guessed at the position of the snorer on the opposite side of the thin partition, placed one of his revolvers within six inches of the wall, and fired. The guess was good and Wes turned over and went to sleep . . . dead men don't snore."[11]

Rather than fire in this deliberate a manner, it is more likely that a drunken Hardin impulsively sent several rounds through the wall as a warning to the offender, a Charles Couger, and one just happened to connect. Far from going back to sleep, Hardin was immediately "gone to Texas."

In his autobiography, Hardin gives an alibi version of this incident, claiming he shot an intruder who broke into his room at night brandishing a dagger and then fled town as he was certain that he would never get a fair hearing.

On October 6, in Nopal, Texas, Hardin got to use the "border roll," the trick he had demonstrated to Hickok, on two black state policemen who tried to arrest him. After Green Paramore and John Lackey recognized him in a small grocery store, Paramore entered the store and said, "Throw up your hands or die!"

Hardin recalls:

> I said "all right," and turning around saw a big black Negro with his pistol cocked and presented. I said, "Look out, you will let that pistol go off, and I don't want to be killed accidentally."
> He said, "Give me those pistols."
> I said, "all right," and handed him the pistols, handle foremost. One of the pistols turned

a somerset in my hand and went off. Down came the Negro, with his pistol cocked, and as I looked outside, I saw another Negro on a white mule firing into the house at me. I told him to hold up, but he kept on, so I turned my Colts .45 on him and knocked him off his mule my first shot. I turned around then to see what had become of No. 1 and I saw him sprawling on the floor with a bullet through his head, quivering in blood.[12]

This killing incensed the local black community, which threatened "with torch and knife [to] depopulate the entire county." Governor Davis offered a $400 reward for Hardin's capture. Hardin says that in September a posse of Negroes came looking for him, but he killed three and the others "returned sadder and wiser."

On February 29, 1872, Hardin married Jane Bowen, then 14 years old, and set up housekeeping in Gonzales, Texas. Hardin described her as "the prettiest and sweetest girl in the country," and fathered three children with her, but he spent very little time at home. "No one knowledgeable would ever call John Wesley Hardin a family man," said Hardin biographer Leon Metz. "He spent most of his adult life sleeping on the ground, on the run or in prison. His children didn't even come to his funeral."[13]

There follow more additions to Hardin's tally. He shot a pair of Mexican bandits while traveling and was not sure whether he killed one or both. In Willis, Texas, "some fellows tried to arrest me for carrying a pistol, but they got the contents thereof instead." After Hardin saw Sonny Speights, a black state policeman, browbeating a white child, he insulted him, and Speights went for his gun; Hardin put a bullet through his shoulder with a derringer he had palmed in his left hand. He shot and wounded Phil Sublet, with whom he'd been gambling, and was seriously wounded in return. When he refused to use some of his gambling winnings to buy James B. Morgan a drink, Morgan took offense and drew his pistol; Hardin was faster and shot him just above the left eye.[14] The early-20th century humorist Irvin Cobb found satirical fodder in Hardin's autobiography: "On such-and-such a day, as he told it, he met-such-and-such a party, killed him and passed on. There is no variety to his narrative, no illuminating touches in his descriptive paragraphs. He might just as well have been swatting flies for all the thrill he was able to get out of the transactions or for all the thrill he was able to impart to his narrative. Toward the last, excepting to a life insurance actuary, the thing grew desperately monotonous."[15]

In April 1873, Hardin became involved in one of Texas's bloodiest and longest-running feuds, the Sutton-Taylor feud. Hardin was on the Taylor side, as he considered the Sutton faction to represent "mob law." In concert with Jim Taylor, he killed John "Jack" Helm, sheriff of DeWitt County and the leader of the Sutton faction, and he vaguely acknowledged having been involved in two other feud killings.

Hardin got word that Charles Webb, a former Texas Ranger and deputy sheriff of the neighboring county, intended to kill him and capture Taylor for the reward; and, furthermore, that he had said that "the sheriff of Comanche, John Carnes, was no man or sheriff because he allowed Hardin and his gang of killers to roam free." On his 21st birthday, May 26, 1874, Hardin attended a carnival in the town of Comanche with a group of friends, including Jim Taylor and Bud Dixon. His horse won a race, and his bets garnered him more than $3,000. The group celebrated by drinking heavily and became increasingly unruly. Hardin and friends were standing in front of a saloon when Webb approached. What followed is described in a newspaper article, in which Hardin's intimidating manner comes through clearly:

Webb came on and started to go into the saloon, passing near Hardin. The latter detained him, asking if he was not the Sheriff of Brown County. Webb replied, "No, I am the Deputy Sheriff."

Hardin then said, "I understand you have papers for me."

Webb responded that he did not know him.

"I am that damned desperado, John Wesley Hardin. Now you know me."

Webb then informed him that he had no papers for him.

Hardin demanded to know what Webb held in his hand [which was behind his back].

The latter exhibited his hand, in which he held nothing but a cigar.

Hardin then said, "I have heard that you said that John Carnes, the Sheriff of this county, is no man and no sheriff."

This Webb also denied.

At this time Judge Thurmond, of Brownwood, who was standing in the street, called to Webb, saying, "Come here, Charlie," at which Hardin turned to Thurmond, saying, "You go on; we are attending to Charlie now."

Webb started to go to Thurmond, but was again detained by Hardin, who remarked, "You are not going away from me in that way."

Webb then stepped back, remarking: "No, Goddamn you, I am not afraid of you," and drawing his pistol at the same time. The pistol fired accidentally as he drew it from the scabbard, and Hardin, Taylor, and Dixon fired at the same time, their balls taking effect, Webb falling to the ground. Webb fired one shot after

> he fell, when Taylor advanced upon him and
> shot him again, killing him instantly.[16]

Hardin's own account of this incident is substantially the same, though he credits himself with an initial headshot that killed Webb and claims Webb's first bullet grazed his side. Hardin and his friends escaped on some horses he cut loose from a hitching post. (He mentioned that he later returned them, priding himself on being no horse thief.)

The reward on Hardin was raised to $4,000, and there followed one of the largest manhunts in Texas history as the rangers scoured the area for him and his gang. After several running gun battles, in which Hardin claimed to have killed two rangers, he escaped the net and fled to Florida. Not so fortunate were his brother Joe, Bud Dixon, and other members of the gang, who were captured and lynched.

Even while on the lam, Hardin found time for mischief. After a black man named Eli was arrested for attempting to rape a white woman in Gainesville, Hardin went with a group of men to the jail and burned it down, killing the suspect. He wrote, "The Negroes were very much excited over the burning, but the coroner set everything all right by declaring that Eli had burned himself up in setting the jail on fire. The coroner himself, by the way, was one of our party the night before."[17]

In his book, Hardin frequently mentions his fear that if he were arrested, he would not receive a fair trial, but be taken by a mob and lynched. Apparently, as long as he was part of the mob rather than its victim, it struck him as rather a good joke.

Hardin's family came to live with him in Florida, and by monitoring the mail to Jane's father, Texas Ranger Jack Duncan figured out where he was. While Hardin was on a train, returning from a high-stakes poker game, four lawmen swarmed him, grabbing his arms and wrestling him to the round before he could reach a pistol hidden in his trousers.

Hardin fought like a demon until ranger John Armstrong smacked him on the head a few times with his pistol.

As he was transported back to Texas, crowds of curiosity seekers gathered at the train depots to see the famous desperado. Those who were permitted to speak with him found him charming and witty. One man, who had ridden from Memphis to Texarkana to meet him, said, "Why, there is nothing bad in your face. Your life has been misrepresented to me. Here is $50. Take it from a sympathizer."

Hardin did his best to ingratiate himself with his captors, Duncan and Armstrong, and to put them at ease. When he was served a meal, he politely asked them to remove his handcuffs so he could eat.

> Armstrong unlocked the jewelry and started to turn around, exposing his six-shooter to me, when Jack [Duncan] jerked him around and pulled his pistol at the same time. "Look out," he said, "John will kill us and escape." Of course, I laughed at him and ridiculed the idea. It was really the very chance I was looking for, but Jack had taken the play away just before it got ripe. I intended to jerk Armstrong's pistol, kill Jack Duncan or make him throw up his hands. I could have made him unlock my shackles, or get the key from his dead body and do it myself. I could then have easily made my escape. That time never came again.[18]

Hardin was tried and convicted of second-degree murder in the killing of Charles Webb. Asked if he wanted to make any remarks before he was sentenced, Hardin delivered a lengthy statement, insisting that he had never threatened any citizen of Comanche and was "incapable of homicide." Unconvinced, the judge sentenced him to 25 years in the Huntsville State Penitentiary.

While in prison, Hardin wrote to his wife and children regularly. In endless, randomly punctuated sentences, Hardin proclaimed his love for his wife, ranted about his innocence, pontificated philosophically, and offered his children moral guidance. The following advice was in a letter to his son, John Wesley Hardin Jr.:

> Son Should any lecherous treacherous Scoundrel no matter what garb he wears or what insignia he boast even if it be the ministerial robe, assault the character and try to debauch the mind and hearts of either of your Sisters or mother, I say Son don't make any threats but just quietly get your gun a double barrel let it be a good gun have no other kind, and go gunning for the enemy of mankind, and when you find him just deliberately Shoot him down like you would a mad dog or a wild beast . . . . Son if it ever becomes necessary to Shield your body from the assassins blow dont wait to be Struc down, to late then but stay the poisonous dagger in uplifted hand with one mighty death blow. Ah my Son it is a Serious affair to kill a man, but to every man it is more Serious to be killed.[19]

In the first five years of his confinement, Hardin made several escape attempts and was punished with solitary confinement and floggings. He eventually accepted his fate and became a model prisoner, spending his latter years studying law.

Hardin was pardoned in February 1894, after 15 years, eight months, and 12 days behind bars. Jane had died in 1892. His children were grown and felt little connection to him.

At the end of March 1895, Hardin drifted into El Paso,

with a set of law books and five revolvers.[20] He set up a legal practice, but soon slipped back into old habits of heavy drinking and gambling.

On the night of May 2, Hardin was throwing craps at the Gem Saloon and losing heavily. When the dealer joked about it, Hardin drew his .41 Colt, and said, "Since you are trying to be cute, just hand over the money I lost here."

The dealer started to give him all the money, but Hardin would only take the $95 he had lost.

As he left the room, he overheard someone make a disparaging remark about his sportsmanship. He immediately returned. As he wrote to the newspaper: "I said to everyone in the house and connected with the play, I understand from the reflective remarks that some of you disapprove my play. Now if this be so, be men and get in line and show your manhood, to which no one made any reply, but others nodded that I was right and they approved my play."[21]

Hardin frequently bragged about his winnings as a gambler, but it seems he owed a good part of his success to his reputation as a sore loser.

El Paso is on the Rio Grande, and is connected to Juarez, Mexico, by a bridge. This made it an attractive locale for marginal characters, as they could slip from one side of the border to the other. One such character was Martin M'Rose, who hid out in Juarez after he was accused of cattle rustling.[22] M'Rose's wife, Beulah, engaged Hardin to help Martin with his extradition fight. A former prostitute, Beulah was considered a beauty by frontier standards, and Hardin soon began mixing pleasure with business. He also dictated his autobiography to her, and she put it in manuscript form. Beulah must have been a fairly literate person, as the style of the book shows a marked improvement over the letters Hardin wrote from prison.

With money borrowed from Beulah, Hardin purchased a half ownership in the Wigwam Saloon and celebrated the venture with a party in Washington Park on July 4, 1895. He demonstrated his shooting ability by setting up playing cards and putting three or four shots into each at a distance of five long paces. He signed and dated the cards, then gave them away or swapped them for drinks. Some of the cards have been preserved and show all shots grouped within an inch or an inch and a half. Evidently, his heavy drinking did not affect his aim.

Hardin once invited Carl Longuemare, an El Paso newsboy, to watch him practice with his pistols in his hotel room. Longuemare said, "Hardin would practice several moves in front of a mirror, repeating the technique as often as necessary to get it right: drawing on someone behind him, drawing on two separate men, drawing in a crouch, drawing from a seated position, and the 'border roll.'"

Longuemare said that Hardin practiced two hours a day and carried his pistols in shoulder holsters under his coat. Another contemporary, range detective Charles Siringo, also referred to a "Wess Harding shoulder scabbard."[23] Others claimed that he kept his pistols in his trouser pockets, used straight-drop or cross-draw belt holsters, or wore a calfskin vest with sewn-in holsters.

Annie Williams, Hardin's landlady, gave another description of his training routine: "Mr. Hardin was certainly a quick man with his guns. I have seen him unload his guns, put them in his pocket, walk across the room, then suddenly spring to one side, face around and, quick as a flash, he would have a gun in each hand clicking so fast that the clicks sounded like a rattle machine. . . . He practiced with guns daily, and I liked to see him handle them when they were empty."

She also observed the strained state of his nerves: "Hardin would just walk the hall for hours at night with a pistol in his hand. I think he was crazy with fear, for no matter who knocked at his door he would spring behind a table where a pistol was lying before he ever said, 'Come in.' He never allowed a living soul to enter his room when he was sitting down."[24]

Hardin had left prison a changed man. He still had his hair-trigger temper and proficiency with weapons but was no longer so ready to risk his life. He allowed himself to be humiliated by U.S. Marshall George Scarborough, who forced him to publish a retraction of remarks he had made while drunk, and he took a public tongue lashing from Chief of Police Jeff Milton.

On the afternoon of August 19, 1895, Hardin confronted Constable John Selman in the street, telling him that his son, another town lawman, was a cowardly son of a bitch. Selman responded, "There is no man on earth that can talk about my children like that without fighting."

Hardin claimed to be unarmed, but added, "I'll go get a gun and when I meet you, I'll meet you smoking and make you shit like a wolf all around the block."

That night, the 42-year-old Hardin was standing at the bar of the Acme Saloon, rolling dice against Henry Brown for drinks, his back to the door. "Brown, you've got four sixes to beat" were his last words before Selman walked in and shot him in the back of the head.

Selman shot him two more times as he hit the floor. "Good gunfighters like Wes Hardin sometimes shoot after they're hit," he explained afterward.[25]

It was a dirty business, but El Paso breathed a sigh of relief. At the inquest, Selman claimed that he had shot Hardin from the front, in the eye, as he went for his gun.[26] When the medical examiner was asked for his opinion on where Hardin had been shot, he answered, "If he was shot in the eye, I'd say it was excellent marksmanship. If he was shot in the back of the head, I'd say it was excellent judgment."

Hardin has been romanticized as a dashing and daring rebel who played by his own rules without fear of the consequences. There is no question that he had courage, commanded respect, and would not tolerate an insult, and that these were the qualities that defined honor in his circle. There is also no question that he was cunning, manipulative, and impulsive; had a grandiose sense of self-worth and a complete lack of empathy; and never accepted responsibility for his actions. These are the qualities that define a psychopath.

NOTES

1. "John Wesley Hardin," *Galveston Daily News*, August 23, 1895, p. 4.
2. *The Last Gunfighter*, p. 297.
3. N.A. Jennings, *A Texas Ranger* (Chicago: Lakeside Press, 1992), p. 310. If the time starts with the first ejected shell, this would require getting off three or four more shots in a second, which is within the realm of possibility.
4. R.L. Duffus, "Some Westerners Who Were Rather Dangerous to Know," *New York Times*, July 21, 1935, p. BR5.
5. *Last Gunfighter*, p. 27–29.
6. *A Texas Ranger*, pp. 314–15.
7. K.S. White, "Kerr County Trail Driver," *Kerrville Mountain Sun*, February 4, 1938, p. 4.
8. *Life of John Wesley Hardin*, 39–42.
9. *Life of John Wesley Hardin,* p. 45. The quoted section is from the original 1895 edition, and parts of it are mysteriously omitted from modern reprints. It doesn't make sense that Hickok would have his pistol in his hand at the same time he was reaching for both of Hardin's; if he had, it is likely he would have shot him. It is more likely Hickok's pistol was holstered. It is also likely that Hickok decided that it was wiser to humor Hardin than to fight him. Many historians have questioned whether such a confrontation actually occurred, but Hardin biographer Leon Metz, who is no great fan of Hardin's, believes it did. Also, it is believed that Hickok called Hardin "Little Arkansas" because Hardin's famed gunfight with the Mexicans was fought near the river of that name.
10. *Dark Angel of Texas*, p. 60.
11. C.L. Douglas, "A Texas Bad Man Dies Suddenly in an El Paso Saloon," *El Paso Herald-Post*, February 24, 1934, p. 1.
12. *Life of John Wesley Hardin*, p. 62. Writing some 24 years after the event, Hardin refers to his "Colts .45," a model which had not yet been introduced. Hardin was probably armed with the .44-caliber Colt Army Model.
13. Ross E. Milloy, "Texas Town Pushes Fight for Remains of Gunfighter,"

New York Times, December 26, 1997, p. A-24.

14. This seems to have been genuine self-defense. However, while Hardin was serving his 25-year sentence, he was convicted of manslaughter for killing Morgan and sentenced to two years, which he served concurrently.

15. Irvin S. Cobb, *Cobb's Cavalcade* (Cleveland: World Publishing Company, 1945), pp. 53–54.

16. "Trial of J. Wesley Hardin, *Galveston Daily News*, October 7, 1877, p. 1.

17. *Life of John Wesley Hardin*, p. 111.

18. *Life of John Wesley Hardin*, p. 121.

19. *Letters of John Wesley Hardin*, pp. 218–19.

20. Shortly after his arrival in El Paso, Hardin purchased a double-action .44-40 Smith & Wesson and a nickel-plated .41-caliber Colt Thunderer with mother-of-pearl grips. Clearly, he was partial to double-action revolvers. At the time of his death Hardin also owned an additional nickel-plated .41-caliber Colt Thunderer with mother-of-pearl grips; a nickel-plated .38-caliber Colt Lightning with mother-of-pearl grips, given to him by "Killing Jim" Miller; and a .45-caliber Colt Peacemaker with a missing ejector rod shroud.

21. *Letters of John Wesley Hardin*, p. 316.

22. There is no explanation for the odd spelling of M'Rose. Martin consistently spelled it that way, though it appeared in print as Mroz, Morose, and Monrose.

23. Charles Siringo, *A Cowboy Detective* (Chicago: W.B. Conkey Company, 1912), p. 145.

24. *Dark Angel of Texas*, p. 254.

25. "Life and Adventures of a Western 'Bad Man'," *New Castle News*, November 7, 1900, p. 5.

26. Examining the records, it appears that Hardin had the Smith & Wesson and Colt Peacemaker on him when he was shot, though some writers claim he was carrying his two .41 Colt Thunderers.

Joseph E. Harrison
(1915–1990)

Writing for *California* magazine in 1984, *San Francisco Chronicle* reporter Mike Weiss profiled a real-life urban vigilante, whom he referred to only by his nickname, the Fat Man. The Fat Man was a San Francisco cab driver who cruised the toughest neighborhoods, picked up people whom no other driver would, and, if they tried to rob him, shot them. After reading the article, I questioned whether this Charles Bronson–type character could be real, but a search of the archives of Bay-area newspapers turned up stories that supported most of the accounts given.

His name was Joe Harrison, and he was born on January 24, 1915, in El Paso, Texas. As a young teenager he got to know the famous Cherokee lawman and veteran gunfighter

Tom Threepersons, who taught him how to shoot. Harrison said that by the time he left El Paso in 1944, he had shot five men, all Mexicans, all of whom were criminals he had caught in the act, including the leader of a gang of thieves operating in the neighborhood where he lived with his mother. Of the men he shot, he had definitely killed one and possibly another, whose body was never found but who left a heavy blood trail. These shootings cannot be verified, and most of them would probably not even have gotten newspaper coverage. Harrison claimed the sheriff of El Paso once said of him, "If he's behind the gun, you're not going to dodge the bullet."

Harrison had resettled in the Bay area by 1961, when he was mentioned in the *San Francisco Chronicle* after he barricaded himself in his apartment and refused to be taken into custody for unpaid parking tickets and moving violations. The article described the cab driver as "an amateur gunsmith and collector of firearms."

Friends called the 5-foot, 6-inch Harrison "the Fat Man" because he was so overweight he got steering wheel marks on his belly. "I didn't drive those cabs, I wore 'em," as he put it.

Harrison bitterly resented Bay-area politicians who issued themselves pistol permits yet denied one to him, despite the fact that he worked every day in neighborhoods into which they wouldn't dare set foot. Obeying a higher law, that of survival, he kept a revolver in a holster strapped to the left side of his seat. He was left-handed, which gave him an advantage in the cab, as he could guard himself with his right arm while swinging his gun over his right shoulder to fire. He shot with an unusual one-handed grip, using his middle finger to pull the trigger while his index finger pointed toward the target. Shooters have experimented with this technique over the years, and Harrison claimed to have developed considerable proficiency with it. He said that it allowed him to shoot without using the sights and helped him retain his gun when wrestling with an opponent.

On January 2, 1969, Harrison took a radio call and picked up Wayne Gatlin at 110 Divisadero Street. Gatlin got into the cab with three others. Immediately becoming suspicious, Harrison drew his 2-inch barreled .38-caliber Smith & Wesson Model 15 and rested it by his left thigh.

The passengers directed him through a series of stops, one getting off at each. There was no conversation. At last, Harrison was alone with Gatlin, who directed him to turn into Elm Street, a dead end, then pressed a pistol against the back of his head and demanded his money. Harrison told Weiss that Gatlin said at least a dozen times, "Ah'm gonna blow your fuckin' brains out."

Weiss was struck by how Harrison's demeanor changed as he told the story, taking on the persona of Gatlin as he repeated the threat, in "a slurry, scratchy black range that seems deadly accurate." (This is often the case when people describe a vivid, searing experience, because in their minds they're reliving it.)

Harrison began laying out $1 bills on the seat beside him, as Gatlin ordered him to hurry up and get to the big ones. Harrison replied that, as he was so fat, it would be easier for him to reach into his pocket if he could just step out of the cab for a moment.

Indicating a brick wall 6 feet away, Gatlin said, sarcastically, "Think you could find that wall?"

Putting a tremor in his voice, Harrison responded, "Watch me, man, because I'm scared shitless. You're not going to have any trouble with me. I'm just a working man, like you."

Harrison told Weiss, "I opened the door far enough to get rid of the goddam nuisance they call an armrest. I got the gun up and over my right shoulder in one movement and *boom boom*."

A brief newspaper article described the incident:

Cabbie Shoots a Passenger
A cab driver seriously wounded a passenger

who held something against the back of his
neck and said, "This is a stickup."

Driver Joseph E. Harrison told police
Friday that he grabbed a pistol from under his
seat and fired five times. The "something"
turned out to be a mock pistol.

The passenger, Wayne Gatlin, 18, a post
office worker, was hospitalized in serious but
not critical condition with wounds in the chest
and shoulder. He was booked on suspicion of
armed robbery.[1]

The shooting was considered justified, and no charges
were filed against Harrison, even though he had no permit for
his pistol. Still, he was not entirely satisfied with the
encounter, particularly as regards the terminal effects of the
.38-caliber round. He began carrying a Smith & Wesson .41
Magnum, which he loaded with mid-power police loads.

Some time later, another robber pulled a gun on Harrison
and got off several shots, one of them grazing his head.
Harrison put a 210-grain lead wadcutter into the gunman's
pelvis. "I caught him in the big joint in his hip, and he came
down like a weighted sack. The bullet went into his prostate.
His sex days were over," he said, with obvious satisfaction.

That incident was not significant enough to make the
newspapers.

Weiss interviewed the commander of the robbery squad,
William Keays. While conceding that cab drivers were frequently targeted by robbers and had a right to defend themselves, Keays said Harrison "was a little different. He looked
like he enjoyed being a victim because of the fact that he could
turn it around and take the guy. I remember one of the inspec-
tors in robbery asked me what to do about [Harrison] carrying
a gun. I said, 'Put it in your report, put all of it in, and refer it
to the district attorney.' So he did. A district attorney saw it.

He said to me, 'Too bad he wasn't a better shot.'"

As a result of this shooting, Harrison was dismissed by his employer, the Veterans Taxicab Company, but he was able to get a job driving for City Cab.

In April 1973, he was eating dinner at Eddie's Soul Food House before driving home one of the waitresses, who was a regular customer. While he sat at the counter, a black man who knew the waitress, burst into the restaurant, pulled a gun, and shouted, "Is that the motherfucker who shoots niggers?"

The restaurant's proprietor quickly grabbed the gunman and wrestled him to the floor.

Harrison realized he had become a target and took precautions: he removed the telephone from his apartment, convinced that even an unlisted number could be tracked down, and in bars and restaurants he sat as far as possible from the door and kept an eye on everyone coming in.

On a rainy night in November 1973, Harrison picked up two men who asked to be driven to Potrero Hill. One seemed nervous and got out before they reached their destination. Harrison flipped his rearview mirror to its night position, a little trick that enabled him to observe everything that went on in the backseat. He saw the remaining passenger take a snub-nosed revolver out of his pocket and slip it into his waistband. The passenger asked to be let out on a dark part of the street and then told Harrison he had no money.

"Sorry, this is the kind of cab you have to pay for," responded Harrison, genially.

Tossing a $20 bill onto the front seat, the passenger said, "Gimme my change."

Harrison knew he was waiting for him to take his wallet out and put his hands in the "prayer position," counting out change. Instead, he pulled out his pistol and shoved it into the would-be robber's stomach, saying, "If you don't think I'll kill you, nigger, just twitch."

Harrison used his radio to call for the police. When officers arrived, the robber claimed he had no gun and refused to submit to a frisking. Before the police could stop him, Harrison kicked the man, knocking him to the sidewalk, where his .32 revolver clattered onto the concrete.

A week after this incident, the City Cab office was held up. When Harrison heard the dispatcher moaning for help over the radio, he immediately sped toward the scene to try to head off the robbers, although he had a passenger in the backseat. With his flashers on, he drove at 70 miles per hour along Army Street while his passenger shrieked in terror. Harrison was too late to intercept the culprits, but he did arrive ahead of the police. He was fast becoming a legend among his fellow cabbies.

On November 28, 1973, near midnight, Harrison picked up Lee Walter Henderson at the corner of Bayshore Boulevard and Oakland Avenue. Henderson was wearing a leather coat several sizes too big for him, which raised Harrison's suspicions. He asked Henderson to sit up front. It was not a cold night, but Henderson asked Harrison to roll his window up. Harrison figured that this was so that no one would hear him call for help.

Again, his left-handedness was an asset. Steering with his right hand only, Harrison drew his .41 magnum and surreptitiously held it against his belly, pointed at Henderson.

Following directions, Harrison drove to the top of Potrero Hill, turned down Coral Road, and stopped. Henderson then pulled a gun and said, "You white motherfucker, you know what this is."

Harrison fired immediately, but the bullet passed harmlessly through an unoccupied part of Henderson's oversized coat. In a brief, furious struggle, Henderson smacked Harrison across the face with his pistol. Harrison dug his right thumb into Henderson's eye, and while Henderson tried to twist his hand back, he got his pistol into position and fired three times, hitting Henderson in the head twice. Harrison recalled the incident as follows: "*Boom, boom*. He just laid his head down on

the radio. There was a fine red spray all over the cab. A mist, a
hot red mist. I said, 'You sonofabitch, you'll never rob anybody
else.' I got out of the cab and kicked his dead ass. He was
already under a river of blood. When you get a guy in the
head, the blood is very thick. I don't know why. Jesus Christ,
it took them a week to clean that cab out."[2]

In researching his article, Weiss contacted a number of police
officials and questioned them about Harrison. The first ones he
spoke to either claimed they didn't know who he was or said
they didn't have time to look into the matter. Clearly, they were
uncomfortable explaining why a citizen who had been involved
in three gunfights with an illegally carried pistol had never faced
charges. At last, Weiss found some officers who were willing to
discuss the situation. Detective Earl Sanders said that it would
have been a waste of time to make a case against Harrison, especially considering that Henderson had a criminal record. "There
isn't a jury in the world that's going to convict this guy on gun
charges. He's got a right to protect himself.

"I don't think he got anybody who was clean, but [Harri-
son] had a phenomenal way of running into these guys. A lot
of cabs won't go to certain neighborhoods, or they'll pass up
certain fares. He was one of those people who loved to play
cop. He worked the way an undercover cop would—you go
through your act and they bite or they don't. It's like fishing in
a certain hole where you know there are fish. In other words,
you put the bait out there. If the person bit, they got shot."

Harrison's bait, said Sanders, was himself. "This guy
doesn't look like a gunman. He looks like easy pickin's, a fat
old white cabdriver."

The assistant district attorney at the time, Walter Giub-
bini, told Weiss, "I recall [Harrison] rather well. He was a
very personable, forceful guy in a certain sort of way. The
cases I was aware of were all investigated by the police. I
assume they arrived at the proper results. I assume that
whatever he did was appropriate under the circumstances."

When Harrison appeared before the Board of Permit Appeals in January 1974, the police taxi bureau insisted he either stop driving a cab or stop carrying a gun. He answered, "If you think I'm gonna spend my life as a paralyzed vegetable, or you're gonna find me in some back alley with my throat cut, or blinded because some goddam nigger wants a few dollars, hell no. I come first and your political bullshit comes so far second you can't even see it. You say I gotta have a permit? And you tell me you pride yourselves on not giving any? Well, I pride myself on taking care of myself."

With his frequent use of the n-word, Harrison comes across as a racist vigilante. However, as Weiss quotes him, he applied that hateful term only to those blacks who attempted to rob him, not to those alongside whom he lived, worked, and socialized. Unlike most drivers, he'd stop his cab for anyone, but was that evidence of an ulterior motive or was he simply giving all riders the benefit of the doubt? Who should a law-abiding black man prefer: a cab driver who won't pick him up out of fear of his race or one who would pick him up at any time, any place, but was prepared to defend himself? Harrison may not have overflowed with the milk of human kindness, but he is not known to have shot anyone without justification.

After the 1974 hearing, the district attorney's office pressured the cab fleets not to employ Harrison. As one fleet operator said, "We just wouldn't give him a shift. He's an insurance risk. In general, you just can't have drivers out there killing people."

Harrison found work as a clerk/security guard at the Liner Liquor Lobby in the section of the city known as the Western Addition. In 1975, he was involved in two shootings. In the first instance, a man attacked him with a bayonet, and Harrison shot him in the groin, destroying his testicles. He said that the police officers who arrived "nearly died laughing," but a hospital nurse said it was the worst wound she had ever seen on a patient who survived.

Near the end of the year, two men came into the store and

stood in front of the chilled wines display. Harrison asked them if he could be of assistance.

"I want some Rob Roy wine," said one.

"I never heard of it," replied Harrison.

"Oh yeah, man. We gets it here. Where that old dude? He order it for us."

"He didn't order you anything. He can't read or write English," said Harrison, no longer with any pretense of friendliness.

One of the men pulled out a long-barreled revolver that Harrison—who described his knowledge of guns as "encyclopedic"—recognized as an Uberti replica of a Remington single-action revolver. He pushed the barrel away as the gunman's accomplice shouted, "Shoot him! Shoot him!"

Harrison hit the gunman with what he described as "the best judo chop he ever landed," and then ducked behind the counter, where he grabbed his .41. The gunman ran toward the door, but then stopped, turned, kneeled, and fired a round that hit Harrison in the stomach. Harrison fell to the floor, but fired back as the robbers fled. The shot went wild, perforating 10 boxes of Tide detergent and a can of Hershey's chocolate syrup. Harrison, who had shot nine men in his life without taking a bullet in return, bitterly regretted missing the man who had wounded him. "I'd give $500 for him even today, and I don't give a fuck what the DA thinks," he told Weiss.

In 1983, when Weiss interviewed him, Harrison had been out of work for some time but was hoping to get another job as a cab driver. And if he did, he didn't deny there might be more shootings. "It could happen again," he said. "If I drive a cab, I pick up everybody. I'm not gonna be cut or shot or blinded. None of those fates are gonna be mine."

According to Social Security records, Harrison died in San Francisco on May 5, 1990.

NOTES

1. "Cabbie Shoots a Passenger," *San Mateo Times*, January 4, 1969, p. 4.
2. Harrison's story is corroborated by the article, "Cabbie Kills Suspected Holdup Man," *Oakland Tribune*, November 19, 1973, p. 13. The article mentions that Harrison had been involved in two previous shootings of robbers.

Kitty Hesselberger & Dorothy Raynes-Simson (20th Century)

*"The chances are they will
not be bothered again, but if
they are they will not run."*
—Robert Ruark

In the early 1950s, a revolutionary movement known as
Mau Mau arose in Kenya, in opposition to British colonial
rule. At first, the Mau Mau directed most of their violence at
their fellow Kikuyu, to intimidate them into supporting them
or, at least, keeping silent. In 1952, the Mau Mau began a
campaign of violence against European settlers by burning
farm buildings and crops and maiming livestock. On October
20 of that year, the colonial governor declared a state of emergency. Two weeks later, the first settler was murdered: Eric
Boyer, who lived alone on a small, isolated farm, was attacked
while in his bath and hacked to death along with his two
house servants.

In late November, Commander Mieklejohn, a retired naval

163

officer, and his wife were attacked as they sat reading after dinner. Mrs. Mieklejohn reached into the pocket of her dressing gown, where she had a pistol, but her wrist was slashed before she could draw it, and her head and body slashed. She survived her wounds, but her husband died the following day.

After the state of emergency was declared, Richard Bingley took to having dinner with his neighbor, Charles Fergusson, and then spending the night at his house for mutual security. Like most Kenyan farmers, they bathed before dinner and then ate in their dressing gowns. On January 1, 1953, moments after the servant had brought the food to the table, a group of Mau Mau burst into the room. Bingley was stabbed to death almost instantly. Fergusson was trying to pull his pistol from his pocket when his hand was chopped off. As one journalist wrote, "The usual demented hacking, severing, and mutilation followed before the gang fled, leaving behind the bloodbath and carnage which by its sheer extent never ceased to astonish and nauseously overwhelm even the most hardened policemen and soldiers when they found it afterwards."[1]

By this time a clear pattern had been established: Mau Mau operated in squads of four to six men armed with *pangas* (heavy-bladed cane-chopping knives) or *simis* (double-edged knives the length of a short sword); they preferred knives to guns for home invasions as gunshots might alert neighbors or paramilitary patrols; attacks were made in the early evening, taking advantage of the darkness and the fact that settlers would be dining or relaxing before bed; and settlers had too little time—barely a second or two—to employ pistols that were holstered or in pockets.

What made the attacks doubly difficult to defend against was that they generally involved the collusion of trusted servants. Through a combination of paternalism and denial, most settlers could not conceive that their servants would turn on them, even when it was known to have happened in previous cases.

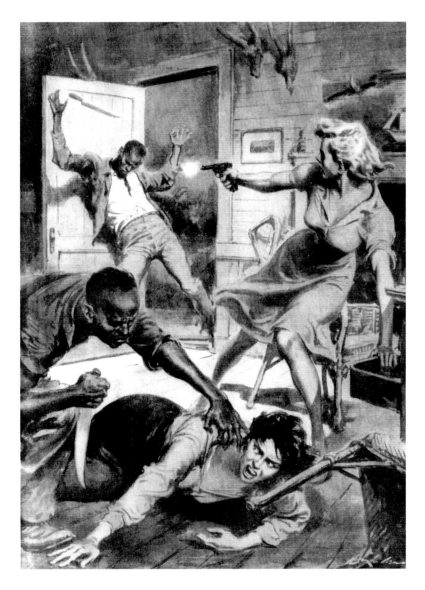

This lurid depiction of the Mau Mau attack in an Italian weekly, La Domencia del Corriere, *transforms the two middle-aged ranchers into pulp magazine cover girls. (Credit: Author's collection.)*

Sometimes a servant would call the man of the house out on some pretense, such as looking at a sick animal, so he could be killed first. More often, a servant would quietly lead the Mau Mau into the home. Ultimately, about 60 settlers were killed, spreading terror through the remote farms.

The night after the attack on Fergusson and Bingley, the Mau Mau struck again. This time, though, they were to suffer a unique defeat, one that made national heroes of the two intended victims, Dorothy Raynes-Simson and Kitty Hesselberger. Raynes-Simson, 40, a divorcée, was a well-known tennis player, who had served with the South African women's forces in East Africa in World War II. Hesselberger, 49, was a widow. Together they managed a cattle farm and riding school 60 miles north of Nairobi.

After the state of emergency was declared, they arranged a distress signal. They kept a lamp burning in the front yard, which was visible for miles. So long as it was burning, the local patrols knew they were all right. If it were turned out, it would be assumed that the Mau Mau had done so.

On the evening of January 2, 1953, the women were in their sitting room, in dressing gowns, listening to the 9 o'clock news on the radio. Both were armed with handguns, and they had two boxer dogs with them. Author Robert Ruark, who knew the women, included an account of this incident in *Something of Value*, his fact-based novel of the Mau Mau uprising. According to Ruark's account, Hesselberger (whom he calls Henderson in the novel) had a .22 automatic while Raynes-Simson (whom he calls Sorrel) had a .38-caliber snub-nosed revolver, with which she was well trained and deadly accurate.

Noticing that her house servant appeared agitated, Raynes-Simson took her revolver from the pocket of her dressing gown and laid it on the arm of her chair, which faced the door. As Hesselberger arose to get some nuts from a bowl about 5 feet from her chair, leaving her automatic behind,

Raynes-Simson glanced up to see four Mau Mau entering the room. One threw Hesselberger back over her chair and began strangling her with a rope while two others ran at Raynes-Simson with pangas. She snatched up her gun and fired two shots at the closest attacker, killing him. (Ruark describes these as shots to the eye sockets.)

As one of the dogs attacked the man who was strangling Hesselberger, Raynes-Simson attempted to get in a shot but, aiming high to avoid hitting her friend, she hit the dog. She fired again and wounded Hesselberger's attacker, who fled the room but dropped dead just outside the house. The other two attackers also ran out. The women followed them, Hesselberger having retrieved her pistol. They fired upon a figure moving in the darkness and killed him.

They returned to the house and reloaded. Hearing noises in the bathroom, they checked the door, which was locked. They fired through it, wounding the man inside. He escaped through the window, leaving a blood trail, and was later arrested. He turned out to be the house servant, complicit in the attack. Of the five men involved in the raid, three were killed, one wounded, and one escaped.

Remembering their distress signal, Hesselberger put out the lamp with a pistol shot while Raynes-Simson brewed a pot of tea. Help arrived within the hour.

The next day, the women hosted a stream of well-wishers and press, and the story made front-page news worldwide. A photo shows the two in the paneled, book-lined room in which the attack occurred, looking cheerful and composed, dressed as for a garden party. Later, Raynes-Simson said that they had been very lucky, as the Mau Mau had entered with the silence of panthers and moved with incredible speed. "Had we been dining, there would not have been time to exchange a knife and fork for a firearm."

One wonders if the sensitivity to the feelings of others that is attributed to women may also have been a factor.

Had Raynes-Simson not noticed the nervousness of her servant, it is unlikely she would have been prepared.

Ruark visited the women some weeks after the event. As he relaxed with them in their sitting room, he noted that when Hesselberger got up from her chair to crack a nut, she wore her pistol.

NOTE

1. *State of Emergency*, p. 117.

Ito Ittosai Kagehisa (16th Century) & Ono Tadaaki (c. 1559–1628)

> *"To try to win is empty and to avoid defeat is essential."*
>
> —Ito Ittosai Kagehisa

When Ito Ittosai Kagehisa drifted ashore near the village of Ito on Honshu, Japan's main island, he looked more dead than alive. The 14-year-old boy had clung to a piece of timber to help him swim the 18 miles from Oshima Island. Something about Kagehisa won the villagers over, and he was allowed to remain with them, sleeping under the village shrine and being given food.

With enough training, a young man might make a name for himself as a swordsman in 16th-century Japan, and this was Kagehisa's ambition. He made himself a wooden sword, practiced with it constantly, and soon no one in the village was a match for him.

When a famous swordsman, Tomita Ippo, passed through

Ito Ittosai Kagehisa.

the area, Kagehisa challenged him to a bout. Ippo was unable to parry his young opponent's blows and was quickly defeated. Shortly afterward, Kagehisa put his skills to a more practical purpose when a gang of bandits raided the village. Borrowing a sword from the head priest of the shrine, Kagehisa single-handedly drove off the half-dozen men.

The local priest was so impressed with his skill and courage that he gave him a fine sword forged by the master swordsmith Ichimonji of Bizen Province. The villagers collected enough money to enable him to travel in search of a suitable master.

Kagehisa traveled first to Kamakura, where he planned to

spend a week praying at the Tsurugaoka Hachiman-gu, a shrine dedicated to the deity of the martial arts. On the seventh night, someone attacked him from behind, under cover of darkness. Sensing rather than hearing his assailant's approach, Kagehisa drew his sword, turned, and slew him with one stroke.

Whether the man was a bandit or a warrior who wanted to test a sword, Kagehisa did not know. He could not explain how he had responded so quickly and effectively to the attack, as he had acted without conscious thought. He would puzzle over this incident for many years until he fully understood it.

Kagehisa traveled to Edo (later Tokyo), where he studied with the great master Kanemaki Jisai. Kagehisa was a fast learner and soon surpassed all of Kanemaki's other students. Though they admired him for his skill, his crude and cocky manner made him few friends. After several years of training, Kagehisa told his master, "I have fathomed the fundamental attitude of swordsmanship."

Though Kanemaki respected his student's ability, he was taken aback by his arrogance and told him he was too young and inexperienced to make such a boast. But Kagehisa, who seemed indifferent to the admonition, replied, "Master, what I call the fundamental frame of mind is related to my own mental condition. It is not part of your teaching. And I think that the attainment of it has nothing to do with the amount of time a man has spent training himself in swordsmanship. If you doubt my words, I would like to prove them to be true."

Angered by his impudence, Kanemaki decided that he would spar with Kagehisa and defeat him with a single stroke. However, the result was quite the contrary: his student defeated him three times in a row. Incredulously, Kanemaki asked, "How have you attained such a mysterious technique?"

Kagehisa answered, "Master, you made an attack on me. All that I did was to instinctively defend myself against your attack. The fundamental frame of mind I have achieved enabled me to do so. To try to win is empty and to avoid defeat is essential."

Impressed by this insight, Kanemaki initiated Kagehisa into the secrets of his style of swordsmanship, the *Chujo-ryu*. Afterward, Kagehisa decided to travel the country in search of swordsmen against whom he could test his skill. He was unable to find anyone who could parry his quick and powerful strokes, and as his fame grew, so did his conceit and rudeness.

Kagehisa settled in Kyoto and opened a fencing school. For the first time he could afford to indulge in some of the comforts of life. This period ended abruptly one summer night when he was attacked while in bed, asleep under a mosquito net. A gang of men had burst into his room with drawn swords and cut the strings that held up the net, so it dropped down and trapped him. As they thrust at him, he thrashed about, avoiding their blows. His sword was not by his side, where it usually was, nor was his mistress in the bed. In league with the assassins, she had taken his weapon and left him defenseless. Not for long, though. Kagehisa quickly wrenched a sword from one of the attackers and used it against the others. After an intense fight, he killed or mortally wounded seven or eight of them. The others fled.

Kagehisa was chastened by the incident. He reflected on the hatred he had inspired in his attackers and the treachery of his mistress. Thinking of how he had boasted of being a matchless and undefeated swordsman, he felt shame. He would no longer brag of his talent, but neither would he allow his trust in other people to leave him vulnerable. Once again he became a wanderer. He was no longer seeking to test his style of swordsmanship, but to find a worthy disciple who might become his successor.

While traveling on the Yodo River, the young ferryman rowing the boat asked him if Kagehisa was a swordsman. When Kagehisa replied that he was, the ferryman asked, "Are you good?"

Annoyed by his impertinence, Kagehisa ignored him.

"Don't ignore me just because I'm a ferryman!" shouted the young man. "Fight me! Then you'll learn. I'll fight with this wooden sweep."

Kagehisa reluctantly agreed. On the riverbank, the two faced off, the ferryman holding his wooden oar at a low guard. Kagehisa had no practice sword with him, so he used his real one, leading with its blunt edge so as not to wound his opponent. The two men studied each other for a long while, each waiting for an opening. Kagehisa was impressed with the ferryman's attitude and concentration, though his talents were undeveloped. When the ferryman raised his oar to strike, Kagehisa dashed in and hit him on the side with the back of his blade.

Though he earned his livelihood as a ferryman, it was Zenki's ambition to become a great swordsman, and he sought a contest with every passenger who was armed. He had never encountered a swordsman of Kagehisa's caliber. "I did not know you were so skillful," he told him. "Please forgive my disrespectful deed."

Kagehisa took Zenki as his disciple.

In the course of his travels Kagehisa is said to have fought 33 duels and won all of them. The most famous occurred while he was staying in Misaki, a castle town on the coast. A Chinese ship had been granted permission to enter the port, and its crew paid a courtesy call at the castle. One of the crewmembers was a martial arts master named Shi-guan, who put on an impressive display with a halberd, whirling it as he performed leaps and somersaults. He challenged any of the castle's samurai to face him in a bout, but none accepted. Some of the samurai said that they thought that Shi-guan could even beat Kagehisa.

Kagehisa was not present for the demonstration, but he soon heard talk of it. Regarding it as shameful that no one had dared accept Shi-guan's challenge, he arranged a duel.

As they met in the palace garden before a throng of spectators, Kagehisa bowed to his opponent and told him, "If you will fight this match with a halberd, I will fight with a fan."[1]

There was a stir amongst the crowd, and when the message was translated to Shi-guan, he was somewhat taken aback, realizing he faced no ordinary swordsman. As Shi-guan raised his halberd, Kagehisa raised his fan until it pointed directly at Shi-guan's face. Each man studied the other, inching first one way, then the other, looking for an opening. This went on for several minutes, and tension built among the spectators.

To the surprise of all, Kagehisa suddenly tossed his fan aside and stretched out his arms in a defiant posture, as if to invite an attack. Still, Shi-guan was cautious. When he took a step forward, Kagehisa took a step back, and vice versa. Each watched the other intently. Finally, Kagehisa sprang at Shi-guan. Shi-guan brought his halberd down, but Kagehisa kicked it away just before it hit him. Disarmed, Shi-guan stood bewildered and exhausted.

Kagehisa named his art the *Itto-ryu* (One-Sword Style), which he defined with the phrase, *itto sunawachi banto*, or "one sword gives rise to ten thousand swords." It incorporated the technique that he had unconsciously employed to defend himself at the shrine in Kamakura, which he called *musoken*, or dream stroke. He had also perfected the technique he had used to ward off the gang that attacked him in his bed, which he called the *hosshato*, or hit-away stroke. No records survive that describe these techniques exactly, but they are related to *kiri-otoshi*, described as the essential technique of the Itto style. It involves the simultaneous action of blocking an attack while dealing a counterblow.

Kagehisa was about 50 years old when he fought Shi-guan. Not long afterward, Zenki asked his master to give him the scrolls that would acknowledge him as his chosen successor. It was not customary for a disciple to make such a request, and Kagehisa, taken aback, did not answer. Instead, he left on another long journey. Each time he stayed at an inn, he put up a sign outside that read, "I will accept a match with any man confident of his swordsmanship, at his request. Ito Ittosai Kagehisa."

In the castle town of Okamoto, in Awa Province, a young samurai named Migogami Tenzen decided to test himself against the renowned master. Armed only with a stick of firewood, Kagehisa defeated Tenzen again and again, knocking his sword from his grasp. As Tenzen's face streamed with tears of frustration, Kagehisa shouted encouragement. He saw true potential in him, and at the end of the match, he accepted Tenzen as his pupil.

After a few years, Tenzen had mastered the *Itto-ryu*, but Kagehisa had still not decided whether Tenzen or Zenki would succeed him. In 1588, he called the two together and announced, "Tomorrow morning, I will permit one of you to succeed me, and I will grant him the scroll of the mysteries of the *Itto-ryu* and my sword. My successor will be the winner of a match that will be fought tomorrow morning in the field at Koganegahara. Fight in accordance with rules of your own making."

The disciples sat, stunned. Zenki then bowed and said, "Master, I have fully understood what you said. I want to fight Tenzen with real swords."

"I also want to have the match with real swords," said Tenzen. "I am prepared to risk my life for the honor of succeeding as the master of *Itto-ryu*."

Kagehisa nodded. Perhaps he felt he could not make an impartial choice and that a match to the death was the only way to resolve the issue.

At daybreak, the three men met on the field. Kagehisa placed an open fan on the ground, and on it he laid one of his swords and the scroll of the mysteries of Itto swordsmanship.

Zenki and Tenzen bowed to each other, and the match began. Each stood at the ready, pointing his sword at the eye of his opponent. They circled each other warily. Both had mastered *Itto-ryu* and were fully aware of the other's technique.

The standoff continued. Suddenly, Zenki bolted to the side, grabbed the scroll, and ran from the field. Tenzen pursued him, catching up when Zenki was slowed by the brush at the field's edge. Holding the scroll in his mouth, Zenki whirled around and assumed a fighting stance. Tenzen brought down his blade, which sliced through a sapling and opened a deep wound in Zenki's shoulder. Zenki collapsed, still clutching the scroll between his teeth. Feeling pity for his disciple, who yearned to have the *Itto-ryu* scroll even in death, Kagehisa told him, "First I give the scroll to you, and then I will give it to Tenzen."

Zenki smiled and then passed away, the scroll dropping from his mouth.

Little is known of Kagehisa's life after this duel. It is said that he entered a monastery and practiced Buddhism until his death at the age of 94.

Tenzen went to Edo and opened a fencing school under his new name of Ono Tadaaki. Soon afterward, a swordsman in a nearby village murdered several people and barricaded himself in a house. Constables were sent to arrest him, but the powerfully built swordsman killed them. The village headman reported the incident to a government official and requested that a master swordsman be sent. The official asked Tadaaki to handle the job.

Taking the sword that Kagehisa had given him, Tadaaki rode to the village and dismounted in front of the house where the killer was holed up. He called out, "Ono Tadaaki of the Itto style of swordsmanship has just come from Edo. If you are confident of your swordsmanship, come out and fight with me."

The killer stepped out of the house, his sword in his hand and an amused smirk on his face. He towered over Tadaaki. "So, you're Ono Tadaaki of the Itto style. You're worthy of my blade."

The fight was brief. With a single movement, Tadaaki par-

·KIRCHNER·

Ono Tadaaki.

ried a blow and then cut both his opponent's arms off below
the elbow. Turning toward an official, Tadaaki asked, "Shall I
behead him?"

The official nodded, and Tadaaki lopped off the killer's head.

This demonstration of his skill impressed Shogun Toke-
gawa Ieyasu so much that he hired Tadaaki as a fencing
instructor for his son Hidetada. As an instructor, Tadaaki was
severe, making no allowance for the fact that his student was
the shogun's son. He didn't hesitate to deliver quick and heavy
blows when sparring, despite the boy's cries of protest.

After Tadaaki had served as Hidetada's instructor for eight
years, the shogun brought in Yagyu Munenori to teach him as

177

well; according to some accounts, Tadaaki himself recommended Munenori. Munenori was a brilliant swordsman, destined to become one of Japan's greatest. He was also far more diplomatic than Tadaaki and quickly rose in the shogun's esteem. He always showed deference to Hidetada and became his mentor, using sword practice as a means to teach him about character and leadership.

Though Tadaaki fought bravely in Japan's civil war, his lack of judgment cost him dearly. At the siege of Ueda Castle, in 1600, Tadaaki left the line to accept a challenge from an enemy warrior. In a short, hard-fought duel, Tadaaki killed the man, a respected retainer of the lord of the castle; but rather than being praised, he was disciplined for having broken ranks without permission. After the Battle of Summer, he was again punished, this time for having called his fellow samurai "cowards" when they failed to respond vigorously to an enemy attack.

Back in Edo, Tadaaki committed another unfortunate blunder. The self-proclaimed master of a sword school was challenging all comers, and Tadaaki went to watch him demonstrate his skill. The amateurish performance made him laugh out loud. Enraged, the master challenged him to a bout with a real sword. Instead of a sword, Tadaaki fought with an iron-ribbed fan and easily defeated the "master" with a single blow to the head. Though Tadaaki thought he had performed a public service in exposing a charlatan, the shogun considered his conduct unbecoming for one in his position and placed him under house arrest.

Many of Tadaaki's troubles came from his inability to make a good case for himself. The only way he knew how to communicate was with the sword. As Makoto Sugawara wrote, "To gain favor, it would probably have been necessary for him to possess some human merits, for example, modesty, which could counterbalance his preeminence in swordsmanship. However, it seems that Tadaaki, who was as self-confident as a simple child, could not even pretend to be what he was not."[2]

Meanwhile, the shogun had increasingly come to rely on the advice of Yagyu Munenori, whose judgment and diplomatic skills were as keen as his blade. The shogun awarded Munenori a yearly stipend of 12,000 *koku* of rice, while Tadaaki's stipend was a mere 700 *koku*.[3]

Tadaaki and Munenori never tested their skills against each other, as both served the shogun and such a match would have dishonored him. However, on one occasion when Tadaaki was giving a demonstration, Munenori told his son Mitsuyoshi to be Tadaaki's opponent. The two confronted each other, but after a few tense moments, Mitsuyoshi bowed and said, "I am no match for you," and returned to his seat.

Munenori asked another of his students to face Tadaaki, but Tadaaki said, "It doesn't make any difference whether my opponent is one or more. Fight with me all together."

Four of Munenori's disciples surrounded Tadaaki with wooden swords. A moment after the start of the bout, all were defeated. One had been disarmed, while another had taken a heavy blow to the head.

Though Munenori had not been involved, this incident is said to have hurt his reputation. To save face, he lavishly praised Tadaaki's skill before the other retainers and the shogun. As for his son Mitsuyoshi, who would become another of Japan's legendary swordsmen, known as Yagyu Jubei, it is said that he sought out Tadaaki and took instruction from him in secret.

There are numerous stories testifying to Tadaaki's skill. According to one, he was on a visit to Satsuma Domain when he was attacked by a gang of swordsmen. He is said to have killed 14 and wounded eight. There is, of course, no way to verify this, but it suggests the level of skill that was ascribed to him.

Most of Japan's master swordsmen saw fencing as a means

of learning about one's true self; Ono Tadaaki saw it only as a means to kill one's enemies. He died in Narita on November 7, 1628. His tomb is on the grounds of Narita's Yoko-ji temple.

NOTES

1. Probably a war fan, an iron-ribbed fan that made an effective weapon.
2. *Lives of Master Swordsmen*, pp. 198–99.
3. A *koku* represents about 5.1 U.S. bushels.

Lozen
(c. 1840–1887?)

"Lozen is as my right hand. Strong as a man, braver than most, and cunning in strategy, Lozen is a shield to her people."
—Apache Chief Victorio

In the latter half of the 19th century, the Apaches waged intermittent war against the United States and Mexico. Although they prided themselves on their fearlessness and ferocity, their fate would be no different than that of other tribes. It was a matter of demographics. Gen. George Crook explained the situation to a Pit River Indian chief: It didn't matter whether the Indians could kill 100 of his men for each Indian brave who died, Crook would still prevail, for in order to replace his braves the chief had to wait for a baby to grow to maturity, while the general had only to request 100 men from Washington and they would be sent immediately. In this twilight struggle, the Apache must inevitably lose.

In rare cases, an Apache woman might become a warrior, and

the most celebrated of these was Lozen. We know of her from James Kaywaykla, a Chihenne Apache who later assimilated into white society and left an account of his early experiences.

He first saw Lozen when he was with a group of Chihenne women, children, and the elderly that had to cross the flooding Rio Grande on horseback. They tossed pieces of turquoise into the raging current to appease it and sang prayers to ensure safe passage, but no one wanted to be the first to plunge in. Blanco, a medicine man, rode along the line of riders, urging them on, to no avail. According to Kaywaykla, "There was a commotion and the long line parted to let a rider through. I saw a beautiful woman on a magnificent horse—Lozen, sister of Victorio. Lozen, the woman warrior! High above her head she held her rifle. There was a glitter as her right foot lifted and struck the shoulder of her horse. He reared, and then plunged into the torrent. She turned his head upstream, and he began swimming."

The rest of the group followed Lozen into the river. Once the crossing had been made safely, she gave them directions as to where to camp and then left to rejoin the warriors of the tribe.

Lozen was the sister of the Chihenne chief Victorio. As a girl she was athletic and it was said that she could outrun any boy. As a young woman she was a beauty, but remained beyond the reach of the men who chased her. She rejected all suitors and her brother declined to press her to marry. An expert rider and roper, a skilled horse thief and sharpshooter, Lozen chose to take her place with the warriors.

Lozen was made a full-fledged member of the council of warriors, perhaps a unique honor for a woman. She willingly took on the most hazardous duties. She rode with the rear guard when the tribe was being pursued. Once, in the middle of a firefight, she ran out from cover to retrieve a saddlebag full of ammunition that had fallen from a US Army pack mule. She also served as an emissary between the Apaches and the army.

Lozen was believed by her tribe to have a special power to

Lozen is believed to be the woman in the center of this 1886 photograph of Apaches being transported to prison in Florida. (Credit: Arizona Historical Society.)

locate enemies. When danger threatened, she would stand, arms outstretched, and slowly turn while chanting a prayer to Ussen, the Apache god. When her hands began to tingle and her palms changed color, Lozen knew that she was facing a foe. The more pronounced the tingling, the closer the enemy. Even as an adult, Kaywaykla never wavered in his conviction that Lozen had this power, for he had seen it demonstrated many times.

In June 1880, Victorio's Chihenne were fleeing U.S. troops near the Arizona border. Traveling with them was a pregnant woman from a different Apache subtribe, the Mescalero, who was about to deliver and had to drop out from the group. Kaywaykla's grandmother wished to stay behind and help her, but Lozen told her to go ahead—she would stay herself. "Take our horses," Lozen told the grandmother, "or else the soldiers will see that we have left the trail and come looking for us."

Lozen took her knife, her rifle, and a pouch containing some dried meat and bean meal. The mother-to-be took a blanket. They hid in a patch of cactus just off the trail.

The tribe broke up into small groups and crossed the Rio

Grande into Mexico. The soldiers followed them to the water's edge and then turned back. "They will ride slowly and may find the tracks leading away from the trail," worried Kaywaykla's grandmother.

The groups of Chihenne traveled circuitously, sometimes returning across the American border to escape the Mexican cavalry, then doubling back into Mexico to escape U.S. Army patrols. When they at last rendezvoused in Chihuahua, they were dismayed to find that Lozen was not among them and assumed she had been killed. As was the Apache custom, her name was no longer mentioned.

As for Lozen and her charge, after the cavalry had passed they left the cactus patch and made their way to a secluded spot. A short time later, the baby was delivered and wrapped in a piece of blanket.

The women camped by the Rio Grande. They had only enough food with them for a few days, but as Apaches they were accustomed to living off the land. It was said that "with a knife, an Apache can survive," and that was necessary, as they couldn't risk a shot for fear of alerting soldiers. Longhorn cattle came to the river to drink, and Lozen sprang upon one and killed it with her knife. She dried its meat for jerky and removed its stomach to use as a water sack. She cut strips from its hide for cord, which she used, along with some willow shoots and the piece of blanket, to fashion a traveling cradle for the baby.

The women needed a horse, as the water holes were too far apart to travel between on foot. There was a Mexican settlement across the river where Lozen might steal one, but the dogs there made a raid difficult. Nevertheless, she was determined to try. She gave the mother all her supplies except her knife and told her how to proceed should she not return.

Before Lozen made her raid, a Mexican cavalry patrol set up camp about a half mile outside the village. This struck Lozen as an opportunity, as the cavalry was not guarded by dogs. While she waited for darkness, she made a halter from rawhide.

In the middle of the night, she swam the river. The troops were sleeping around a campfire, wrapped in their serapes, their heads resting on their saddles. Behind the sentry's back, Lozen snuck in among the horses, which shuffled nervously in their hobbles. She picked out the most powerful-looking one and fastened the halter onto it. When she cut its hobbles, it snorted and bucked, awakening the Mexicans. She leapt onto its back and turned it toward the river. The troops shot at her as she plunged over the bank and into the water, but she wasn't hit. The horse scrambled onto the opposite bank, and within seconds Lozen was out of sight.

Lozen and her charges were now able to cover more ground. They planned to camp near the water holes along their route, but as Lozen cautiously reconnoitered the first of them, she found it guarded by the U.S. cavalry. The troops who had chased Victorio into Mexico had received reinforcements and were watching every water hole in the region.

Lozen went back into Mexico in hopes of reentering the United States some distance to the west. She killed another steer with her knife and made a bag from its hide, in which the women carried the cactus fruit they gathered as they traveled. They needed an additional horse, but most of the ranches they passed were well guarded. At last they came upon the isolated camp of three vaqueros, consisting of a corral with a small adobe shed in it. At night the vaqueros slept on the ground while their herd of horses grazed the surrounding range. They kept a few mounts penned in the shed, so that they could mount up in the morning and round up the horses they wanted. On a night with a full moon, Lozen snuck into their camp. In the morning, after one of the vaqueros had opened the corral gate, he was startled to see the door of the shed fly open and a saddled horse burst out, with Lozen lying flat against its back. Before the men could mount a pursuit, she had picked up the mother and baby, who had hidden nearby, and disappeared.

The women had two horses, but only one saddle, until a lone cavalryman confronted them. Lozen shot him and took his rifle, ammunition, blanket, shirt, and canteen. The women were now well equipped for both travel and defense.

Meanwhile, the Chihenne were feeling the absence of Lozen. The Mexican army had killed Victorio along with 77 members of the tribe while they camped at Tres Castillos. Sixty-eight women and children had been taken prisoner. Seventeen escaped. The survivors were sure that had Lozen been there, her power to detect the enemy would have protected them.

Lozen learned of her brother's death when she delivered the Mescalero mother and child to their tribe and set out to rejoin her people. Days later, at the Chihenne camp, a lookout announced the approach of a solitary rider, armed with a rifle and leading a packhorse. Lozen rode into the camp as if there were nothing extraordinary about her arrival.

In the autumn of the following year, the Chihenne and Chiricahua met at a Sierra Madre camp they called the Stronghold. It was the greatest assembly of Apaches since the time of Cochise. After the killing of Victorio, the tribe had launched a series of punitive raids on Mexico. Many had played a part in the vengeance, including Lozen. At a ceremonial dance, the chiefs and warriors were each introduced to the gathering and applauded. Lozen hung back until the Chihenne chief Nana called her before the group, reminding the men that there was another great warrior to be honored. "She whom we had mourned as dead has returned to her people. Although she is a woman there is no warrior more worthy than the sister of Victorio."

Nana asked Lozen to determine if an enemy was near. Her arms outstretched, palms up, Lozen slowly turned and sang:

> Over all in this world
> Ussen has Power.

Sometimes He shares it
With those of this earth.
This power He has given me
For the benefit of my people.
This Power is mine
For locating the Enemy.
I search for that Enemy
Which only Ussen the Great
Can show to me.

"No enemy is near," she told the group.

Lozen was with Geronimo in his last breakout from the reservation in 1886, when his small group of Apaches eluded more than 8,000 troops of the United States and Mexico for five months. After their surrender, she was sent by railroad with the rest of his band to an Alabama military base for confinement. There, along with many of her tribe, she contracted tuberculosis and died.

Chuck Mawhinney (1949–)

> *"I was never ashamed of what I did. I was proud of it. I didn't go over there to kill people. I went to save lives— my guys' lives."*
>
> —Chuck Mawhinney

Upon graduating high school in 1967, Charles Benjamin "Chuck" Mawhinney joined the Marine Corps. An avid hunter, he chose to delay his entry until mid-October so that he wouldn't miss deer season. He did a 13-month tour in Vietnam and then extended twice, spending a total of 21 months in-country. In 1970 he returned home to rural Oregon, got married, and started raising a family. He worked for the Forest Service for 27 years. In his leisure time he hunted, fished, and trapped. He didn't talk much about his experiences in Vietnam to his friends and coworkers, feeling that war stories are for "wannabes and bores." He didn't read books or watch movies about the war. "It was over," he said. "I just wanted to forget about it and get on with my life."

Mawhinney at his base posing with his M-700 sniper rifle. (Courtesy of Chuck Mawhinney.)

In 1991, a book was published entitled *Dear Mom: A Sniper's Vietnam*, Joseph T. Ward's memoir of his experiences as a Marine sniper. Ward described being briefly partnered with the sniper who had the highest number of confirmed kills in the division, and recalled the total as 101; in fact, the number was 103, with 216 probables. The sniper was identified as Chuck Mawhinney.

Many people who were knowledgeable about military sniping reacted skeptically. Since the publication of *Marine Sniper* in 1986, Carlos Hathcock's record of 93 confirmed kills was considered to be the highest achieved by any Marine. After reading Ward's account, Peter Senich, an expert in the field, looked into the claim about Mawhinney with the intention of debunking it. However, he discovered that it was true. When he tracked Mawhinney down, Senich found him reluctant to receive any publicity. He wrote, "Here was a seasoned combat veteran who had managed to do something no other Marine had in over 200 years of Marine Corps history and he could care less if anyone knew about it, or believed it, for that matter."

However, law enforcement and military snipers were very interested in the lessons Mawhinney had to teach, and he was eventually persuaded to give up his anonymity. He now lectures at the Camp Pendleton Scout-Sniper School, helps police forces set up sniper teams, and trains snipers for agencies such as the FBI, the DEA, and the BATF. He has served as a range master, safety officer, and referee at international police-sniper competitions.

After his story came out, some of his neighbors looked at him in a different light. "I went out and people didn't want to talk to me," he told one interviewer. As far as his friends, he said, "I think they were hurt because I never told them. It wasn't, 'We can't imagine you doing this stuff.' It was more, 'Why didn't you tell us? Didn't you trust us?' But it was honestly not that big a deal to me. I was asked to do a job and I did it. I mean, who really wants to go around telling friends they've killed over 300 people?"

Born in 1949, Chuck Mawhinney grew up on a small ranch in the town of Lakeview, Oregon. His father, a Marine veteran of World War II, taught him to shoot "the Marine way" when he was 6 years old. As a boy, "anything that flew or crawled was fair game," he said. He particularly enjoyed shooting flies off fences with a BB gun. Later, he hunted with his father, his favorite deer rifle a pre-64 .270 Winchester with a Redfield 4-power scope.

In his sixth week of boot camp, Mawhinney went to Camp Pendleton for rifle training. Qualifying as expert on the M14, he accepted an offer to attend the newly formed Scout-Sniper School. There he learned the finer points of long-range shooting, as well as stalking, fieldcraft, camouflage, and day and night land navigation.

Mawhinney arrived in Vietnam shortly after the Tet Offensive. When he got to his unit, Lima Company, 3/5th Marines, he was told that they didn't need a scout sniper, they needed riflemen. The company was down to 65 people, less than half strength, and so Mawhinney spent his first three months in Vietnam as an ordinary grunt. In retrospect, he realized that this was a valuable experience, as it gave him time to learn how to get along in an infantry squad, how to move in the country, and what gear to carry. Still, he was determined to do the job for which he had been trained, and to be reassigned he had to get to the Fifth Marine Regiment combat base at An Hoa. He faked a toothache so convincingly that he was allowed to go there to see a dentist, but instead met with Master Gy. Sgt. Mark Limpic, who headed the Scout-Sniper Platoon, which rotated sniper teams through infantry companies in the area. After three days of pleading his case, Mawhinney got the assignment he wanted.

Snipers worked in two-man teams. The experienced sniper was the team leader and made the shots. The new man served as a security backup and a spotter, using binoculars or a 20-power spotting scope to search for targets and call shots. The apprenticeship normally lasted about two months, during which time the spotter would be allowed to take progressively more difficult shots until he was qualified to become a team leader with a spotter of his own.

Mawhinney was training under Cpl. Cliff Albury when he

Mawhinney shooting from a sitting position. (Courtesy of Chuck Mawhinney.)

made his first kill. Albury told him, "That wasn't a man you just killed; it was an enemy. This is our job. This is what war is all about. You screw up, you die."

Mawhinney trained six or seven snipers during his tours, and he gave every one of them the same lecture.

When Mawhinney became a full-fledged sniper, he was issued a new, accurized Remington Model 700 bolt-action rifle, serial number 221552, mounting a Redfield 3-9x variable scope. It was chambered for the 7.62mm NATO cartridge, and while on a mission Mawhinney carried about 40 rounds with him. He took care of his rifle, as he put it, "like a mother with a newborn baby. The rifle was carried with caution, cleaned after shooting, lubricated properly, and tucked in at night."

His spotter carried an M14, along with five or six 20-round magazines in case sustained firepower was needed. For nighttime use, the M14 could be fitted with the Starlight scope, an optical device that amplified ambient light 60,000 times. It was heavy and awkward, but it served its purpose: Mawhinney made 30 to 40 percent of his kills with the Starlight scope.

Mawhinney sighted in his rifle for 500 yards. For distances up to 700 yards, he would hold over to compensate for the drop of the bullet. Beyond that he would "dial in dope"[1] for 1,000 yards and then hold over or under as necessary for the range. He was an expert at range estimation, using the "football field" technique, i.e., calculating 100-yard increments by how many football fields would fit between him and his target. He and his spotter practiced range estimation constantly. When on patrol, they would pick a distant landmark they were walking toward, estimate the distance, and then count their paces to see how accurate they had been.

The 3/5 Marine Scout-Sniper Platoon operated within a 20-mile radius of An Hoa, encompassing Arizona Territory, Liberty Bridge, and Go Noi Island. Twenty miles southwest of Da Nang, and near the Lao-Cambodian border, this area was home to three Vietcong (VC) battalions. It was also ideal sniping terrain, being mostly flat, with rice paddies and rolling hills.

Anyone carrying a weapon or wearing a North Vietnamese Army (NVA) uniform was considered a legitimate target. Kills were confirmed by an officer, who then signed the sniper's "kill sheet," the Fifth Marine Regiment Scout-Sniper Log. Generally, officers required that the body be inspected and its weapon and any documents retrieved, but they would usually accept confirmations from helicopter pilots. Often, the enemy carried away their dead, and those kills could not be confirmed.

Scout-sniper teams were rotated through different companies as needed. Upon arrival at a new assignment, Mawhinney would first introduce himself to the company commander and explain to him the ways that the team could be useful to him.

These included helping guard the perimeter at night, using the Starlight scope; accompanying patrols at a 200- or 300-yard flanking distance and providing fire in the event of an ambush; or, if the company was going to make a sweep of a *ville*, the scout-sniper team could head out a couple nights beforehand, conceal themselves at a vantage point, and spend a day looking for signs of suspicious activity.

Mawhinney and his partner also made it a point to establish good rapport with the troops. "I wanted to be as tight as I could with the company, because if we were 600, 700, 1,000 yards from the company and we got compromised, and all of a sudden there's automatic weapons fire going on, I didn't want the people in the company to go, 'Huh, snipers just screwed up.' I wanted those guys on the run; I wanted a squad coming to get my butt out of there. It happened a couple of times, and it was very, very helpful being in tight with them."

The sniper team regularly set up ambushes in areas

Louie Mackey, Mark Limpic, and Mawhinney beside the .50-caliber Browning atop the sniper tower at the Liberty Bridge Artillery Base. (Courtesy of Chuck Mawhinney.)

where they thought they might spot enemy activity. Camouflaging themselves with face paint and vegetation, they traveled by night and stayed off the trails and out of the rice paddies. If they were spotted by villagers, they immediately aborted the mission.

Once in position, they wouldn't move. Mawhinney recalled one night when he was sitting in position and a snake slithered across his legs. He whispered to his partner, "Don't move, I've got a big snake crossing me." The snake was about 15 feet long and he figured it was a cobra. He recalled, "I don't know how long it was in real time, but it seemed like an hour to me. . . It just kept crossing, and crossing, and crossing."

Mawhinney said he actually felt safer when he was out in a hide than when he was within the perimeter, because he knew he wasn't being watched.

After he took a shot from a hide, he generally left the scene immediately. The second shot would give away his position, enabling the enemy to set up an ambush between him and his company. He would try to return with a squad to inspect the body and recover weapons and documents.

Mawhinney was confident he could make a kill out to 800 yards, but he occasionally took longer shots. Once, while at a hilltop staging area near Liberty Bridge, he spotted movement in the rice paddies about 1,200 yards away. Through the scope he could make out four VC, standing in a group, looking toward the base. He had a sandbag rest and the breeze was light, so he decided to take a shot. He put "dope on the scope" for 1,000 yards and held over one of the VC. His first shot missed, but his spotter told him where the bullet had hit, allowing him to correct his aiming point. Though the VC had all dropped to the ground, Mawhinney could see them lying in the grass. He fired a second time and hit one. He shot twice more, killing one of the VC, at which point the remaining two jumped up and ran toward a tree line. A chopper was dispatched to finish them off.

After the door-gunner did his work with the M60, the helicopter landed and crew members picked up the weapons of the two Mawhinney had shot. They told him the distance was closer to 1,500 yards than the 1,200 he'd estimated. It was the longest confirmed kill he got. He was surprised not only that he had hit his targets, but that the bullets retained enough energy to kill them.

Mawhinney was accompanying a squad on patrol when they ran into NVA regulars as they were sweeping through a ville. The NVA scattered and ran, and as Mawhinney chased them between the village huts, scattering chickens left and right, he ran smack into one. As both men jumped back, the startled North Vietnamese hesitated before raising his AK-47. Mawhinney didn't hesitate and fired his rifle into the enemy's chest at a distance of about a foot. This was his shortest-range kill.

On another occasion, a squad Mawhinney was accompanying drew sniper fire as it moved into an open area. The Marines hit the dirt, but no one was able to see where the fire was coming from. Mawhinney and his spotter carefully crept off to the flank until they reached a vantage point. Observing the area, Mawhinney saw a patch of ground move—it was the lid of a spider hole, a foxhole with a well-camouflaged lid that allowed a rifleman to pop up, fire a round, and immediately disappear. The range was about 300 yards. When the next VC raised his lid, Mawhinney shot and killed him. Seconds later, a short distance away, another lid popped up, and Mawhinney fired, again with success. After a few seconds, another lid cautiously opened and the last of the VC snipers looked around to see what was happening. Mawhinney put a bullet into his forehead. The situation reminded him of a typical prairie-dog hunt.

Mawhinney considered the Remington/Redfield system first rate. His only problem was with the Marine armorers who sometimes "adjusted" his rifle while he was on R&R, despite his explicit instructions to leave it alone. One time, after he had just returned to base, he decided to take some sighting-in shots. He took a sitting position near the perimeter, and immediately saw a Vietnamese step out of the trees about 300 yards away and look toward the base. Mawhinney studied him to see if he had a weapon. The man walked forward and stepped up on a dike. As he did so, the muzzle of a rifle, slung low along his side, briefly swung out. He was a valid target, and it was an easy shot. Mawhinney put his crosshairs over the man's belt line and fired. The man looked startled but wasn't hit. Mawhinney knew then that the armorer had been adjusting his rifle. The sights were off, and he had no idea how to correct for it, as he didn't have a spotter to tell him where the rounds were hitting. As the VC stood stock still, trying to decide which way to run, Mawhinney aimed to the right of him and squeezed off another round. Again, a miss. He shot to the left, he shot high, and he shot low, as the VC ran off to fight another day. Fate had intervened on his behalf, in the person of a Marine armorer who had removed Mawhinney's scope to make sure the base mounting screws were tight. The rifle was shooting 5 feet high and to the right.

Mawhinney still expresses frustration over the incident: "I can't help thinking about how many people that VC may have killed later, how many of my friends, how many Marines. He fucked up, and he deserved to die. That still bothers me."

While that was the sniper's nightmare, Mawhinney also experienced the sniper's dream, a perfect setup.

On February 14, 1969, he was working with Delta 1/5. The company had dug in for the night about 300 to 500 yards from the banks of the Thu Bon River. Just before dusk, an observation plane flew over and reported a large concentration of enemy on the other side of the river, moving toward Delta's position. Mawhinney and his partner set themselves up at a point where high water had cut away the wall of the riverbank, leaving a sniper's nest that offered cover as well as concealment. Keeping watch through the Starlight scope on the M14, they settled in and waited. After a few hours they detected movement on the far bank, about 100 yards from their position. An NVA scout crawled down to the river and slipped into it soundlessly. He was evidently scouting a crossing point. He walked across the river, which at its deepest reached only to his neck. Mawhinney kept his sights trained on him as he came out about 20 or 30 yards away, so close that Mawhinney could hear the water dripping off him. As the scout walked to the edge of the elephant grass, Mawhinney thought he would have to shoot him, as he couldn't afford to let him get between him and Delta Company. But the scout stopped, stood a moment, returned to the river, and crossed back. Mawhinney whispered to his partner, "You know, this might get real interesting."

Half an hour later, a column of NVA soundlessly came out of the brush and began crossing the river in single file, about 10 feet apart. They were in full battle gear, holding their rifles above their heads. As the point man left the water, Mawhinney put the crosshairs on his head and fired, and then picked off the column one by one as it stood paralyzed, not sure whether to keep going or pull back. He fired 16 times, all head shots.

Occurring on February 14, this exploit was inevitably dubbed "the Saint Valentine's Day Massacre." The NVA never did cross the river that night, preventing what might have been a large-scale engagement, and once again demonstrating the sniper's ultimate purpose—saving American lives. Ironically, these kills never counted toward Mawhinney's total, as the bodies all floated away.

Joseph Ward was partnered with Mawhinney on Mawhinney's last patrol. About an hour into it, the point man spotted some NVA troops moving across an open area 900 yards away. The squad crouched down, and the call went out: "Snipers up." Mawhinney raced across a rice paddy to reach a small rise about 25 yards away. Seconds later, he was in kneeling position and getting his breathing under control as Ward took a spot two feet behind him and looked through his binoculars. *Bam.*

"Hit," said Ward, as an NVA at the center of the column collapsed. The rest of the NVA started running. *Bam.*

"Hit," said Ward as a man toward the front of the column dropped. One of the NVA, who had been running in the wrong direction, turned to rejoin the others. That was a mistake. *Bam.*

"Hit," called Ward.

These were Mawhinney's last three kills. He was at the end of his first extension and had been given a different assignment for his second. He gave Ward his Remington 700, serial number 221552, with the words, "Take care of my baby."

Ward said the rifle could have passed for new.

Mawhinney tried to extend a third time, but a chaplain who talked to him decided he was suffering from combat fatigue, a diagnosis that Mawhinney rejects. His motives for wanting to remain in Vietnam were several. He had a four-year enlistment, and he preferred to spend it in Vietnam than at a base back in the United States, where he would be subject to the spit-and-polish routine that he disliked. He had become accustomed to the country, knew how to move around in it, and knew he was effective. Mostly, he didn't like the idea of going home when he had friends in Vietnam who were still being shot at.

After returning Stateside, Mawhinney was made a rifle instructor at Camp Pendleton. However, shortly afterwards, the military began withdrawing forces from Vietnam, resulting in a shortage of housing at the base. Mawhinney was offered an early discharge, and he took it.

In 16 months as a sniper, Mawhinney had 103 confirmed kills and 216 probables. He attributes his success to several factors: his Marine Corps training; the area in which he worked, which was a true "target-rich environment"; the support of such higher-ups as Mark Limpic and the company commanders who let him do his job; and "last but not least," said Mawhinney, "were the thousands of brave young Marines that I worked with that made our job happen, because without them we couldn't have done anything."

NOTE

1. The expressions "dialing in dope" and "puttting dope on the scope" refer to adjusting the elevation setting on the telescopic sight to compensate for the drop of the bullet.

"Paddy" Blair Mayne (1915–1955)

"Paddy was the best professional killer I have ever seen."

—Sgt. Frederick "Chalky" White

As the commanding officer of the 1st SAS Regiment, "Paddy" Blair Mayne said, "I have a mental blueprint of the ideal SAS man. No one fits it exactly, but when I look at a man and listen to him, he must come close to it."

Mayne himself came as close to the ideal as any man could. Born on June 15, 1915, in Newtownards, Ireland, he studied law at Queen's University of Belfast. Standing 6-foot-2 and weighing 210 pounds, he was the heavyweight-boxing champion of the Irish Universities in 1936, and after graduating played on the British Rugby Touring Team. He enlisted in the army when the war broke out and joined the Commandos as soon as that elite force was created.

On June 7, 1941, while with No. 11 Commando,

Lieutenant Mayne led part of a large amphibious landing behind the Vichy French lines at the Litani River in Syria. He described the battle in a letter to his brother, which included the following passage:

> It got hilly and hard going and Frenchies all over the place. Eventually, we came to a path which we followed and came on a dozen mules and one knew that there must be something somewhere and we came upon it just around the corner. About thirty of those fellows sitting twenty yards away. I was round first with my revolver,[1] and the sergeant had a tommy gun— were they surprised! I called on them to "jettez-vous à la planche" [raise your hands] but they seemed to be a bit slow on the uptake. One of them lifted a rifle and I'm afraid that he hadn't time to be sorry. This was a sort of HQ place, typewriters, ammunition, revolvers, bombs and, more to the point, beer and food. We had been going about six hours and we were ready for it.
>
> While we were dining the phone rang. We didn't answer but followed the wire and got another bull—four machine guns, two light machine-guns, two mortars and fifty more prisoners. We lost only two men (sounds like a German communiqué).[2]

For his courage at Litani, Mayne was honored by being "mentioned in despatches." Within weeks, though, his unit was scheduled to be disbanded, and, looking for more action, Mayne requested a transfer to North Africa.

He arrived at a fortuitous moment, as Lt. David Stirling had just been authorized to create the special commando force

"Paddy" Blair Mayne. (Credit: British Library.)

known as the SAS (Special Air Service Brigade).[3] The SAS would conduct commando raids against German airfields located along the populated coastal area, using the "Great Sand Sea" of the Sahara as a staging area. Stirling envisioned small teams of commandos being parachuted into the desert some distance from their objective and making their way to it on foot. After performing as much destruction as possible, they would escape into the desert and rendezvous with the Long Range Desert Group (LRDG), a motorized unit that conducted reconnaissance missions. The unit started with 60 men led by six officers.

Stirling, who was impressed by Mayne's performance with No. 11 Commando, wanted him for the SAS. According to legend, he had to recruit Mayne out of jail, where he was being held after decking his commanding officer, Lt. Col. Geoffrey Keyes. While it is true that Mayne had knocked Keyes to the floor for interrupting a game of chess in which Mayne was engrossed, Mayne had not actually been arrested.

The SAS conducted its first mission on November 17, and it was a disaster. Parachuting in high winds, the men were scattered widely, with several badly injured upon landing. The supplies were lost or destroyed. Of the 63 men taking part in the operation, only 22 made the rendezvous with the LRDG, the rest having been either killed or captured. Clearly, parachute drops were not the right approach.

On December 18, 1941, the SAS mounted another mission, this time going in and out with the LRDG. Four teams attacked four airfields simultaneously. One team was led by Bill Fraser, one by Jock Lewes, one by Stirling, and one by Mayne. In addition to their weapons, they carried special bombs invented by Lewes. Realizing that the standard 5-pound satchel charges were too heavy for a hit-and-run group, Lewes concocted a mixture of plastic explosive, engine oil, and thermite, and molded it into 1-pound sticky bombs detonated by a time pencil.[4]

Mayne led the raid on Tamet, Libya, accompanied by Reg Seekings, Bob Bennett, Johnnie Rose, and Dave Kershaw. They approached the airfield in darkness, splitting into two teams. Mayne and Seekings placed bombs on the wings of 14 planes and destroyed the instrument panels of 10 others.[5] They had activated the 30-minute fuses at the outset of the raid so that the explosions would be simultaneous.

When they were done, Mayne and Seekings saw some soldiers walking along a road and decided it would be worthwhile to follow them. After the soldiers entered a prefabricated hut from which came the sounds of talking and laughter, the SAS men walked up and opened the door. It was the officer's mess, and inside were some 30 German and Italian pilots talking, drinking, and playing cards. The party must have come to a dead halt at the sight of the two men standing in the door, holding Thompson submachine guns with 50-round drums. Then the shooting began, and the wounded scrambled over the dead, screaming, seeking whatever cover they could find. With a last burst, Mayne blew out the lights, and then tossed in a few grenades. He and Seekings left the hut in flames.

As they headed toward their rendezvous point, they came across a Messerschmitt that they had overlooked. Seekings said, "There wasn't a bomb left for the last plane and Paddy got so pissed off that he climbed up to the cockpit and demolished it with his bare hands. What a feller!"

In fact, Mayne ripped out the instrument panel with sheer brute force and took it with him as a souvenir.

The first bomb went off before the reunited group was clear of the airfield. "We had to stop and look, didn't we? What a sight—flames and muck all over the place," said Bob Bennett.

Sporadic machine gun fire erupted from the base. In his after-action report, Mayne dismissed it tersely: "The guards were slack and when alarmed wasted many rounds in misdirected fire."

They reached their pick-up point and returned to base.

Only Mayne's and Fraser's teams had achieved success, but their success was impressive: they had destroyed 61 aircraft and 25 trucks, without a single casualty of their own. The SAS had proved its worth and lived up to its motto: Who Dares Wins. Mayne was awarded a Distinguished Service Order (DSO) for his actions.

There followed a series of such raids, with the raiders sometimes returning to an airfield only a week or two after they had attacked it previously. There were many close calls. In June 1942, Mayne was driving a truck accompanied by Stirling, three other SAS men, and Karl Kahane, an Austrian Jew who spoke German fluently, when suddenly they found themselves at a roadblock manned by 10 or 20 Germans. Counting on bluff, Kahane began shouting at the guard in German, "Some fool put us on the wrong road. We've been driving for the past two hours and then you so-and-so's, sitting on your asses here in Benghazi, in a nice safe job, stop us. So hurry up, get that ——— gate open!"

Mayne wrote:

> But Fritz isn't satisfied, so he walks to about three feet from the car on my side. I'm sitting there with my Colt on my lap and suddenly I remember that it isn't cocked. So I pull it back and the Jerry has one look and then orders the gates to be opened. Which they did and in a chorus of "Guden Nachtens" [sic] we drove on. We thought later that he came to the conclusion, the same one that I had come to, that if anyone was going to be hurt he was going to be a very sick man early on.

Johnny Cooper, who was in the backseat, recalled, "Paddy cocked his Colt .45 automatic and the German stiffened; the rest of us instantly followed suit with a series of clicks. The German NCO must have realized that he would be the first to be gunned down if he tried to detain us."[6]

Mayne's account continues:

> We drove on at any rate and came on a lot of tents and trucks and people (at Lete), got our machine-guns up from the bottom of the truck and started blowing hell out of them,

short, snappy and exhilarating. The story is far too long and I am fed up with writing, at any rate we cut into the desert, chased by armoured cars. We climbed the escarpment. We had 40 lb of explosives which blows when set off by our own delayed action fuse. The fuses had got set off by the bumps but it is so fixed that after it cracks there is twenty seconds' safety fuse and we made the most of that twenty seconds. We all got out at any rate. But there is no use writing this stuff, people think you are shooting a line—the most fantastic things happen every time we go out.[7]

Stirling wrote of the unit's success: "By the end of June 'L' Detachment had raided all the more important German and Italian aerodromes within 300 miles of the forward area at least once or twice, and a few of them even three or four times."

The SAS was expanded to 100 men, and now had its own vehicles: American jeeps armed with two sets of twin Vickers "K" guns or, alternately, one set of twin Vickers in the rear and a single Vickers and a .50-caliber Browning in the front. The .303-caliber, air-cooled Vickers guns were normally used in aircraft and had a very high rate of fire—about 1,000 to 1,200 rounds per minute. They fed from 100-round drums that were loaded in an alternating sequence of tracer, armor piercing, and incendiary.

In the raid on Bagoush on July 7, 1942, the team was about to leave a German airfield when it realized that half the Lewes bombs had failed to detonate. "Damn," said Mayne. "We did 40 aircraft, [but] some of the bloody primers must have been damp."

Stirling suggested using the Vickers guns. "Paddy was all for it and we decided simply to drive onto the field and shoot the beggars up," recalled Stirling. "It was amazingly easy—it was a total surprise to the Jerries. We used only the Blitz Buggy[8] and one Jeep. We did a circuit of the perimeter and poured down as much lead as we could. We left the whole place littered with burning planes."[9]

They had destroyed an estimated 34 planes, inspiring Stirling to plan a massed jeep raid on the airfield at Sidi Haneish for July 16. Eighteen jeeps would take part, driving in a box formation. Rather than attempt a surreptitious entry, the SAS would count on the massive firepower of the machine guns to overwhelm any defense that the enemy might mount.

Malcolm Pleydell, the unit's medical officer, wrote, "It must have been a terrifying experience for the enemy. At one moment the airfield had been a hive of German efficiency, with everything running to schedule—at the next, there had been utter chaos and confusion. Sudden hell had been let loose. Tracer and incendiary was whipping past in every direction. It is true that the ground defences opened up in reply, but they were overwhelmed and quickly quieted."[10]

At one point Mayne called a halt, ran out of his jeep, and tossed a bomb onto the wing of a Heinkel—apparently he couldn't resist leaving a calling card. The SAS jeeps roared off the field, leaving aircraft burning and bombs detonating from the heat.

In an attempt to guard against the SAS, the Axis forces assigned a soldier to sleep beside each plane. Subsequently, after a raid on the Fuka airfield, Maj. Gen. Lloyd Owen asked Mayne how things had gone. "A bit trickier tonight," Mayne replied. "They had posted a sentry on nearly every bloody plane. I had to knife the sentries before I could place the bombs."

"And he had, too," said Owen. "He must have knifed about 17 of them."[11]

Mayne seemed to enjoy his work. Pleydell recalled him saying, as he headed off on a raid, "There should be some good killing tonight."

Pleydell observed, "Paddy was a bit different from the others—this sort of fighting was in his blood; he thrived on it. There was no give or take about his method of warfare, and he was out to kill when the opportunity presented itself. There was no question of sparing an enemy—this was war, and war meant killing. . . . Neither did I hear him complain when his friends were killed; but I always felt . . . that a friend's death meant so many enemy lives in a form of personal revenge, a wiping off of the debt as it were."[12]

By the end of September, the SAS had to call a halt to its airfield raids. For one thing, the Luftwaffe had become more effective at tracking down and destroying the raiders; after a failed raid on Benghazi Harbor, on September 4, Stirling lost 75 percent of his vehicles and 25 percent of his men. Also, by the end of the year, the British advance had pushed the Axis forces into a small section of Tunisia. Their airfields were now concentrated in a narrow coastal strip, surrounded by German troops, and the old-style raids were no longer practical. Still, in less than two years, they had done considerable damage, destroying at least 367 aircraft, tons of ammunition, thousands of gallons of fuel, and many repair facilities.

In January 1943, Stirling was captured while out on patrol and spent the rest of the war in POW camps. He escaped four times, but his unusual height made it hard for him to blend in among the populace and he was always recaptured. The Germans finally placed him in Colditz Castle, the maximum-security prison for persistent escapers. Fortunately, Stirling had an able successor in Paddy Mayne, who took command of the unit.

On July 10–12, 1943, Mayne led a raid to destroy coastal defense guns in Sicily and to capture and hold the town of Augusta. In the course of the 36-hour mission, the SAS men destroyed two shore batteries, took nearly 500 prisoners, and killed or wounded 200 of the enemy, with a loss of only one killed and two wounded on their side. At one point, walking alongside Sgt. Maj. Johnnie Rose, Mayne suddenly turned and fired two rounds from his Colt .45, killing an Italian soldier who was about to shoot Rose in the back. He muttered, "Mr. Rose, be more careful."

For his success, Mayne earned a second DSO, or, more precisely, a bar for his DSO.

On October 3, Mayne led a landing at Termoli, on Italy's Adriatic coast. When a machine gun held up his unit's advance, he grabbed a Schmeisser[13] and killed the three Germans manning it. The next morning, during a German counterattack, a mortar round landed in an SAS troop truck and killed 29 men. Mayne reacted to this tremendous loss with grim silence. Later that day, German troops again dropped mortar rounds on the SAS, from a position entrenched in a ravine. Paddy managed to get on their flank and killed the mortar crew with a grenade. He finished off 12 others with single shots from his Bren gun.

During an R&R after this operation, Mayne took a bit of drink, which, as always, triggered a violent mood. He tore the iron railings from a balcony, broke up the officer's mess, and threw Phil Gunn, the unit medical officer, against a wall, injuring his shoulder. He meant no harm—he and Gunn got along very well. When sober, Mayne was a reserved, soft-spoken man, who was shy around women, and enjoyed relaxing with a book of poetry. When drinking, his eruptions of temper terrorized his comrades. He would pick men up and fling them across the room, or empty his .45 in their general direction. It was sheer luck that he never killed any of them.

Mike Sadler, a long-time SAS member, said of his commander, "When the pressure was off, it was the violent element which attracted him. He wasn't happy unless he was involved in something which resulted in violence."

"In action he was superb," said another SAS man, Johnny Wiseman. "Out of action we were terrified of him. He was completely unpredictable. Particularly when we were hanging around. It wasn't a blind fury. He wasn't particularly cross. He just became destructive. Especially after several days solid drinking without a single bit of food."[14]

After the Normandy invasion, the SAS performed a variety of missions in German-held northern France. Operating from secret bases established in forested areas, it ambushed patrols, raided logistics centers and troop concentrations, and destroyed bridges and railways. Mayne was behind enemy lines for four months. Though his superiors would have preferred he remain at his base, directing actions, Mayne saw himself as a combat soldier and personally led many raids.

The SAS troops were armed with M1 carbines, .45 automatics, and Sykes-Fairbairn fighting knives. Each jeep carried a Bren gun with ten 30-round magazines. The Bren was a fully automatic weapon, but Mayne didn't like it to be used that way. "Paddy never allowed a Bren to be fired automatic— *ever!* It had to be single aimed shots," said SAS veteran Capt. Johnny Wiseman. "If you hadn't something to aim at, you did not fire."[15]

On September 1, 1944, Mayne was on patrol with Lt. Monty Goddard when he heard the rumble of heavy vehicles. After they pulled into cover by the road, the SAS men were surprised to find themselves in the midst of a group of Resistance fighters (Maquis) who were planning to ambush the approaching Germans. Seeing that the Maquis weren't adequately armed for the task, Mayne told Goddard to take the single Vickers out of the jeep, along with plenty of ammunition. Mayne took the Bren gun and requisitioned several grenades from the belt of one of the Frenchmen.

As the German column came within 50 yards, Mayne opened up, firing single shots and "double taps" from the Bren. Goddard ran at the column, firing bursts from the Vickers, which he held at his hip. As the German troops spilled into the roadside ditches for cover, Mayne ran to a position that allowed him to fire on them in enfilade. Goddard was killed by a cannon shot from one of the trucks. Enraged, Mayne emptied a full magazine into the truck, killing all its occupants. He dropped to the ground as a machine gun opened up on him. Switching the Bren to his left hand, he rose up and threw a grenade into the ditch where the Germans were sheltering, while keeping up a covering fire with the Bren. After throwing another grenade, he retreated to the forest and made his way back to the base. Mayne would later refer to this engagement as "just a scrap." It was only one of many such ambushes in which he participated. In late April, Mayne, L/Cpl. Billy Hull, and Paddy Williams ambushed a German troop convoy. Hull recalled that Mayne was smiling and enjoying the power of the Browning as he pumped .50-caliber bullets into the Germans scrambling from their half-tracks.

Paddy's men were in awe of his hair-trigger homicidal instincts. "He went straight from perception to action—not a second's hesitation," said Capt. Derrick Harrison.

Williams and Hull were dozing in a jeep that Paddy was driving when they were shaken awake by a sudden acceleration. Ahead of them was a German machine-gun position in a roadside ditch. Its three-man crew froze as Mayne bore down on them. "I felt the vibrations as the vehicle plowed over the three Germans," Hull said. "Paddy reversed it, the Germans were writhing on the ground. He stopped the jeep, reached across, took hold of the Schmeisser and fired several bursts into the wounded men. There wasn't much left."

He then turned to his companions and said, "In the future, keep your eyes open."[16]

Mayne's quick-wittedness was displayed in other less blood-soaked ways as well. When Patton's Third Army liberated the French city of Le Mans, Mayne drove through it with his twin Vickers firing into the air in celebratory fashion. For American soldiers who thought the fighting was over in that area, the sound of the full-auto fire must have created a panic. Mike Sadler described what happened: "We drove through Le

Mans and into the countryside where we were apprehended by the Yanks. . . .We were then taken back to Le Mans and led in front of the General. Paddy knew we were in trouble, but he carried it off beautifully. He said to Patton, 'I hope we didn't frighten your men.' There was nothing even Patton could do but reply that of course we hadn't done that."

On April 9, 1945, Mayne earned the third bar to his DSO after he got a radio message that one of his squadrons was in trouble. It was pinned down along a road, taking heavy fire from Germans situated in two nearby houses and a wooded area, and its commanding officer had been killed. Mayne sped to the scene in a jeep. The citation reads, in part:

> From the time of his arrival until the end of the action Lt Col Mayne was in full view of the enemy and exposed to fire from small arms, machine guns, sniper's rifles and panzerfausts. On arrival he summed up the situation in a matter of seconds and entered the nearest house alone and ensured that the enemy here had either withdrawn or been killed. He then seized a Bren gun and magazines and single-handed fired burst after burst into the second house killing and wounding all the enemy here and also opening fire on the wood. He then ordered a jeep to come forward and take over his fire position, he himself returning to the forward section where he disposed the men to the best advantage and ordered another jeep to come forward. He got in the jeep and with another officer as rear-gunner drove forward past the position where the squadron comman- der had been killed a few minutes previously and continued to a point a hundred yards ahead, where a further section of jeeps were

halted by intense and accurate enemy fire. This
section had suffered casualties in killed and
wounded owing to the heavy enemy fire and
the survivors were unable at the time to influ-
ence the action in any way until the arrival of
Lt Col Mayne. The Lt Col continued along the
road all the time engaging the enemy with fire
from his own jeep. Having swept the whole
area very thoroughly with close-range fire, he
turned his jeep round and drove back again
down the road, still in full view of the enemy.
By this time the enemy had suffered heavy
casualties and were starting to withdraw.
Nevertheless they maintained an accurate fire
on the road and it appeared almost impossible
to extricate the wounded who were in the ditch
near the forward jeeps. Any attempt at rescu-
ing these men under these conditions appeared
virtually suicidal owing to the highly concentrated and accurate fire of the Germans.
Though he fully realized the risk he was taking
Lt Col Mayne turned his jeep round once again
and returned to try and rescue these wounded.
Then by superlative determination and by dis-
playing gallantry of the very highest degree and
in the face of intense enemy machine gun fire
he lifted the wounded one by one into the jeep,
turned round and drove back to the main body.
The entire enemy position had been wiped out,
the majority of the enemy having been killed or
wounded, leaving a very small remnant who
were now in full retreat. . . . From the time of
the arrival of Lt Col Mayne, his cool and determined action and his complete command of the
situation together with his unsurpassed gal-

lantry, inspired all ranks. Not only did he save
the lives of the wounded but also completely
defeated and destroyed the enemy.[17]

Those who were present agreed that the arrival of Mayne
turned the tide, but the claim that Mayne rescued the
wounded while still under enemy fire was exaggerated. In
fact, Mayne rescued the wounded when the Germans had
already retreated; to do otherwise would have been stupid
and foolhardy. Those who wrote up the citation embellished
the point in the hope that it would earn Mayne Britain's
highest honor, the Victoria Cross (VC). Most of his comrades
felt that Mayne deserved the VC in any case, and certainly
for his overall career. That he was never awarded it, they
were convinced, was due to the regular army's disregard for
unconventional forces.

Mayne left the service as one of the most highly decorated
soldiers in the British Army. He had received the DSO with
three bars, one of only seven servicemen to achieve that dis-
tinction in World War II. In addition, the postwar French government awarded him the Legion d'honneur and the Croix de
Guerre with Palm for his work with the French Resistance. He
was the first foreigner to receive both honors.

Mayne returned to the legal profession, but he did not
adapt well to civilian life. He maintained his hard-drinking
habits and frequently got into bar fights, which he generally
won by knockouts. On one occasion, he and two friends were
attacked by seven men; Mayne laid out four of them.

His friend George Mathews recalled a challenge Mayne
once put to him at his home. Setting his unloaded Colt .45 on
a table, Mayne walked to the door of the room and said,
"When I come through that door, grab it."

Mathews played along. When Mayne came through the
door, Mathews reached for the gun, but before he knew what
had happened, he was looking down its muzzle. "You're dead,"

said Paddy. "It's just a question of moving quicker than the other man."

On December 14, 1955, shortly after 4 A.M., Mayne was driving home from Mathews' home, where he had been drinking, when he slammed into a parked truck and was killed. His funeral was the largest ever held in his hometown of Newtownards.

Col. David Stirling wrote this about Mayne: "It is always hard to pin down the qualities that go to make up an exceptional man and Paddy could be exasperatingly elusive because his character was such a mixture of contrasting attributes. On the one hand there was his great capacity for friendship: his compassion and gentleness displayed during the war in his deep concern for the welfare of all his men . . . . On the other hand, there was a reverse side to his character which revealed itself in outbursts of satanic ferocity."[18]

On the 50th anniversary of his death, his supporters mounted an effort in Parliament to award Paddy Mayne the Victoria Cross he had been denied. It failed to pass.

NOTES

1. Mayne carried a Colt 1911 but, like many Britons, consistently referred to the semiautomatic weapon as a revolver.
2. *Rogue Warrior of the SAS*, p. 23.
3. The name was selected as part of a disinformation campaign to make the Germans think there was a British airborne brigade in Egypt.
4. The time pencil consisted of a spring, a striker, a capsule of acid, and a retaining wire. When the capsule was broken, the acid burned through the wire, released the spring and striker, and so detonated the bomb. The time lag between setting and detonation depended on the thickness of the wire.
5. As their technique evolved, the SAS always placed bombs on the port wing to prevent parts from one plane being cannibalized to repair another. The bomb would ignite the fuel tank within the wing.
6. Johnny Cooper, *One of the Originals: The Story of a Founder Member of the SAS* (London: Pan Books, 1991), p. 56.
7. *Rogue Warrior of the SAS*, pp. 44–45.
8. The Blitz Buggy was a Ford V-8 convertible modified to resemble a

German staff car, though it had the winged sword emblem of the SAS painted on its doors.

9. Alan Vick, *Snakes in the Eagle's Nest: A History of Ground Attacks on Air Bases* (Santa Monica: RAND, 1995), p. 54.

10. Malcolm James, *Born of the Desert: With the SAS in North Africa* (London: Greenhill Books, 1991), p. 160.

11. *Rogue Warrior of the SAS*, p. 50.

12. *Born of the Desert*, p. 80.

13. The Schmeisser was the German MP40 submachine gun.

14. *Rogue Warrior of the SAS*, p. 89.

15. *Rogue Warrior of the SAS*, p. 78.

16. *Rogue Warrior of the SAS*, p. 195.

17. Stewart McClean, *The History of the Special Raiding Squadron: Paddy's Men* (Stroud, UK: Spellmount, 2006), pp. 140–1.

18. *Rogue Warrior of the SAS*, p. xii.

Lewis L. Millett
(1920–)

Lewis Millett was born on December 5, 1920, in Mechanic Falls, Maine, and joined the National Guard in 1938, while still in high school. His yearbook described him as the class member "most likely to become a soldier of fortune." He enlisted in the U.S. Army Air Corps and after basic training was trained as an antiaircraft machine gunner. With war raging across the Atlantic, Millett thought he would soon be in the thick of the action, but the United States remained isolationist, content to let Europe thrash out its own difficulties. After a year without combat, he could stand it no longer. He went AWOL, traveled north, and joined the Canadian Army. He was sent to London, where he went through the British Army Commando School.

Lewis L. Millett.

When American forces began arriving in England in the summer of 1942, Millett transferred to the 27th Armored Field Artillery Battalion of the 1st Armored Division. In November, he participated in the invasion of North Africa and saw his first combat near Tunis. When German shells set fire to a haystack under which were concealed two half-tracks loaded with ammunition. Millett knew they could explode at any moment. At great risk, he drove both vehicles to safety, for which he was awarded the Bronze Star.

Early in 1943, during the counterattack at Kasserine Pass, Millett's unit was strafed by an Me-109. Millett jumped onto a half-track and fired at the plane with its twin .50s. "The plane was strafing down the road and I shot right through the windshield, hitting the pilot. He went straight into the ground. I was promoted to corporal for that," he said.

Millett was fighting in Italy when the AWOL charge finally caught up with him. His company commander informed him that he had been convicted of desertion. Millett protested that he hadn't even been invited to appear at his own trial, but considering that the penalty was a mere $52 fine, he decided not to contest it. "Then a few weeks later they made me a second lieutenant!" he recalled years later. "I must be the only Regular Army colonel who has ever been court-martialed and convicted of desertion."

While fighting in the Appians, north of Rome, Millett earned a second Bronze Star when he called artillery down on his own position to halt a German attack.

Millett was discharged at the end of the war and transferred into the National Guard. He attended Bates College for three years, but with the outbreak of the conflict in Korea, he requested active duty. He was called up in January 1949, six months before he would have graduated. He was assigned to the 27th "Wolfhound" Regiment of the 25th Division.

While stationed near Hwanggang-ni, Millett awoke one night to discover a battalion of Chinese troops marching through the American lines. Armed with his M1 rifle and the six grenades he always carried, he fell in at the end of the line of enemy troops. Making his move, he threw his grenades among them as quickly as he could and emptied his semiautomatic rifle. He then climbed behind the phosphorous gun on a nearby truck and began firing, scattering the troops and lighting up the night.

For his actions, Millett was awarded a third Bronze Star.

On November 27, 1950, Millett's leg was torn open by mortar fire. Persuaded to get it properly treated, he boarded a convoy taking wounded troops to the rear. A doctor told him to leave his rifle behind, as the Geneva Convention forbade weapons in ambulances. "I'm a soldier, not a lawyer. Where I go, my rifle goes," replied Millett.

When the convoy was ambushed, Millett rolled out of the truck and into a ditch. With his M1 he opened a path through which he and two other GIs were able to make their way out of the kill zone. Millett ended up at a MASH unit. "People were moaning and suffering everywhere," he recalled. "I took my bandage off and I wasn't bleeding anymore. I figured these people were hurt worse than I was, so I left."

While Millett's leg was healing, he served as an aerial observer, flying in the passenger seat of an L-4 Piper Cub. On one occasion, he and his pilot, Jim Lawrence, spotted a P-51 that had been shot down. They landed and were met by the pilot, John Davis, a South African. As the L-4 couldn't carry all three men at once, Millett volunteered to stay behind until Lawrence could come back for him. Lawrence returned for Millett just as a Chinese patrol was approaching the scene, and they took off in a hail of bullets. Millett earned no medal for this action, but the South Africans awarded him a bottle of Scotch.

When his leg had fully recovered, Millett volunteered for the infantry, and in January 1951 he was put in command of Easy Company, 27th Infantry, of the Wolfhounds, which had lost its former commander a few weeks earlier. During a relentless Chinese onslaught, Capt. Reginald "Dusty" Desiderio killed and wounded dozens of the enemy until a shell from a tank cut him down. He was awarded a posthumous Medal of Honor. "There'll never be another one like

Dusty," the soldiers of Easy Company told each other. Granted, the tall and powerfully built Millett, with his steely gaze and bushy red handlebar mustache, looked every inch the warrior; still, he had large shoes to fill.

Millett oversaw Easy Company's retreat from the Yalu River to the 37th Parallel, where it went into reserve. During the next few weeks, he began an intensive training regimen to toughen up his troops. He ran them up and down the frozen, rocky hills with full field packs and taught them the hand-to-hand combat techniques he had learned in his British Commando course. To increase the company's firepower, he obtained an additional Browning Automatic Rifle (BAR) per squad and issued each man four to six grenades rather than the customary two. He also taught a lesson on grenades, explaining that a man would be safe lying on the ground near the blast, as the explosion went outward and upward. To demonstrate, he pulled the pin on a grenade, tossed it a few feet away, lay down, and plugged his ears. After the explosion he stood up, dusted himself off, and continued to lecture.

A Chinese report had been intercepted that stated that American troops had no stomach for hand-to-hand combat, particularly when they faced cold steel. Millett said, "When I read that, I thought, 'I'll show you, you sons of bitches!'"

Bayonets were no longer routinely issued, but Millett requisitioned, scrounged, and horse-traded to get enough for Easy Company. They came with a dull edge, so he paid Korean women to hone them. Millett ran his men through two days of intensive bayonet training, using bundles of straw and mud banks as targets. First he indoctrinated them in the principles: *Get the blade into the enemy. . . . Be ruthless, vicious, and fast in your attack. . . . Seek vital areas, but don't wait for an opening. Make one.* Then he taught them the moves: the slash, jab, smash, vertical butt stroke, horizontal butt stroke, parry right, and parry left. They ached from the unfamiliar workout, but Millett was determined that they master the weapon in the brief time he had to train them. "From now on bayonets will be fixed any time we attack," he told them. "You're going to use them to kill commies."

His battalion commander told him he was wasting his time.

With the launching of Operation Thunderbolt in February 1951, the 8th Army started moving north, riding atop mud-spattered Pershing tanks. Just south of Osan, on February 5, Easy Company came under fire from Chinese troops on a hillside. As bullets zipped by, Millett ran toward the base of the hill, shouting, "Fix bayonets, men! Follow me!"

He headed up the slope, shouting "*She-lie, sa-ni!*" which he understood to be Chinese for "I'm going to kill you with a bayonet!"

As Millett's men charged up the hill, bellowing at the top of their lungs, the Chinese troops retreated from their positions. By the time the platoons reached the crest of the hill there were only a few Chinese left, and they were quickly mopped up.

The bayonet charge had been a spectacular success. The battalion commander, who had witnessed it, congratulated Millett on his courage and started the paperwork to get him the Distinguished Service Cross. Little did he know that Easy Company's captain was just getting warmed up.

On February 7, Easy Company was the point unit for the battalion. Accompanied by three tanks, it was approaching a saw-toothed ridge identified as Hill 180, the number referring to its height in meters. Millett planned to bypass it until one of his men saw movement in the thick foliage at its top. It was covered with Chinese troops, their guns covering the Americans' approach.

As the Chinese opened fire, Millett got his tanks off the road and his platoons behind the cover of a paddy dike, and began organizing an attack. He didn't want to give these Chinese a chance to melt away as the others had.

As a second Chinese machine gun opened up, catching E

Company in a crossfire, Millett ordered his tanks to fire at the top of the ridge until his men were halfway up the slope. He roared, "Get ready to move out! We're going up the hill! Fix bayonets! Charge! Everyone goes with me!"

He ran across the ice-covered ground to the base of the hill, bullets zipping past him, then waited under the cover of a rocky outcropping while the 13 men who had followed him caught up. Two were armed with BARs.

Hill 180 was made up of three separate knobs. The center knob was set back and rose 20 meters higher than those on either side. Millett and his men started up the lowest knob. Spotting eight dug-in Chinese, he and one of his men killed them with grenades and rifle fire, while his BAR-man cleaned out a machine-gun nest. Within minutes, the knob was theirs.

Once his men were in position, Millett ordered: "Attack straight up the hill!"

With Millett in the lead, the men raced 250 yards up the slope through heavy fire.

When they reached the first line of enemy foxholes, they plunged in, bayonets first, and cut a bloody swath through the Chinese.

Millett was at the point, far ahead of the main body, and grenades were being thrown at him from several directions. He escaped injury from most of the explosions, but one blasted shards of hot steel into his back and legs. Though soaked with blood and in intense pain, he continued to lead the attack, shouting to his men, "Let's go! Use grenades and cold steel! Kill 'em with the bayonet!"

As they got within 30 feet of the crest of Hill 180, they began taking fire from a Russian Simonov 14.5mm antitank rifle that had been put into an antipersonnel role. They put it out of action with rifle fire and a few well-placed grenades.

Millett spotted three enemy soldiers in a slit trench, tossing strung-together clusters of grenades. "I figured that every time they threw grenades, someone had to stand up. And that would be the best time to jump in the hole with them. When I saw an enemy soldier again, I jumped into his hole and jammed my blade into his chest."

A second soldier rushed at him. Millett slashed his throat open with his bayonet as the third man turned toward him with a submachine gun. "But," said Millett, "I guess the sight of me, red-faced and screaming, made him freeze."

Millett lunged forward and thrust his bayonet into the man's forehead, later expressing his surprise that it went in so easily: "I thought a head was harder than that. There was no resistance in the bone. It was like stabbing a cantaloupe." However, it did not come out as easily; Millett had to fire a round to dislodge the blade.

Millett leaped out of the trench and joined his men as they streamed past, screaming in the grip of a battle frenzy as they assaulted the dug-in positions at the top of the hill. They fired bursts, threw grenades, and ripped into the enemy with their bayonets. "We were ready for a bayonet battle and we went berserk, crazy. It was a fighting frenzy. A red haze came over us, and time stood still. We lost control of our actions."

Millett later described one of his men, Victor Cozares, repeatedly bayoneting a dead opponent; another, Takashi Shoda, laughing hysterically as he fired bursts from his BAR. Within minutes the Chinese who had not fled were eliminated from every foxhole, trench, and bunker. Millett stood atop the ridge pumping his rifle up and down to signal that he had taken the hill.

Brigadier General S.L.A. Marshall, who visited the scene the following day, called the action the "greatest bayonet attack by US soldiers since Cold Harbor in the Civil War." By his count there were 47 Chinese and North Koreans killed, over a third of them by bayonet. Millett said the toll was closer to 100, as Marshall saw only the bodies that were still exposed, and that many who had been killed in their foxholes had been covered over with dirt.

Millett later told Easy Company that he had watched them at work, and not one of them had used the strokes he had taught them, but just jabbed and slashed every which way. Cozares responded, "I watched you too, Captain, and you didn't make one stroke correctly either."

Millett spent several months recuperating from his wounds, and on July 5, 1951, received the Medal of Honor at a White House ceremony. He remained in the army as one of its top experts on commando, paratroop, and guerrilla operations. He attended the Infantry Advanced Course and Ranger School at Fort Benning. Afterward, he was assigned to the 101st Airborne, and founded their Recondo School. In 1960, he went to Vietnam, where he helped develop the South Vietnamese Army's Ranger program. He served as an adviser to the Phoenix Program in Laos from 1968 to 1970, and then returned to South Vietnam until the war ended. As a paratrooper, he made 11 jumps in Vietnam and five in Laos. He left the army in 1973 as a full colonel, disgruntled over the Vietnam War because "we quit."

Millett volunteered for duty during Operation Desert Storm, but was turned down due to his age.

In his 35-year military career, Millett received four Purple Hearts, three Bronze Stars, one Silver Star, the Distinguished Service Cross, two Legions of Merit, three Air Medals, the Army Commendation Medal, and the Medal of Honor. He remains active in veterans' affairs.

"I am not a hero," says Millett. "I am a warrior."

Jeff Milton
(1861–1947)

In a life that spanned 85 years, Jeff Milton experienced all
the adventure the American West had to offer, having worked
as a cowboy, Texas Ranger, saloonkeeper, deputy sheriff, Wells
Fargo express messenger, prospector, hunting guide, range
detective, and border patrolman. His meandering career left
him with little in the way of wealth or possessions, but a great
deal in the way of reputation. Those who needed a man of
proven reliability, integrity, courage, and deadliness knew they
had one in Milton. He was considered "a good man with a
gun" by friend and foe alike.

People were always curious about Milton's gunfights, but
he did not care to discuss them. He would enthusiastically tell
about a time he spent weeks trailing an outlaw through the

Sonoran desert, but not bring the tale to a conclusion. When the listener asked, "But what happened to the outlaw?" Milton would reply, in his soft Southern drawl, "Why, he's still there."

Late in life, when he was a married man, his wife once asked him who gave him the bullet wound beneath his jaw. "A man who is no longer alive," he responded quietly.

Asked about an incident where he was supposed to have killed four men who waylaid him, Milton waved the question away, saying, "That was a-way back yonder."

He did sometimes talk ruefully of the many men he *ought* to have killed. These were usually blustering bullies who, when he stood up to them, begged for mercy. "Well, you just can't kill a man like that," Milton would say, shaking his head.

The historian J. Evetts Haley wrote an excellent biography of Milton, but he got little detail on these incidents from his subject. However, he did persuade Milton to deny or correct accounts he had gathered from newspapers and eyewitnesses.

Jefferson Davis Milton was born in Sylvania, Florida, on November 7, 1861, the youngest son of the state governor, John Milton. An ardent supporter of the Confederacy, John Milton committed suicide after the defeat of the South.

At 16, Milton went to Texas and found work as a cowboy. At 18, standing over six feet tall and sporting an impressive mustache, he lied about his age to enlist in the Texas Rangers, which required that a man be 21. He carried a Winchester .44-40 and a Colt .45 and was known to throw tin cans in the air and hit them with pistol shots. His peers found him a comfortable man to be with in a fight.

On May 16, 1881, Milton and two other Rangers were patrolling Colorado City when a drunken cowboy named W.P. Patterson began shooting up the town. The Rangers grabbed Patterson's arms and demanded his pistol. Patterson wrenched himself free and took a shot at the Rangers. Milton killed him on the spot. Patterson was a popular local figure,

Jeff Milton. (Credit: Author's collection.)

and the shooting caused Milton some difficulties, but he was tried and acquitted.

Milton spent three years with the Rangers and then left to pursue other ventures.

He served briefly as deputy sheriff in a rough cow town called Murphyville. When he heard that a group of cowboys in the saloon were bragging that they were going to run him out of town, he stepped in through the back door with a ten-gauge shotgun. As he covered them, he ordered, "Boys, every one of you get your six-shooters off as fast as you can or I'll kill every damned one of you right here."

He later explained, "I made quite a talk to them, like a man would talk to men. I told them they all wanted to be gentlemen when they came to town . . . . It had quite an effect on them. Never had no more trouble—not a word."

Milton briefly tried running his own Murphyville saloon. His bar was supported on three posts, and on each post he affixed a holstered pistol so that one would always be within easy reach. On the day he opened, some rowdy cowpunchers came in and one immediately broke a glass. Milton quietly reminded him that glasses were hard to come by.

"Hell, I'll just break 'em all," answered the cowboy, and raised his arm to sweep them onto the floor. Before he could complete his move, he was looking down the barrel of a Colt .45. "If you do, you're a dead 'un," said Milton. He shooed the cowboys out the door and was locking the place up when a friend showed up wanting a drink. "Nothing doing," said Milton, "I'm closed. No need to be in a business where you got to kill a man for nothing."

The saloonkeeping venture had lasted less than two hours.

In 1884, Milton was working as a deputy in Socorro, New Mexico. He was riding the Gila River with his friend Jim Hammil when assailants hidden in the brush suddenly fired upon them. A bullet killed Milton's horse and then passed through his leg from above his knee down through his calf. He pulled out his Winchester, and "there was a lot of shooting."

After it was over, he treated his wound with turpentine and plugged the hole with a rag. Some time later, back in Socorro, the sheriff asked him if he knew about some trouble on the Gila River that had resulted in the death of three Mexicans. "'Tweren't nothing," Milton told him. "No trouble at all."

Milton took a job as a conductor with the Pullman Company in 1890. This would seem to have offered a peaceful interlude, but while working the El Paso to St. Louis route, he had some trouble with a burly Pullman porter who had beaten up several conductors previously. When Milton confronted him for sleeping on the job, the porter lunged at him. "I did not want him to beat me up," Milton said. "I just took my time, as I knew exactly where to hit him. I tapped him a couple of times with my six-shooter just as the train was checking down. Then I got him by the collar, dragged him into the aisle, out on the back platform, and dropped him off on the ground about the time the train was stopping. And we went on without the gentleman."

On August 10, 1894, Milton was appointed Chief of Police in El Paso. This didn't sit well with John Selman, a rustler, robber, and killer who was then serving as constable. Selman let people know he intended to shove Milton's gun up where the sun don't shine and kick off the handles. He was in a saloon laying out this plan when a firm hand dropped onto his shoulder and spun him around. "Hello, Uncle John," said Milton, "How about that six-shooter? I've got it on me. Think you might want to use it on me?"

Startled, Selman quickly backed down.

John Wesley Hardin drifted into town in 1895, after his release from prison. By no means did Milton underestimate the danger Hardin posed. He cached five Burgess slide-action 12-gauge shotguns at various places around town in case he should need one in a hurry.

Milton was present during a heated altercation between Hardin and an enemy, Tom Finnessy. In an instant, Hardin had slapped Finnessy, drawn his gun, and stabbed it into Finnessy's belly. Milton quickly grabbed Hardin's revolver and forced its muzzle to the side while he persuaded him to put it away. Afterward, Milton said, "Hardin is the fastest thing I ever saw in my life with a gun. There is nobody that is a match for him as far as that is concerned. Before I could get my gun, he had pulled his and had it in Finnessy's belly."

Another dangerous local character was Martin M'Rose, a rustler, horse thief, and reputed killer. As there was a $1,000 reward on his head, he stayed in Juarez, across the river from El Paso.

Deputy Marshall George Scarborough, who was considerably interested in collecting the $1,000 reward, started working his way into M'Rose's confidence. On the night of June 29, 1895, he got Milton and a Texas Ranger, Frank McMahon, to conceal themselves near the American end of the bridge connecting El Paso and Juarez. Scarborough then enticed M'Rose to accompany him across the bridge. As they neared the American end, Milton and McMahon jumped out and ordered M'Rose to raise his hands. Instead, M'Rose pulled out a snubnosed Colt .45 and was immediately shot in the chest, either by Milton or Scarborough. He fell, but got back up and fired a shot before he was shot down again for good.

The first shot had hit him in the heart, but, remarkably, he had been able to get up and fire his own weapon before he was finished off with six more shots, including a second one to the heart.

Beulah M'Rose had hired Hardin to help her husband fight extradition, and the two had become an item. After M'Rose was killed, Hardin spread a story that he had hired Milton and Scarborough to get him out of the way. This didn't sit well with Milton, who never let a lie, an insult, or a threat go unchallenged. "Settle your troubles at once and go on about your business," was his credo. According to a witness, Milton approached Hardin on the street, told him he was a goddamned liar, and demanded he admit it.

"Why, Captain Milton, I don't let any man talk to me that way," responded Hardin.

"I'm telling you that in fighting talk," said Milton. "If you don't like it, help yourself. But you're going to say it."

"I don't want to have any trouble with you," said Hardin.

"Well, you took a damn poor way to keep from it," said Milton.

As Hardin continued to protest, Milton said, "The trouble with you, Hardin, is that your nerve's failed you. You're not only a goddamned liar, you're a goddamned lying son of a bitch, and you are now going to tell these gentlemen you are."

To the group of men who had gathered to watch this confrontation, Hardin choked out the admission that he had indeed been a "goddamned liar" when he told the story.

Milton later told a friend that he was relieved at the outcome, saying, "He's so much faster with a gun than I am, that if he had gone for his gun, I wouldn't have had a chance."[1]

On the night of August 19, as Hardin stood at the bar of the Acme Saloon, he was shot in the back of the head by John Selman. Within the year, John Selman pushed his luck and tried to get the drop on Scarborough in the alley next to the Wigwam Saloon. Scarborough killed him with four quick slugs.

Milton and Scarborough liked to work together as they knew they could count on each other. That was not always the case with other men who were brought in to assist them. Early in 1898, the two lawmen were leading a posse in search of a gang of train robbers led by Black Jack Ketchum. As they neared a cabin where they thought the outlaws might be hiding, one of the posse members said, "Mr. Milton, I've got a wife and children and I can't afford to go."

The two other posse members then recalled that they too had family responsibilities and would also have to beg off. Exasperated, Scarborough exclaimed, "I'm married, I got a wife and a lot of children, and damned if they can't take care of themselves!"

In July 1898, Milton and Scarborough were searching for a couple of murderous train robbers named Bronco Bill Walters and Bill Johnson, who had assembled a small gang. After a long and difficult pursuit, the lawmen came upon their camp near a horse ranch in the White Mountains.

Milton called out to Walters, who jumped onto his horse, pulled his revolver, and put two shots between Milton's legs. With his Winchester, Milton put a bullet into Walters' shooting arm. The bullet entered at the elbow, plowed up the arm (shattering the bone), passed through his chest, and lodged under his left arm. Walters fell from his horse.

Johnson and another member of the gang, Red Pipkin, shot at Milton and Scarborough from the other side of the canyon. The lawmen shot the horse out from under Pipkin, and it is said that "wounded in the seat of his pants, [he] jumped off into the thick brush and never did stop running until he got into Utah."[2]

Johnson jumped behind a tree and shot at the lawmen with his rifle.

A shot from Scarborough hit the bark of the tree near Johnson's face, which caused him to duck back reflexively, exposing his hips on the other side. Milton put a bullet through Johnson's lower quarters, which dropped him, writhing in agony.

Milton scribbled out a succinct note and gave it to a cowboy to deliver to the nearest town. It read, "Send me a doctor and one coffin, Milton." (This note became part of Western lore and Milton was sometimes kidded about it, but he observed, "What else was there to say?")

Johnson died that night. Milton buried him, chiseled his initials on a rock, and placed it on top of the grave. He later said, "I felt pretty sorry for Bill Johnson. Wasn't no use being sorry for those fellows but I couldn't help it."

Walters survived. The doctor splinted his shattered arm and, though in tremendous pain, Walters rode forty miles with Milton and Scarborough to the nearest train depot.

When the train stopped at Solomonville, a crowd gathered on the platform to stare through the window at the notorious outlaw. Disgusted by their ghoulish curiosity, Milton whispered to Walters, "Do you suppose if I raised your head you could say 'boo'?"

"I will try to say it to the sons-a-bitches," Walters answered.

Milton raised him, Walters shouted "Boooo!" and the crowd fell over itself as it recoiled in terror. The lawman and outlaw shared a good laugh.

In this, and in other cases, Milton showed a certain sympathy for the men he arrested, or, in some cases, shot. He captured one fugitive who was wanted on a murder warrant and after traveling with him a few days, decided that he was quite

JEFF MILTON

a decent fellow. "A lot of nice men have had to kill people, you know," he observed.

Not long after breaking up the Walters and Johnson gang, Milton was contacted by Wells Fargo. It had a shipment of several million dollars in gold and asked him if he would accompany it, along with some extra guards. Milton said he'd take the job, but only if he could do it alone. He reasoned that he knew what he could do, but was not sure what to expect from anyone else. Wells Fargo accepted his terms. Packing some jugs of water, food, and his bedroll, and armed with a Colt .45 revolver, a rifle, and a semiautomatic shotgun, Milton guarded the gold from El Paso to San Francisco. So pleased was the company that it hired Milton as a guard on the regular run between Guaymas, Mexico, and Benson, Arizona.

Meanwhile, a renegade lawman, Burt Alvord, had formed a gang and successfully pulled off a train robbery—he even had had the audacity to ride back to town and lead the posse looking for the culprits! Alvord plotted another train robbery, carefully arranging it for a day when Milton was off duty. He did not intend to take part, but gave the job to five associates: "Three-Finger" Jack Dunlap, George and Louis Owens, Bravo Juan Yoas, and Bob Brown.

Unbeknownst to Alvord, the scheduled guard got sick and Milton agreed to fill in for him. As darkness fell on February 15, 1900, the train pulled into the station at Fairbank, Arizona, and as usual a crowd was waiting for it. Milton was standing in the open door of the express car, handing out packages, when he heard, "Hands up!"

He thought it was a joke until a shot knocked his hat off. Milton grabbed the short-barreled shotgun he kept by the door, but he couldn't use it as the bandits were standing behind a screen of bystanders. They opened up on him with their rifles and several shots hit him in the left arm, knocking him to the floor.

Assuming he was out of the fight, the gang rushed for the

door. Milton raised himself up and fired his shotgun one-handed, hitting the lead man, Dunlap, in the chest with 11 pellets. Yoas caught a pellet in his buttocks and fled the scene.

"Look out for the son of a bitch, he's shooting to kill!" shouted Dunlap as he fell.

Losing blood rapidly, Milton took the keys to the safe and threw them into a pile of packages at the other end of the car. He then tore off his sleeve, made a tourniquet around his arm, and collapsed unconscious between a couple of trunks. Milton later recalled, "I felt myself going, but I enjoyed it. I heard the most beautiful music—the most wonderful band—that I ever heard in my life. I wonder if every man does."

Meanwhile, the three remaining bandits fired round after round through the door and walls of the car to be sure Milton was dead. When they entered the car and looked at his limp, bleeding body, they were confident they had succeeded. However, with no key to the safe and no explosives to blow it, they were forced to leave empty-handed, taking the mortally wounded Dunlap with them.

Milton was taken to the hospital, where he spent eight months recuperating. He rejected the doctor's recommendation that the arm be amputated, and eventually regained partial use of it.

Sometime later, he dropped into Tucson and heard that Alvord was in town, telling everyone he would finish off Milton. Milton took a shotgun with him to the hotel and, when Alvord walked in, leveled it at him.

Alvord stopped dead in his tracks and begged Milton not to kill him.

Others on the scene shouted, "Kill the son of a bitch!"

Instead, Milton grabbed him by the ear, spun him around, and kicked him into the street, telling him never to return to Arizona. Thinking back on the incident years later, he said, "He had murdered a bunch of men and I should have killed him. But you just hate to shoot a man when he's hollerin'!"

Milton never forgot that he was a gentleman of the Old South, and there are things a gentleman does and things he does not do. Among the things he does not do is sully himself with the blood of a contemptible coward.

Milton worked regularly as a guard or lawman, but there was a line he wouldn't cross. When the copper magnate Bill Greene was having trouble with the Mexican workers at his mine in Cananea, he began hiring gunfighters. When he approached Milton, Milton asked him what he was expected to do.

"Just hang around," said Greene.

"What'll you pay?" asked Milton.

"I'll just write a note to my treasurer and let you fill it [in]," said Greene.

That kind of work didn't appeal to Milton. If he had signed on, he probably would have participated in the great Cananea shootout of 1906, when Greene's hired guns crushed an uprising of Mexican workers.

In 1904, the rising problem of illegal Chinese immigration led Sam Webb, Customs Officer at Nogales, to look for a man to patrol the border. He immediately thought of Milton, whom he considered the best pistol shot in the country and a man of utter fearlessness. Milton took the job and would later be dubbed "America's First Border Patrolman."

The job required riding through the desert between Yuma and El Paso, a distance of over 500 miles. This was work that suited Milton fine; in his younger years he would sometimes spend three months at a time without human contact, living off the land. He never felt lonesome when he was in the wild.

In 1915, Milton and a friend were sent to the San Francisco World's Fair to represent the Immigration Service. As a souvenir of the trip, Milton brought home a revolver he had snatched from a thug who tried to rob him with it.

Milton bought a stripped-down Model T and used it to perform some of his duties. On November 3, 1917, he rode into

Tombstone and heard that the bank had just been robbed and its manager, T.R. Brandt, had been killed. The robber, Fred Koch, had fled on foot. Milton and a friend took off after Koch in the Model T, Milton armed only with a .38 automatic. As they closed to within 100 yards of Koch, Milton shouted at him to halt. When he didn't obey, Milton shot him in the arm, causing him to surrender.

Brandt had been a popular figure in town, and when Milton brought in Koch, there was considerable sentiment for lynching him. Though Brandt and Milton had been good friends, the lawman wouldn't stand for this.

At Koch's trial, Milton was asked if he was "shooting to kill" when he fired at Koch, and he acknowledged that he was. The courtroom erupted in laughter; the idea that Milton would have hit a man in the arm when he had intended to kill him was considered very droll.

On another occasion Milton was out driving when he was stopped by two men who meant to rob him. Milton burst out laughing. "I'll tell you what to do," he told them. "Just go down this road and ask the first person you meet how safe it would be to hold up Jeff Milton."

Then he drove on.

On June 30, 1919, Milton married Mildred Taitt, a frail New York schoolteacher who had come West for a rest cure. He was 58 years old and she was 40. The deeply religious Mildred had her concerns about this "terrible man" who had "been in many a gun fight and broken a few laws," but she was won over when she found out he baked a pan of cornbread every day to feed the birds.

Mildred once asked him, "Jeff, didn't you ever have a feeling of fear in a fight?"

"Yes," he admitted, "I was afraid of what I would have to do to the other fellow. But after he had taken a couple of shots at me I got over it."

Jeff Milton died on May 7, 1947. In accordance with his

wishes, his widow spread his ashes among the saguaro cacti southwest of Tucson.

NOTES

1. *The Last Gunfighter*, p. 235.
2. Frank L. King, *Pioneer Western Empire Builders* (Pasadena: Trail's End Publishing Co., 1946), p. 161.

Moros

"[The Moro] is absolutely fearless, and once committed to combat he counts death as a mere incident."
—Gen. John J. "Black Jack" Pershing

Europe received its rude introduction to the Moros when Magellan stopped in the Philippines during his circumnavigation of the globe. He was able to form alliances with several tribes, but was rebuffed by Chief Lapu-Lapu, headquartered on Mactan Island. Through messengers, Magellan warned him that he and his people would be killed unless they gave him tribute, bowed to the authority of the king of Spain, and converted to Catholicism. The chief's response boiled down to "shut up and fight."

On the morning of April 27, 1521, Magellan landed on the beach of Mactan Island, accompanied by 48 soldiers in helmets and breastplates, and armed with Toledo swords. A large force of Moros encircled the Spaniards, undeterred by the fire from arquebuses and crossbows in the ships anchored off-shore. Magellan was wounded in the face by a lance, and then in the leg by an arrow. As he ordered his men to fall back, he suffered a severe leg wound from an islander's sword and fell facedown in the surf. Unable to come to his aid, his men watched as he was hacked to death by Chief Lapu-Lapu and his warriors.

A trio of well-armed Moros. (Credit: National Archives.)

The Spanish dubbed these Muslim inhabitants of the southern Philippines "Moros," after the Moors they had only recently driven from their homeland. The Moros had been converted to Islam by Arab missionaries in 1380. They had a spiritual leader, the Sultan of Sulu, but were far from a unified people. They lived in small tribes and fought among themselves almost constantly.

In 1565, the Spanish sent a fleet to conquer the Philippines, and within 11 years they controlled the northern islands, which accounted for half the total land mass. What remained were the southern islands of Mindanao, Basilan, and the Sulu Archipelago, which comprised some 300 smaller, scattered islands, the principal one being Jolo, home to the Sultan of Sulu. Never would the Spanish have guessed that these territories would defy conquest for as long as they held the Philippines.

Father Francisco Combés left an account of a Moro attack on a Spanish landing party in 1663:

> The Moros were so eager to display their valor as well as confident of humbling ours that scarcely had our troops reached land when the Moros came to meet them, so resolute that, taking no account of the bullets or sword, they struggled from five directions to penetrate our troops . . . and like mad brutes they hurled themselves to their death, not fearing wounds. The sword made no impressions on them and they laughed at the arquebuses.[1]

After many such encounters, the Spanish elected to leave the Moro islands largely alone, except for a few isolated garrisons that were under almost constant siege. Coastal towns on other islands were fortified in order to protect them from the depredations of Moro pirates, who regularly raided them in search of slaves.

Relying on weapons of obsidian and copper, the Aztec and Inca failed to stop the Spanish conquest. With weapons of good steel, the Moros succeeded. A Moro man always had one or two edged weapons on his person. Even when sleeping he kept a blade close at hand, often tethered to his wrist.

The basic blade types were the *kris*, *barong*, and *campilan*. The *barong* is a heavy, single-edged, leaf-shaped cleaver with a blade two to three inches wide and 12 to 18 inches long. The *kris* is a narrow, double-edged sword, which may be straight or wavy, and can vary significantly in length. The campilan is a heavy, two-handed sword with a single-edged blade, 35 to 40 inches long. It is wider at the tip than at the hilt and can deliver a devastating cut.

These blades were often laminated from iron and steel in a manner similar to that used by Japanese swordsmiths, though Filipino blades were not produced to the same level of finish. They were of excellent quality and there are numerous accounts of a blow from a barong or kris taking off a man's head, or his arm at the shoulder. A blow from a campilan could cleave a man from collarbone to waist.

The kris and barong were tucked into the sash that Moros wore around their waist, with the hilt of the weapon positioned in easy reach. An American officer observed, "Nothing could be more rapid than the way a Moro gets into action. His barong or kris slips in or out of its scabbard like oil, it is nicely placed to his hand, and the swing of drawing it plunges it into his victim."[2]

Because of its size, the campilan was often carried across the back in a wooden sheath made in two halves, secured by lashings of jute. When necessary, a blow could be delivered without unsheathing the blade, as its edge could cut through these lashings without slowing down.

Male children were trained in the use of the blade by older warriors who were themselves veterans of numerous encounters. This training was deadly serious: live blades were often

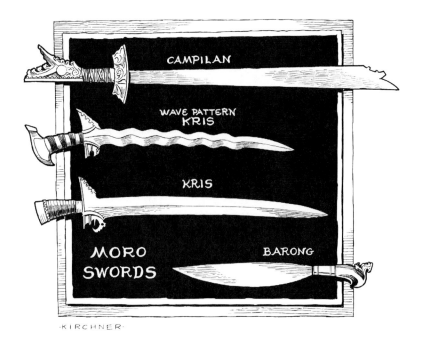

·KIRCHNER·

Typical Moro weapons.

used, which imparted a healthy respect for the damage they could do. It was rare to encounter an adult Moro who did not bear the scars of hand-to-hand fighting. The Spaniards called the Filipino fighting style *escrima* after their word for fencing.

According to one expert, "The Moro fighter used lightning-fast, agile movements, sometimes consisting of a series of pumping and darting maneuvers to confuse his opponent. These allowed the warrior to close the gap between them rapidly. When he had reached striking distance, he made short work of his enemy by way of sophisticated cutting and slashing movements with his sword."[3]

Captain Robert Hamilton reported that "in a fight, the Moros always aim to cut or sever the tendons and muscles of the body, thus leaving their victims to suffer intense agony."[4]

Major R. L. Bullard wrote, "[The Moros] are all of one profession—arms. As children their first toys are wooden arms; their first instruction, the play of the sword and spear. Whatever else as men they may be, priest, farmer, robber, pirate, merchant, lawyer, they are always, first, soldiers."[5]

In the late 19th century, the Spanish finally made progress in their campaign to bring the Moros under control. With new steam-powered gunboats they were able to suppress Moro piracy, and in 1876 they captured the walled town of Joló for the fifth and final time. It was in this period that the Moros adopted a new tactic rooted in the Islamic tradition of jihad—the suicide attack. The Spanish term for such an attacker was a *juramentado*, meaning "one who has sworn an oath." His oath was to kill as many infidels as possible until he was killed, after which he would ascend to the seventh level of paradise on a white horse, where, in addition to the 72 sloe-eyed virgins allotted him, every infidel he had killed would serve him as a slave.

Contributing to the terror of the attacks was the juramentados' remarkable resistance to gunshot wounds. This was due to adrenalin, fanaticism, and certain physical preparations, such as wrapping their abdomen tightly in bandages and binding their main arteries to slow blood loss.

Juramentado attacks were often well planned. As Moros were not permitted to carry weapons within the walled city of Joló, they smuggled them in food packages or hid them down their trouser-legs. On one occasion a Moro checked his barong with the guards at the gate, conducted his business in town, and after he returned and picked it up, generously passed out cigarettes to the guards. After several of the soldiers put down their rifles to light up, he went to work. According to the account, "Quick as lightning he snatched his barong from its sheath, beheading one of the soldiers with a continuation of the same movement that drew the knife. The man's head rolled 15 feet away. Before the stupefied guardians recovered from their surprise two more of them had received fatal injuries, while a third was crippled for life, but the Sergeant was too quick for the Moro and blew his head off."[6]

A French doctor, Joseph Montano, described an attack by *juramentados* in the village of Tianzgi on the island of Sulu in 1883. Eleven of them entered the town, concealing their weapons in loads of fodder that they pretended to be selling.

> After stabbing the guards they rushed up the street, hacking at everyone they met. The soldiers in the garrison, hearing the cry "*Los juramentados!*" seized their guns and advanced to meet them.
>
> The mad Mahometans rushed blindly on them, cutting and slashing right and left. Again and again, though shot and shattered by the hail of bullets, they rose and flung themselves upon their enemies. One of them, though transfixed by a bayonet, remained erect, struggling fiercely to reach the soldier that had impaled him. Nor would he cease his furious efforts till another soldier had blown his brains out with a pistol. Before all of the *juramentados* could be killed, they had hacked fifteen soldiers to pieces, besides wounding many others.
>
> "And what wounds!" says Dr. Montano; "the head of one corpse is cut off as clean as if it had been done with a razor; another soldier is cut almost in two. The first of the wounded to come under my hand was a soldier of the Third Regiment, who was mounting guard at the gate through which some of the assassins entered. His left arm was fractured in three places; his shoulder and breast were literally cut up like mince meat; amputation appeared to

be the only chance for him; but in that lacerated flesh there was no longer a spot from which could be cut a shred."[7]

Describing events of this period, Dean C. Worcester wrote:

> I have known [a Moro] when bayoneted to seize the barrel of the gun and push the bayonet through himself in order to bring the man at the other end within striking distance, cut him down, unclasp the bayonet and, leaving it in the wound to prevent hemorrhage, go on fighting. I have known two Moros armed with bamboo lances to attack a column of two thousand soldiers armed with rifles. It is an historic fact that Moro *juramentados* once attempted to rush the walls of Jolo and kept up the fruitless effort until they blocked with their dead bodies the rifle slits, so that it became necessary for the Spanish soldiers to take positions on top of the walls in order to fire. I have known a Moro, shot repeatedly through the body and with both legs broken, to take his *kris* in his teeth and pull himself forward with his hands in the hope of getting near enough to strike one more blow for the Prophet.[8]

It is reported that during the last eight years of Spanish rule more than 300 soldiers were killed by juramentados in Joló alone.

After defeating Spain in 1899, the United States took over the Philippines, provoking a war for Filipino independence. Though the main insurrection was crushed within three years, resistance from the Moro minority, which numbered at most about 300,000, continued until 1913.

Like the Spanish, the Americans were struck by the ferocity of their opponents. General John "Black Jack" Pershing, a veteran Indian fighter, declared the Moros a far fiercer and more determined foe than the Apache, writing, "The nature of the Moro is such that he is not at all overawed or impressed by an overwhelming force. If he takes a notion to fight, he will fight regardless of the number of men he thinks are to be brought against him. You cannot bluff him."[9]

Many American soldiers considered their .38 Colt revolver inadequate. To underline that point, Captain F. C. Marshall described the following juramentado attack, which occurred on March 12, 1903, in an article for the *Cavalry Journal*:

> This time the Jolo market was the scene, at seven o'clock in the morning. Three Moros, with their *barongs* hidden under the folds of their sarongs, bearing loads of native produce to sell, entered the market, which, since the cholera scare, has been held in a cocoanut grove near the village of Jolo. On getting into the thick of the crowd they threw down their loads, drew their *barongs* and started. They killed three Moros, one East Indian, and wounded a Filipino and his Moro wife, before the crowd scattered. Captain Eltinge and Lieutenant Partridge, Fifteenth Cavalry, with a detachment of eleven men of Troop III of that regiment, were just leaving their stables for target practice. Hearing the commotion, they rushed to the market and were at once charged by the three Moros most desperately. Of course the cavalrymen being mounted, could easily keep out of the way and could shoot the men down at their leisure, but it was noticed that the stopping effect of the bullets was very

small, and only when hit by bullets that entered the skull did the men stop their desperate attempt to get at the soldiers. The last Moro to die, while on his knees, threw his *barong* at a mounted man, fully twenty feet away, striking him in the pit of the stomach with—most fortunately—the hilt.[10]

Major Robert L. Bullard described an attack that occurred in September 1903:

> In a fight by boat last year with the Sultan of Toros on Lake Lanao, I suddenly heard a death groan and a fearful struggle behind me. I turned to find a Moro, kris in hand and the awful fire of murder blazing in his eye. One stroke of his deadly knife had half severed the head from the body of my soldier steersman, and the flashing blade was raining blows into the bottom of the boat at the prostrate writhing form and flying legs of the soldier oarsman who had occupied the place between me and the steersman. The latter, his head fallen sadly forward on his breast, sat bolt upright in his place, dying. Too fast to tell, I poured four shots into the mad Moro, but to my consternation they seemed wholly, wholly without effect; and in desperation and bitterness of heart, cursing such an arm and the fate that had given it to the soldier to fail him in his hour of need, I spared the last two shots, springing forward in the last hope of shoving the revolver's muzzle against him, and so to blow out his brains or heart. In that hundredth part of an instant, he stooped to clear a bamboo bow that looped

the narrow boat over the body of the fallen
oarsman; I thrust my muzzle against the top of
his close-cropped head and fired. Then at last
he felt the .38, and sank forward upon his own
weapon and the legs of the soldier whose head
was against my feet.[11]

In his classic study on gunshot injuries, Col. Louis A. La
Garde, who had been a U.S. Army doctor in the Philippines,
wrote, "In 1907 a Moro charged the guard at Joló, P.I.
[Philippine Islands]. When he was within 100 yards, the entire
guard opened fire on him. When he reached within five yards
of the firing party he stumbled and fell and while in the prone
position a trumpeter killed him by shooting him through the
head with a .45-caliber Colt's revolver. There were ten wounds
in his body from the service rifle. Three of the wounds were
located in the chest, one in the abdomen and the remainder
had taken effect in the extremities."

In describing the death of the rebel leader Hassan, Gen.
Hugh Lenox Scott wrote that Hassan absorbed 32 Krag
rounds and was still attempting to use his barong on an
American soldier when the latter dropped him with a .45 slug
between his ears.

Some ascribed this bullet-resistant quality to some physio-
logical peculiarity; General Scott wrote, "The Moro seems to
have a nervous system differing from that of a white man, for
he carries lead like a grizzly bear and keeps coming on after
being shot again and again."[12] Colonel G. V. Fosberry, who
won a Victoria Cross in action against the Hindustanis in
1863, facetiously ascribed the difficulty to ignorance: "With
the civilized man, who knows to a nicety the location of his
principal organs and something of the effects that the presence
of foreign bodies in his interior may be expected to produce, a
comparatively slight wound will often suffice to set him thinking of his spiritual condition or his other personal interests,

rather than the business in which he may be engaged." But, he explained, this is not the case of the fanatical native, who "will make his rush, having his mind fully made up to kill you or to be killed by you, and he knows as little about his own insides as a tiger does."[13]

However, most placed the blame on the M1889/1895 revolver, chambered for the anemic .38 Colt round. Major Bullard wrote:

> Whatever, theoretically, may be its capabilities and uses, actual service has found for the revolver but one practical use which justifies its retention and covers the trouble of its carrying in war, namely, to destroy suddenly and effectively, to kill dead, an enemy threatening at close quarters, within, say, twenty paces. This is its one practical paramount use, and to this purpose its caliber should conform. This is the use of which in the days of the Wild West developed and made the revolver preeminently the weapon of the fighting American, and made it, let me say, not of toy caliber, but a real "gun," which means a .45 and nothing else. . . . Now at close quarters you must kill your enemy and kill him quick, or he will do as much for you. It is not enough simply to knock him down, not enough to wound, even to wound him badly; because, over the souls of men fighting and falling at close quarters, even wounded unto death, but not dead, comes a fierce rage and thirst of revenge, an awful desire to kill and sweep their slayers with them into eternity, and often they do it. It is but the crook of a finger, perhaps. Whenever, therefore, we really come to a fight with the revolver, it is

An Army poster showing the Colt .45 in use against the Moros. (Credit: U.S. Army.)

necessary to have a revolver that will kill. This
the .38 does not.[14]

Troops demanded that the tried-and-true .45-caliber
revolver be brought out of retirement. In 1901, 500 refur-
bished Colt Single Action Army revolvers were shipped to the
Philippines and the following year saw shipments of a double-
action .45-caliber revolver dubbed the "Philippine Model."[15]

Shortly thereafter was begun the search for an automatic pistol in .45 caliber which culminated in the adoption of the model 1911.

Though a bigger bullet is more effective than a smaller one, the notion of "stopping power" is generally misunderstood. Contrary to popular opinion, the .45 automatic will not bowl a man over or knock him down with a hit to the shoulder. To drop a man in his tracks you must either shut down his central nervous system with a shot to the brain or spine, or break his pelvis. Here the .45 caliber round has an advantage over the .38 Colt, in that it has the power to get through the body and inflict this kind of damage. However, shot placement matters more than the caliber.

It should be noted that even in the hand-to-hand combat for which they were renowned, Moros sometimes got more than they could handle from an American. A case in point was the assassination attempt on Capt. Vernon L. Whitney. Whitney was a large, powerful man, a decorated veteran of the Philippines Constabulary whose sciatic nerve had been severed in battle, causing him to limp. As a reward for his service, he was appointed governor of Joló. On August 21, 1913, he was walking alone along the street of a small village, having sent his aide ahead to make ready his steam launch, when two Moros approached and saluted him respectfully. As they passed, they suddenly drew their barongs and rushed him. Whitney grabbed one and tucked him under his powerful left arm, and at the same time drew his revolver and shot the other twice in the head, killing him. He pumped the four remaining rounds into the body of the Moro under his arm, but the Moro continued to hack at his back with his barong. Whitney had to wrestle it away from him and kill him with it.

Whitney's back was laid open in five places and his shoulder arteries severed, but he recovered from his wounds.[16]

Though in hand-to-hand fighting the Moros were formidable, in open combat they were no match for American troops, with their superior weapons and tactics. This was dramatically demonstrated when the United States mounted punitive expeditions into the islands' interiors, seeking the Moros out in their jungle fortresses and attacking them with machine guns and mountain artillery. Though the Moros fought desperately, their losses were wildly disproportionate to the casualties they inflicted. In the battle of Bud Dajo, in March 1906, between 600 and 1,000 Moros were killed for American losses of 15 killed and 52 wounded. In the battle of Bud Bagsak, in June 1913, more than 500 Moros were killed, while American losses were 15 killed and 25 wounded. This was the battle that broke the back of the Moro resistance. The Sultan of Sulu, the Moros' spiritual leader, surrendered to General Pershing.

The Japanese invasion at the beginning of World War II once again aroused the Moros to fierce resistance. Two weeks after Pearl Harbor, news accounts read, "Moro leaders have expressed a desire to organize their followers for a fight to the death against the Japanese and the war drums are throbbing through the wild hinterland inhabited by these fierce tribesmen."[17] In March 1942, these leaders pledged to General MacArthur: "We have prepared our bladed weapons because we lack firearms, and with sharp *kris, barong, campilan, tabas,* and spear, we will attack or defend as ordered. We have over 10,000 already sworn upon the Koran and additional fighting men are being sworn every day. We Lanao Moros have fought for many generations: we know how to fight. . . . We want you to know, and the President of the United States to know, that we Lanao Moros are loyal and will fight all the enemies of the United States."[18]

Throughout the war, the Japanese could only maintain a few well-defended garrisons on Moro-populated islands.

In 1945, as American forces retook the Philippines, the Sultan of Sulu held a welcoming ceremony for Col. William J. Moroney, commander of the 163rd Infantry Regiment. This was the same sultan who, as a young man, had surrendered to

General Pershing 23 years earlier. When the meeting ended, the sultan rather openly hinted that he would appreciate a gift from the Americans, and his eye was focused on Moroney's .45 automatic. A news article states, "Moroney silently unstrapped his pistol belt and handed the weapon and belt to the sultan. It must have caused both Moroney and the sultan to smile inwardly. For the sultan was one of the few men responsible for the creation of the .45 caliber pistol. During the Moro uprising, American troops learned—the hard way— that a .38-caliber pistol wouldn't stop a Moro's charge."[19]

NOTES

1. Maj. Gen. Ernesto B. Calupig, "Piracy and Its Historical Background in the Philippines," October 24, 2000, Internet resource.
2. "Revolver and Its Holster," p. 138.
3. *Moro Swords*, p. 12.
4. *America at War*, p. 216.
5. "Among the Savage Moros," p. 268.
6. "When Moros Run Amuck," *Washington Post*, January 14, 1912, p. M3.
7. Ramon Reyes Lala, *The Philippine Islands* (New York: Continental Publishing Co., 1899), pp. 112–13.
8. Dean Worcester, *The Philippines Past and Present* (New York: MacMillan Company, 1914), pp. 654–55.
9. *Muddy Glory*, p. 27.
10. "Revolver and Its Holster," pp. 137–8.
11. "Caliber of the Revolver," p. 302.
12. *Memories of a Soldier*, p. 316.
13. G.V. Fosbery, *Journal of the Royal United Service Institution*, 40 (1896), p. 1470.
14. "Caliber of the Revolver," pp. 300–01.
15. Based on the 1878 Colt "Frontier" Model, the Philippine Model had a large trigger guard to allow diminutive Filipinos to use two fingers to pull its double-action trigger.
16. "Victim Slays Moro Assassins," *Chicago Daily Tribune*, August 22, 1913, p. 2.
17. "Bolo Swinging Moros Ready to Join in War on Japan," *Los Angeles Times*, December 21, 1941, p. 1A.

18. "Guns Lacking, They'll Wield Cold Steel," *Washington Post*, March 3, 1942, p. 2.
19. Richard C. Bergholz, "Sultan of Sulu, Who Surrendered Moros to Pershing in 1913, Greets Americans Loyally This Time—and Gets Another Gun," *Washington Post*, May 20, 1945, p. B3.

Rich Owen
(1880–1948)

"Nobody I electrocuted ever held it against me. At least not beforehand."

—Rich Owen

When the topic of *The Deadliest Men* comes up, people have asked me if I include killers such as Timothy McVeigh, who was responsible for 168 deaths in the bombing of the Federal Building in Oklahoma City. I explain that I'm not writing about mass murderers, but people who were able to dominate a violent environment and hold their own against overwhelming odds. McVeigh does not qualify, but the second most prolific killer in Oklahoma history, Rich Owen, does. By the time he died at 67 years of age, Owen had killed 75 men. Of these, nine were in one-on-one encounters involving guns, knives, and, in one case, a shovel, but he allowed as how that might be an undercount, as "I never count peckerwoods." He killed the other 66 in his official capacity as executioner for

Owen assaulted by two inmates at McAlester State Penitentiary. (Credit: New York Public Library.)

the Oklahoma State Penitentiary, a post he held for 29 years.
Richard Ernest Owen was born in Joplin, Missouri, on
January 19, 1880. He was 13 when he shot his first man, a
thief who was stealing his father's horse. In 1900, when he
was working as a coal miner in Heavener, Oklahoma, he killed
a man in a knife fight. Later, as a coal-mine hoisting engineer
in McAlester, he was attacked by a miner he had fired. When
the man came at Owen with a gun, Owen pulled his own pistol and killed him. Details of Owen's personal affrays are
sketchy, but he was tried for murder four times and acquitted
in every case.

When a strike at the mine put Owen out of work, he spent
much of his time working with a couple of bloodhounds he
had raised as a hobby. In April 1909, after a prisoner escaped
from the newly built McAlester State Penitentiary, Owen took
his dogs out and soon captured him. As a result, he was
offered a job as guard, at $75 a month, and he took it.

All prisons are rough, but the one at McAlester was excep-
tionally so. Oklahoma had only been granted statehood in 1907;
before that, it was considered Indian Territory and had served
as an outlaw sanctuary through much of the 19th century.

On November 2, 1913, Owen was taking part in the manhunt for John Cudjo, who had shot and killed a Deputy
Sheriff, when he ran into some trouble:

> Sheriff McEwan of Mcintosh county and
> Rich Owen of McAlester arrived Sunday night
> to assist in the pursuit of the fleeing negro.
>
> As the posse was searching for Cudjo
> Sunday evening, four negroes were met in the
> road in the Little River district. Peter Carolina,
> one of the negroes, threw down his gun in line
> with Deputy Sheriff Wiseman. Officer Owen
> commanded the negro to drop the gun.
> [Carolina] turned and attempted to point his

weapon at Owen. Instead, that officer fired, shooting Carolina through the heart.[1]

On December 10, 1915, Oklahoma executed its first prisoner in its new electric chair. Mack Treadwell, the prison electrician, handled the duty with the assistance of Owen, who assisted on nine subsequent executions. When Treadwell left the job, a new man was hired, but the second time he was needed he was too drunk to pull the switch.

Interviewed by journalist Ray Parr in 1948, Owen recalled:

> The warden nodded to me and said, "Can you pull it, Rich?"
> I didn't say a word. I just walked over and slapped it to him like I'd been doing it all my life. I didn't think much about it. Somebody had to pull it as the fellow was already in the chair waiting. I never feel a man should have to wait any longer than he has to.

From then on, in addition to his regular duties, Owen handled executions. For each one the state paid him a $100 fee, plus $50 for every additional man he might have to electrocute the same day. Some nights he made $200.

Owen took his job seriously. He would soak the hood and the leg piece in salt water. As he told Parr:

> It makes for a good clear connection. Then I see that they shave his head and legs. I want a good smooth skin because hair burns and smells. The trouble with a lot of fellows, they try to electrocute a man too quick. I always run up to about 40 seconds. When the switch hits 2,300 [volts] I roll her back to 1,700 and then I work up to 2,300 again. If you turn the juice on real strong and leave it on it won't kill as quick as if you

turn it down some. The blood has to have time to cook
in the heart, the way I figure it . . . . I take 40 seconds
because this gives me more time and I don't burn a
man half so bad. I hardly ever blister him. I watch a
man right close and when I see smoke begin to rise out
of him, I roll 'er back and let him cool down a little,
and then turn 'er back up. . . . I guess I've electrocuted
50 or 60 men and I've never had no complaint whatever . . . . I never had 'em take one out and have to put
him back in again.

Along with these tricks of the trade, Owen learned not to
touch a body too soon, as it stored a residual charge. Instead,
he would roll a Bull Durham cigarette and smoke it while the
charge dissipated. Owen's expertise got him work in neighboring states: he electrocuted three men in New Mexico, two in
Arkansas, and two in Texas.

Owen supervised one hanging, that of kidnapper Arthur
Gooch on June 19, 1936. It did not go well; the knot slipped
behind Gooch's head and he dangled for 15 minutes before he
was pronounced dead. Owen bristled at any insinuation that
his work had been shoddy. He explained, "You pull a chicken's
head off and he flops around like everything. That's the way it
was with Gooch. He just had to have time to die."

Owen's regular duties were as boss of a prison work gang.
Like all guards who worked within the walls, he carried no
weapons. This put him in constant danger of attack, but Owen
was known as a dangerous man to cross. Lean and powerfully
muscled at 160 pounds, he was a formidable middleweight
boxer. He had a hard face and his blue-gray eyes burned with a
"strange, fierce fire." Convicts used to say that if you looked in
those eyes, you could see little devils jumping out of them.
One former inmate, Percy Parnell, stated unequivocally that
"Rich Owen was without a doubt the toughest, most feared
guard that ever stalked the halls of Big Mac."

In 1948, shortly before his death, a reporter wrote:
> Rich was not afraid of death. He had faced
> it too many times, in bloody prison riots, per-
> sonal fights, and in the death chamber.
>
> "I never was afraid of dying," he said. "I'm
> not now. I just figure every man has such a
> time to go. When it comes, he goes. I never give
> it a thought.
>
> "When it gets a little rough, like it has a few
> times, I just laugh to myself and say this might be
> the time. I might go. I either win or go down."

One time, while working in the prison twine plant, Owen was attacked by "six peckerwoods." A convict who was a friend of Owen's grabbed a board "and we whipped all six of them. They never jumped on nobody else."

On November 27, 1936, Owen was in the prison tool shed when he was jumped by two long-term inmates, Harlan Welles and Roy Glasby, who were trying to break out.

Glasby was armed with a short knife fashioned from a piece of file, and Welles with a hatchet. Welles hit Owen with the blunt side of the hatchet and knocked him out for a few minutes. When he came to, his hands were tied behind his back with barbed wire. The convicts told him they were going to use him as a hostage and break out. Owen told them they might as well kill him then and there, because he was going to kill them if they didn't. "I'm not asking you for any mercy, and if I get out of here don't you ask me for any," he warned them.

Owen described what happened:

> We started walking. They had that knife in
> my back almost three inches. They'd turn it to
> steer me, like a bridle on a horse. They was cut-
> ting out a pretty good space in my back. It
> made a bad sore.

When Watkins [the tower guard] sees something is going on, I yell up at him— "All right, Pat, go to shooting, the fight's on."

With that I jerked away and spun around right quick. I kicked the fellow who had the knife in the groin and butted the other with my head. We all went down rolling in the ditch, me still a-kicking and a-butting.

He hit at me twice with that hatchet, but I ducked and he ran. When I rolled in that ditch, the wire came loose from one of my hands and I grabbed the blade of that knife. He was stabbing at me trying to cut my head off.

I was hanging on to that blade with him a-yanking it. You can still see the scar here. I shook him loose and Pat shot him. That bullet missed my belly about half an inch.

I believe I would eventually have come out without Pat shooting him, but it helped a lot when he did. It knocked him loose of the knife.

By then I had my other hand loose. I grabbed that so-and-so by the hair and socked that knife in to the neck bone. And I didn't pull it straight out. I just ripped 'er out and let 'er slice clear across. Then I kicked him a couple of times in the mouth and said, "Now die, you so-and-so and go to hell with the others."

You just should have seen how that so-and-so looked.

I went in the tool shed after that other one. He began to cry for mercy— "Oh, Mr. Rich, oh, Mr. Rich, don't kill me."

I said, "You so-and-so, I said I'd kill you if you didn't kill me. I told you not ever to ask me for mercy."

> He jumped through the window and a
> guard shot him in the knee.
> He went down bellering and I finished him
> with a long-handled shovel. I sure smashed his
> brains out.

When Warden Jess Dunn, a good friend of Owen, arrived on the scene and saw the man Owen had killed with the knife, he asked, "Well, Rich, why don't you go ahead and cut his head plumb off? You damn sure nearly did."

Dunn told Owen to go get his wounds treated, but Owen said he preferred to wait until his shift was over in half an hour. He returned his attention to the work party he had been supervising.

> I turned to the rest of those peckerwoods,
> who'd just been standing around waiting to see
> me get killed, and I says, "Now go on to work.
> Me and them has had our fun. I'll tell you fel-
> lows when to quit."
> You just ought to seen them picks begin to
> fly. They dug more dirt in 10 minutes than they
> had all day. We sure got lots of work done in
> the next 30 minutes.

On August 10, 1941, four convicts took Warden Dunn hostage, got rifles and pistols from the guards, and drove out of the prison in Dunn's automobile. Owen shot out two of the car's tires, and a deputy sheriff opened fire on the convicts. Three of the convicts were killed, but not before they fatally shot Dunn. Hiram Prather, the only prisoner who survived the shootout, was convicted of Dunn's murder. As he was strapped into the electric chair on July 14, 1943, Owen leaned over and told him, "I'm going to fry you like bacon."

He turned the dial up to 2,300 volts and left it there.

Owen and his family lived in a frame cottage he had built in 1908 on a dirt street three blocks from the prison. Due to the many death threats he had received over the years, it was surrounded by a high board fence with a sign on it reading "Bad Dog." Inside were two savage bulldogs.

"If I had to kill one of those dogs, it would hurt me a lot more than it hurts me to execute a criminal," Owen told one reporter. "An execution is more like killing a chicken—just a job. I'm never nervous during one, and I can come right home and go to sleep afterward. It's not the dead convicts I have to worry about, but some of the live ones."

At 67 years of age, Owen was diagnosed with liver cancer and returned home to die. It was at this time that Ray Parr, reporter for the *Daily Oklahoman*, interviewed him. As Parr passed by the guard dogs, Owen said with a grin, "Great dogs, those bulldogs. You can kill 'em but you can never whip one of 'em."

Like owner, like dog.

NOTE

1. "Killings in Seminole," *Evening News* (Ada, OK), November 3, 1913, p. 2.

Frank Pape
(1909–2000)

"Everybody I shot and killed deserved it. I slept like a baby after every one."
—Frank Pape

Dubbed "the toughest cop in America," Frank Pape achieved legendary status in his 39-year career with the Chicago Police Department. It is said he never lost a case in court, put over 300 men in prison, and sent six to the electric chair. He was in 16 shoot-outs in which nine criminals were killed and 14 wounded.

Pape was born on February 13, 1909, in the Bucktown section of Chicago. He was a toddler when his father died and he became the man of the house early, taking care of his mother and sister. He dropped out of high school after two years to become a sheet metal worker, but when the Depression hit he lost his job. He thought about working for the police department; the security of it looked good to him. Standing five-feet-

Detectives Rudy Friedl and Frank Pape (right) examine sawed-off shotguns used by two suspects in 23 tavern holdups. On the table are two .32-caliber revolvers, a .380 automatic, and assorted ammunition. (Courtesy of Jerry Pape.)

ten but weighing only 147 pounds, Pape had to stuff himself with bananas and drink a gallon of water to meet the minimum weight requirement of 150 pounds. He was sworn in on March 25, 1933.

Pape first made the news in 1937. He was in an unmarked car, with a partner, working plainclothes, when he spotted four suspicious-looking young men drive by. As the officers followed, the car suddenly pulled to the side of the street and the occupants ran out of it. Pape chased two of them, firing a warning shot. The men shot back at him and Pape returned fire. One of the men fell; he had not been struck by a bullet, but had tripped. The other man ran into the Chicago River, continuing to fire at Pape until his gun was empty. "It was the first time I had ever been shot at," said Pape. "I could hear the bullets hitting the mortar on the buildings. This guy was really trying to kill me."

Pape arrested the two men who, after a short period in the interrogation room, identified their accomplices and admitted they had stolen the car for a planned series of robberies. In this case, as in many others after it, Pape acted upon an instinct that "something wasn't right" about a person or group of people and was proven correct.

Pape took the sergeant's exam in 1942. His grade, along with the efficiency points he had earned for his many arrests in the Robbery Unit, got him the promotion.

On June 5, 1945, Pape was driving with detectives Morrie Friedman and Rudy Friedl, with whom he had been partnered for seven years. Friedman, ten years his senior, had long been a friend and mentor to Pape. As they went south on Clark Street, Pape saw a convertible heading northward. For some reason he didn't like the looks of its three occupants, two men and a woman.

As always, Pape was armed with his bone-handled .38 caliber Colt Police Positive, which he kept in a canvas-lined front pants pocket. As he circled around to follow the convertible, he opened the glove compartment and took out his backup gun, a long-barreled Smith & Wesson .44 Special, and laid it on the front seat.

The police pulled alongside the convertible and nosed it to the curb. As it was forced to a stop, one of the passengers, Lyman Heiman, 37, got out and hurriedly walked away. Friedman ran after him. For some reason that he later could not explain, Friedl grabbed Pape's backup gun and followed.

Pape remained behind, covering the other two people in the convertible.

Friedman rounded the corner after Heiman and fired a warning shot into the air. Heiman was standing behind a parked Cadillac sedan, a .32 automatic in one hand and a .38 revolver in the other. He immediately fired on Friedman, mortally wounding him with his first shot.

Friedl fired at Heiman and the two men began circling the car, ducking and shooting. Each had two guns and more than 20 shots were exchanged. As Heiman knelt behind the fender to try to get a steady firing position, Friedl shot him in the head. Not certain that he had finished his opponent, he ran up and fired three more shots into him.

On Heiman's body were his Army discharge papers, which indicated that he had been awarded a Silver Star, Bronze Star, Purple Heart, and Good Conduct Medal for his service in the North African and Sicilian campaigns. He and his accomplices were wanted for two grocery store robberies in Indiana.

Friedman was taken to the hospital, where he died shortly after he was admitted. After this, Pape adopted a new rule: no warning shots.

On the evening of October 19, 1945, Pape and Friedl were cruising with their new partner, John Moss, when Pape spotted an expensive Buick being driven by five young men. He had a hunch that something wasn't right and he was correct. The car had been stolen from a garage less than an hour before, after one of the gang, Victor Puzzo, had beaten the attendant uncon-

scious with the butt of his revolver. He was accompanied by
Phillip Puzzo, Charles DeCola, Charley Simeni, and Frank
Randazzo. They were looking for a store to rob. The squad car made a U-turn to follow the Buick. The
Buick sped away, with the police now in hot pursuit. Driving
through an alley, the police vehicle hit a pothole that tore its
muffler loose and broke a front spring. Friedl, who was driving, kept the pedal to the floor despite the deafening racket.
The Buick failed to make a turn before the El tracks and
slammed into a telephone pole. The five hoodlums piled out
into the alley, guns blazing at the detectives. The detectives
charged at them, firing back. Losing heart, Phillip Puzzo dived
under the car. Simeni was hit twice in the side and collapsed.
Randazzo was hit in the leg and fell. Victor Puzzo was hit
twice in the head and once in the chest and died with a burning cigarette still between his lips. As Pape advanced, DeCola
fired at him from behind an El pillar. Pape heard *click, click,*
click as DeCola's hammer fell on empty chambers. The 19-
year-old DeCola put his hands in the air and shouted, "I surrender, I surrender!"

As Pape stepped out from behind a garbage can, DeCola
dived to the ground to pick up another gun. "Fuck you, surrender," said Pape, as he shot him.

The outcome: two dead, two wounded, and one prisoner.
None of the detectives had been hit. Two automatics and three
revolvers were recovered at the scene.

At the inquest, DeCola's parents shouted "Murderer, murderer!" at Pape. DeCola's father insisted that Pape had no right
to shoot his son, as his son's shots hadn't hit anyone. He told
Pape he knew where he lived and he would pay for what he
did. Pape responded, "If you come within one block of my
home, or near any member of my family, there's going to be
another goddamn funeral and it won't be mine."

In the autumn of 1945, Chicago police were after a gang
called the Bookie Bandits, which specialized in robbing illegal

betting parlors. Its members included Lawrence "Tiny" Mazzanars, "Chris the Greek" Perres, James "Red" Kelly, and Renoro Lolli.

In December, on a tip from an informant, the Robbery Unit picked up Lolli. He had a large cache of weapons in his apartment, including six revolvers, a rifle, a sawed off double-barreled shotgun, an M3A1 submachine gun, and hundreds of rounds of ammunition.

Lolli played dumb, so Pape threatened to call some "syndicate boys" and let them know who had been robbing the bookies. Lolli cried, "For God's sake, what are you trying to do to me? I get whacked either way, there's no way out for me."

Pape smiled at him and said pleasantly, "Rule number one: Don't make your problems my problems. Rule number two? Don't cry. You want to be a tough guy, do stickups, shoot people, steal money? When the jig's up, don't cry. I hate crybabies. You don't want me to make that call, I want a list of all the scores you've put down, I want to know the identity of your partners. I want to know everything about everything, and then, when I'm satisfied you've told us the truth, I'll decide what to do with you." [1]

Lolli talked. He even told Pape that Mazzanars and Perres had a job planned for the following day, and he gave them the address of the garage where they had parked the Cadillac they had stolen for the purpose.

Pape and his partners took Lolli with them to look at the garage on West Lyndale Avenue. As Pape and Moss approached it, two men left it and walked toward a nearby alley.

"Police officers! Put your hands in the air!" shouted Pape.

The two men turned and shot at them, then ran through an alley, with the two detectives in pursuit.

Friedl, waiting in the car with Lolli, heard the gunshots. Suddenly a man with a gun ran in front of the car.

"That's Mazzanars!" said Lolli.

Friedl drew his gun and fired through the windshield.

Mazzanars was hit in the shoulder, staggered across the street, and collapsed.

Meanwhile, Perres was running up Lyndale Avenue, firing wildly back at Pape. Pape returned fire and dropped Perres with a bullet in his head.

Still enraged that Mazzanars had shot at him, Pape walked over to where he lay wounded and said, "I'll kill you right now, you son of a bitch!"

Friedl bumped him with his shoulder and said quietly, "Frank, there's people gathering on the street and on the porches."

Pape holstered his revolver.

The gang was broken. The only loose end was James Kelly. No witnesses were able to identify him and he had to be released. That loose end would not be tied up for another six years.

In December 1947, Chicago saw what newspapers called its most indiscriminate, sadistic killing since the St. Valentine's Day Massacre, perpetrated by a trio of young thugs: Thomas Daley, Lowell Fentress, and James Morelli. Three months earlier, they had invaded a woman's home, pistol-whipped her, and escaped with a modest amount of cash and jewelry. Shortly afterward, they were arrested and let out on bail. Daley was convinced that he knew who had tipped off the police: John Kuesis, an ex-con and a garage owner who worked on Daley's car. On the night of December 12, the gang entered the garage. There they found not only John Kuesis, but his brother Nick; Frank Baker, a part-time mechanic; Emil Schmeichel, another part-time mechanic; and Theodore Callis, a customer who was working on his car. Daley confronted Keusis, accusing him of being a stool pigeon. While Morelli held the other four at gunpoint, Daley and Fentress began hitting Kuesis. Kuesis was no pushover, though, and soon was getting the better of both of them. At this point Daley pulled out a gun and shot him in the head.

Fentress later gave the following confession to the police:

> After Daley shot Kuesis we decided the others would have to be killed because they saw the shooting, and so we pushed them into our car.
>
> We drove west, and Daley and Morelli climbed into the front seat where they could cover the four piled in the back. They made Nick Kuesis curl up on the floor because they figured he'd be the most dangerous, since he'd seen his brother shot.
>
> As we drove, Daley played a kind of game with them by hiding his gun and pulling out the clip so they couldn't see it. He'd then point his gun at one of them and pull the trigger. He'd do it over and over again, so they didn't know each time if he had bullets in the gun. Morelli also kept jerking his gun as though he was going to shoot any moment.
>
> All were very frightened, and sweating, although it was cold. In a little while they were pleading with us not to shoot them, and promising they wouldn't do anything about John Kuesis' death. We didn't think we could take a chance.
>
> Out in Brookfield, Daley leaned over the front seat and fired at Nick Kuesis, saying "That's one Greek less." We stopped and pulled Nick out, and then Frank Baker. Daley shot him twice. Daley was wild and crazy drunk.[2]

Kuesis and Baker were dumped in a roadside ditch. Though seriously wounded, both men only feigned death until the car drove away. Nick managed to crawl to a nearby house and notify the police. Meanwhile, the gang stopped the car again, took Schmeichel out, and shot him twice, killing him. Fentress said, "By this time, Callis was so scared he couldn't talk. We took him to a dump at 39th St. and Central Ave. in Stickney, where he was shot in the back of the head as he was walking away from Daley and Morelli."

Daley wanted to go after the detectives who had arrested him, but Fentress and Morelli persuaded him to wait until the following day.

Daley dropped Fentress off at his apartment. As he walked in the door, he was surrounded by four detectives pointing guns. Frank Pape was called in. As Charles Adamson, Pape's biographer, wrote, "Frank wasn't exactly on his best behavior . . . So after Fentress picked himself up off the floor several times, he decided he'd better tell Pape exactly what he wanted to know."

After learning where Daley and Morelli lived, Pape's squad descended on the building. While the other officers guarded the escape routes with shotguns and Thompson submachine guns, Pape and Friedl entered. The two detectives were inching their way down a darkened hallway toward Morelli's third-floor apartment when they heard shotgun blasts and a burst of automatic fire from outside. "Go down there and find out what the hell is going on," Pape told Friedl.

As Pape stood alone in the hallway, he suddenly heard movement inside the apartment. "I knew I was going to get shot," he recalled later. "I could feel the bullets tearing into my stomach. It wasn't a good feeling."

He kicked open the door. Inside, it was completely dark. With his pistol in his right hand and his flashlight in his left, held well away from his body, he moved through the apartment. The beam of light hit a young woman sitting up in bed with a panicked look on her face. Pape turned to look into a room on his right. Daley was standing against its back wall, a gun in each hand, and as he raised them Pape fired five times fast, striking him twice in the head and three times in the chest. "The adrenaline was blasting through my body. I could hardly hear my gun going off, so I just kept pumping at this guy, waiting to get hit myself," Pape recalled.

Daley was dead when he hit the floor.

The gunshots Pape had heard seconds earlier had come from detectives shooting at Morelli as he fled the apartment. Morelli escaped, but turned himself in two days later, ending the hunt for what the press had dubbed "The Mad Dog Killers."

Morelli was executed on November 26, 1949. Fentress was sentenced to 199 years. He escaped the electric chair because he had cooperated with police.

During the 1940s and 1950s, Pape achieved national celebrity as "America's toughest cop." Detective magazines published 49 articles about him and many episodes of the television series "M Squad" were based on his cases. Pape made good copy even when he wasn't shooting bad guys, as in this anecdote he told a reporter:

> The warden of the state penitentiary called and said he heard two guys were getting out and they were going to pay some other guy $5,000 or $10,000 to hit me. Well, that didn't bother me too much because what else do these cons have to do down in the stir but talk like that? But when these two got out of prison, I had my dicks go pick them up at their homes.
>
> "So I got these two jokers in my office and I said, "I understand you two are cooking up some plan to try and get me, and let me tell you something. If I thought there was any merit in it, I'd fill you so full of .45s it would take a tow truck to pick you up off the street. Now get out of here."
>
> And out they flew and that was that.[3]

On May 23, 1951, the career of James Kelly, formerly of the Bookie Bandits, was brought to an end. An informant had told police that Kelly was going to rendezvous with accomplices at an alley near Washington Boulevard and then rob a currency exchange.

Pape took four detectives and staked out the alley. As each suspect showed up, the detectives took him into custody.

Pape was across the street when Kelly pulled into the alley and honked his horn. Detective Moss pulled the squad car into the other end of the alley. Spotting him, Kelly threw his car into reverse, but Pape stepped out in front of him, gun in hand. When Pape saw Kelly's arm move to the seat beside him, he didn't hesitate, but fired two shots through the windshield. Both bullets hit Kelly in the head. On the seat beside Kelly were two revolvers, hidden under a newspaper.

In January 1952, Pape took the exam for promotion to lieutenant. He had mixed feelings about it because a promotion would mean he'd have to spend most of his time in the office rather than on the street. Nevertheless, he passed, and was soon made Commanding Officer of the Robbery Unit, vowing to run it the best way he knew how. He had little patience with police bureaucracy, believing that it diluted orders and responsibility. "Every time you go through a level of command, an order loses its effectiveness. If I had a problem with a man I would go and talk with him. I wouldn't write him little love notes and put them in a book for others to read."

He knew the personal problems of his men and would often intercede with higher-ups to see that they were treated properly.

Although it wasn't expected of him, Pape also continued to work the street when he felt it was necessary. He sat in on a 35-hour stakeout with a 10-man detective detail on September 23-24, 1954. They were waiting for Chris Kanakes and Spiro Demitralis to show up in an alley for an appointment. The two were wanted in 15 armed robberies.

At 4:00 P.M., Kanakes and Demitralis entered the alley. Three detectives followed them, and ordered them to halt. The robbers turned, drew guns, and fired, and then ran towards Pape's position, where he waited with a Thompson.

"This was the first time I used a machine gun," Pape told reporters afterward. "We were 11 men against two today. They decided to shoot it out, and that's where they made their mistake."[4]

As the news account put it, "It was not known definitely whether Pape could add another two notches to his gun, since a detail of 11 men participated in the gunfight. However, Pape wielded a machine gun in the battle and Demitralis had 13 bullets slammed into him, while Kanakes was hit by nine."[5]

Pape's last shootout occurred a month later. Events had been set into motion earlier that year, when a twice-convicted burglar, Gus Amedeo, had broken out of the Criminal Courts Building with a gun smuggled to him by his girlfriend, Delores Marcus. He managed to elude arrest for months, but detectives spotted him as he sat in a Northside bar on October 21. As they moved in on him, Amedeo drew a .45 automatic and shot Detective Charles Annerino, mortally wounding him. After a fierce struggle with the two other detectives, Amedeo broke free and ran into the street, with the detectives in pursuit. They fired at him, inflicting a superficial wound on his arm, but they lost him in the darkness.

After outrunning his pursuers, Amedeo got rid of his jacket and the .45, then broke into the apartment of a crony, Robert Tuefel. Amedeo threatened him and his family with death if they didn't allow him to stay the night.

The following morning Amedeo left, and a few hours later the Robbery Unit showed up, as detectives had heard the two knew each other. Tuefel recognized Frank Pape. "You're going to kill him, aren't you?" he asked.

"You got that right," said Pape.

It was known that Amedeo frequented a certain restaurant owned by the Del Genio family, one of whose daughters was his girlfriend, Delores. Detectives installed a wiretap on the restaurant's line and within a few days recorded a phone call from Amedeo to Dorothy Del Genio, Delores's sister. He asked her to deliver a car he owned to him. The police contacted the Del Genios, and they agreed to cooperate.

On the day of the meeting, Pape set up an ambush. More than 50 detectives flooded the area, disguised as workmen, taxi drivers, and store clerks. Dorothy waited at the meeting place but Amedeo never showed up. Pape figured that this was a test, so that Amedeo could see if Dorothy had tipped off the police. Apparently, he hadn't spotted any of the undercover men, as the next day he called and arranged another meeting. Again, the detectives were in place.

At about 9:20 P.M., on October 29, Amedeo walked out of a movie theater and crossed the street toward the car. A detective shouted, "Gus, stop right there!"

Amedeo pulled a .32-caliber nickel-plated revolver from his pocket. Pape, armed with a 30-30 rifle and positioned in a second-floor window across the street, fired the first shot, breaking Amedeo's right arm and knocking him to the pavement. After playing possum a few seconds, Amedeo sprang to his feet, fired two wild shots, and tried to run. He staggered crazily under a fusillade of shots and collapsed in the gutter.

Pape called headquarters and announced, with quiet satisfaction, "We got him."

Amedeo had been hit by 18 bullets. In an irony captured by a press photographer, one of them passed through a tattoo on his arm that bore the slogan, "Death Before Dishonor."

Pape was promoted from Commander of the Robbery Unit to Deputy Chief of Detectives in 1957. It seemed his star was continuing to rise, but a year later he would be involved in a case that cast a shadow over his career. Following the robbery-murder of Peter Saisi, an insurance salesman, his wife pored over mug shots and identified James Monroe as the killer. Within a month, it was learned that she and her lover were actually responsible for her husband's murder, but at the time, Pape had to follow up the lead. Monroe, an African American, had previously been arrested for robbery, burglary, and auto theft, so he seemed a likely suspect. Without an arrest or search warrant, Pape led 12 detectives in a predawn raid on his apartment.

What followed was a matter of dispute. Pape claimed there had been nothing unusual about the raid and that Monroe, his wife, and six children were all treated with a reasonable amount of respect. However, Monroe charged that he and his family had been humiliated and terrorized by Pape and his detectives. The case was dismissed in the lower courts, but, pushed by civil rights advocates, *Monroe v. Pape* was heard by the Supreme Court in 1960. On February 20, 1961, the Court ruled against Pape in a landmark decision that permitted the federal government to bring civil rights actions against police officers in local cases. *Time* magazine reported Monroe's most lurid charges as if they were fact, without using the term "alleged." "The police," wrote *Time*, "broke through two doors, woke the Monroe couple with flashlights, and forced them at gun point to leave their bed and stand naked in the center of the living room. The officers roused the six Monroe children and herded them into the living room. Detective Frank Pape struck Mr. Monroe several times with his flashlight, calling him 'nigger' and 'black boy.' Another officer pushed Mrs. Monroe. Other officers hit and kicked several of the children and pushed them to the floor. The police ransacked every room, throwing clothing from closets to the floor, dumping drawers, ripping mattress covers."

As most of these accusations had been rejected in civil court, Pape sued *Time* for libel. This case too went to the Supreme Court, and Pape again lost, the Court deciding that in reporting unsubstantiated charges *Time* was not guilty of the "actual malice" necessary to constitute libel against a public figure.

Pape had been promoted to Captain in 1959, and had been considered for Police Commissioner. However, after *Monroe v. Pape* he became a political liability. In 1961, he took a leave of absence to work as Chief of Security at Arlington Race Track. He returned to the department in 1965 and retired in 1972.

Upon his retirement, the *Chicago Tribune* wrote, "Somewhat disappointed and disillusioned, and feeling like a stranger to the Chicago Police Department that had been his home for 35 of the last 39 years, Capt. Frank Pape has said goodbye to police work."

In an interview he gave in 1994, Pape said, "The police force is our peacetime army, but they are getting no support anymore from John Q. Public. Today, every move a policeman makes is scrutinized by the public, more so than the criminal. . . . Because of the scrutiny, because the public wants to talk about crime but not do anything about it like we did in my day, these policemen are retreating from crime rather than going forward and confronting it. They are doing this because their jobs are in jeopardy. It hurts me to see this. It takes guts to fight crime, but it takes everyone to have guts. Policemen today have lost the support of the people, and because of that the people have lost control of their country. Damn shame, really."[6]

Pape died on March 12, 2000, at age 91. He was survived by Kitty, his wife of 68 years, and two children.

NOTES

1. Charles F. Adamson, *The Toughest Cop in America,* 1st Books Library, 2001. All quotes are from the Adamason biography unless otherwise noted.

2. "Gang Massacre of 3 Is Told By Gangster," *Chicago Daily Tribune,* December 14, 1947, pp. 1, 2.

3. "Toughest Cop in Town," p. 1.

4. "Police Kill 2 Robbery Suspects in Trap," *Chicago Daily Tribune,* September 24, 1954, p. 1.

5. "Three Killed, One Hurt by Chicago Police," *Oshkosh Daily Northwestern,* September 24, 1954, p. 9.

6. "Toughest Cop in Town," p. 1.

George S. Patton (1885–1945)

> *"Of course we are willing to die, but that is not enough. We must be eager to kill, to inflict on the enemy—the hated enemy—wounds, death, and destruction. If we die killing, well and good, but if we fight hard enough, viciously enough, we may kill and live."*
>
> —Gen. George S. Patton

George Smith Patton was born on November 11, 1885, to a family of distinguished military tradition, and from boyhood aspired to glory of his own. His consuming fear was that he might prove unworthy, show cowardice in the face of danger, and "betray his blood." He was assured by his father that "while ages of gentility may make a man of my breeding reluctant to engage in a fistfight, the same breeding made him perfectly willing to face death from weapons with a smile."

After high school, Patton entered the Virginia Military Institute (VMI), the third generation of Pattons to do so. When his sizes were taken for his uniform, he learned that he had exactly the same measurements as his father and grandfather before him. A firm believer in destiny, he took this as a

In Bourg, France, Lt. Col. George S. Patton poses in front of a Renault tank in July 1918. (Credit: National Archives.)

sign that he might, after all, "measure up." After a year at VMI, he received a sought-after position at West Point.

After graduating in 1909, Patton competed at the 1912 Olympics in Stockholm in the pentathlon, the event comprising the martial skills of running, swimming, riding, pistol shooting, and fencing.

Patton was an excellent pistol shot, but placed twenty-first in the event for reasons still subject to speculation. Although other competitors used .22 caliber weapons, Patton used a military .38, which he felt was more in keeping with the spirit of the event. In practice the day before, Patton had shot a world's record. In the competition, Patton shot out the bull's-eye with all nines and tens, but there were two shots unaccounted for. It seems entirely possible that these shots had gone through the existing holes, but the judges scored them as complete misses. Patton did not protest, considering that to be unbecoming to a sportsman. (However, at the end of World War II, Patton returned to Sweden, met with his old competitors, and in an informal rematch scored much higher than he had in 1912.)

On March 9, 1916, Pancho Villa raided Columbus, New Mexico, killing 17 Americans. Pulling some strings, Patton, then 30, got himself posted as an aide to General Pershing for the retaliatory incursion into Mexico. Shortly before the incursion, Patton had purchased a Colt Single-Action Army revolver, engraved and nickel-plated. Its ivory stocks were engraved on the right with his initials and on the left with an eagle. It was to become his signature sidearm in World War II.

On May 14, Lieutenant Patton led a motorized patrol to a ranch belonging to Julio Cárdenas, one of Villa's officers. Leaving six men to guard the cars, Patton split the remaining nine men into three groups, which approached the ranch from different directions on foot. A farmhand who saw them dropped what he was doing and ran into the house, as if to sound the alarm, and then returned to his task. The Americans had no idea how many of the enemy might be in the house, a large adobe compound built around a central courtyard.

As Patton rounded a corner toward the main gate, he saw four Mexicans skinning a beef. He was on the verge of speaking to them when three Villistas armed with rifles rode out of an arched gate from the corral at the rear of the compound, heading away from him. They opened fire, showering Patton with chunks of adobe from the wall over his head, and narrowly missing his scout, Emil L. Holmdahl, and his driver, Leonard Hudnall, who had come up behind him. Patton raised his Colt and fired five times at the leading rider, putting one bullet into his arm (breaking it) and another into the belly of his horse. His pistol now empty, Patton ducked behind a wall to reload.[1] The wounded rider, who turned out to be Cárdenas, wheeled his mount and rode back through the gateway, followed by the others.

Patton had reloaded by the time the second horseman spurred his mount and made another dash out the gate. He rode diagonally across the ranch yard to the left of Patton and his party, firing over his shoulder.

"I remembered then," Patton relates, "what an old Texas ranger had told me. That was to kill a fugitive's horse, which was the surest way of stopping him."[2]

Patton put a pistol bullet through the hip of the fleeing Villista's horse, dropping it about ten yards away. "Impelled by misplaced notions of chivalry," as he later put it, Patton waited until the Villista extricated himself and rose to fight. Lieutenant Patton, Holmdahl, Hudnall, and the two enlisted men all shot at once, killing the Villista instantly.

Another of the three Villistas was spotted about 150 yards away, running along a stone wall that ran southeast of the ranch house. Patton and four or five of his men opened fire on him, Patton firing three times with his rifle. The Villista pitched forward, dead.

Two enlisted men spotted Cárdenas as he slowly and painfully made his way along a stone wall that stretched away from the ranch to the north. He was bareheaded and bleeding, his broken arm dangling, but he was still armed with a rifle and a pistol, and he exchanged shots with the enlisted men as they closed in on him. He kept firing until he was too weak to raise his gun; then he sank down, mortally wounded.

An enlisted man signaled to Patton that Cárdenas was finished. Holmdahl approached him to take away his weapons, but Cárdenas was still game. When the scout was within 20 feet of him, Cárdenas rested his pistol over his broken arm and

A familiar image of Gen. George S. Patton in World War II. (Credit: National Archives.)

fired. He had decided to die fighting. Holmdahl accommodated him with a shot to the head.

Examination of Cárdenas showed he had been hit four

times in the body before the final *tira gracia* (mercy shot) killed him instantly.[3]

Patton got a ladder and with four enlisted men checked the flat roof of the hacienda. From that vantage point he saw a strange sight: the four farmhands who had been skinning a beef when the Army cars first came up were still doing so. Apparently, they had realized that if they kept busy with heads bent, they would not be shot at. Patton forced them to walk ahead of his group as he made a careful room-by-room search of the hacienda. He encountered no one except a few women, who stared silently or cursed him.

Patton took Cárdenas' silver-mounted saddle and weapons as souvenirs, and had the three bodies strapped to the fenders of his car like deer carcasses. As the Americans prepared to leave, they saw some 50 Villistas approaching them on horseback, and exchanged shots with them as they drove off. Patton's group passed through the town of Rubio, a Villa stronghold, without incident. Upon his return to Pershing's headquarters, Patton proudly presented the bullet-riddled corpses to his astonished commander.

He wrote his wife, Bea: "I have at last succeeded in getting into a fight. . . . I have always expected to be scared but I was not, nor was I excited. I was afraid they would get away. . . . You are probably wondering if my conscience hurts me for killing a man: it does not. I feel about it just as I did when I got my swordfish, surprised by my luck."

Patton was probably responsible for one of the deaths, possibly two. During a World War II visit with the King and Queen of Great Britain, he recounted this adventure, showing them the two notches he had carved in his pistol's stock. Evidently he had given himself the benefit of the doubt.

Patton once said that he never expected to reach 60 years old. He died on December 21, 1945, just 40 days past his 60th birthday, from injuries sustained in a car accident in occupied Germany. Some 20,000 GIs requested to serve as his pallbearers.

NOTES

1. A Colt single-action six-shot revolver was normally only loaded with five rounds so the hammer could rest safely on an empty chamber.
2. The Texas Ranger Patton referred to is Dave Allison.
3. "Cardenas's Family Saw Him Die," p. 5.

John Purcell
(c. 1740–1822)

In *Bowie Knife*, author Raymond Thorp wrote that the
greatest knife fight he knew of was fought not by Jim Bowie,
nor even with a bowie knife, but rather, by a septuagenarian
landlord armed with a carving knife. He added, "If there is
any comparable single-handed victory in Bowie-knife history,
it has been strangely unreported."[1]

Highfort House stood in a secluded area about seven miles
south of Charleville, in County Cork, Ireland. It had been built
by the Purcell family and occupied by them for centuries. In
1811, it was home to John Purcell, a strong and active gentleman in his seventies who had large land holdings in the area. At
this time there was no law enforcement except for detachments
of soldiers stationed in the small towns, and the countryside fre-

quently erupted in violence, particularly by "Rockites," insurgents who attacked and robbed rural landlords.

On March 11, after spending the day collecting rent, Purcell returned to his home late in the evening with a considerable sum. He asked for a supper of cold meat and bread to be brought to his room and then dismissed his servant for the night, telling him he could remove the tray in the morning. He worked on his books, and retired around 11 P.M.

Purcell's bedroom was on the ground floor, adjoining the parlor. There was a door connecting the two rooms, but it had been nailed shut and chairs and a table placed in front of it. Purcell used a side door, which opened into a hallway.

He was awakened at 1 A.M. by the sound of someone forcing open a window in the parlor. He heard men climbing through it and dropping onto the floor. There were nine in all. Determined to defend his home, Purcell realized to his dismay that his pistols were in a small office on the other side of the parlor, and that all he had was the steak knife on his dinner tray. As he heard the men pushing aside the table that blocked the door, he picked up the seven-inch knife. As the door was smashed in, Purcell saw a crowd of men with faces blackened, many of them bearing firearms. He put his back against the wall next to the doorway and waited. He had one advantage over his assailants: he was completely in the dark, while they were illuminated by moonlight, which reflected off the snow-covered ground and poured through the broken window.

The leader of the gang loudly demanded Purcell's money or his life, and one of the members approached the door. Purcell afterwards stated that "at this moment I only hesitated to decide whether a back-hand or a right-forward blow would be the most powerful," and, deciding upon the former, he plunged his knife into the man's chest. The robber cried out, "I am killed," fell back into the parlor, and expired.

Another man came through the door and was stabbed just like his predecessor.

Author's rendering of the only known portrait of John Purcell. Note the famous knife.

The leader gave orders to fire into the room, and a musket was thrust through the doorway, its barrel pressed across Purcell's stomach. Purcell pushed against the barrel in order to convince the gunman that he had solidly aimed at center mass. As the gunman fired, the slugs passed harmlessly by Purcell, who then stabbed the gunman in the arm. The gunman jumped back, screaming.

Taken aback by Purcell's resistance, the bandits were about to retreat when the strongest man of the party forced his way into the bedroom, exclaiming triumphantly that he would finish the job. Purcell struck him with his knife and wounded him, but at the same time the man struck Purcell on the head with a sword. The two grappled. Purcell shortened his grip on his knife and continued to stab at his opponent. The floor had become slippery with blood, and they both fell, still struggling.

Purcell noticed that his thrusts didn't seem to be hitting home. Running his finger along the knife's edge, he found, to his shock, that its point had been bent back. At the same time, he realized that his opponent was losing his strength. In a minute or two the man's grip relaxed as he slumped back. The knife had done its job.

Purcell took the sword from his attacker's hand and gave him several blows with it.

At this point, the robbers, seeing so many of their number dead or injured, lost heart. Placing chairs against the wall under the window, they climbed out, dragging their wounded with them. Purcell stepped back into the shadows, sword in hand, and let them retreat.

After they left, he called out to his servant, who had remained huddled in his bed throughout the fight, and cursed him for his cowardice.

Two bodies were found at the scene. Three of the attackers had been severely wounded, and one of them died shortly afterward. Purcell thought he recognized one of the gang,

Maurice Noonan, and constables found him at home convalescing, with stab wounds in his arm. The gun he had fired at
Purcell was under his bed. Purcell identified it by the string
used to hold the barrel to the stock. Noonan was hanged on
September 9, 1811.

According to the record in the *History of the Munster
Circuit Court*, "The news of the attack and gallant defence
spread far and wide, and men of all ranks, creeds, and classes
came to offer their expressions of abhorrence at the attack and
of admiration at the courage, bravery, and skill with which Mr.
Purcell had acted."

On June 18, 1811, Purcell was knighted in recognition of
his "unexampled bravery and resolution."[2] Newspapers
dubbed him "the Knight of the Knife."

Purcell continued to reside at Highfort until his death in 1822.
He was survived by his wife, three sons, and two daughters.

After reading the account of this incident, it's hard to
ignore the difference between Britain then and now. Purcell
received a knighthood for an act that would now earn him an
indictment and, in all likelihood, jail time. Over the past 80
years British courts have whittled away the right of self-
defense to the point that a victim who injures a criminal is
often treated more harshly than the criminal himself. This has
resulted in a population so cowed that more than half of all
residential burglaries in Britain are committed while the victims are at home.

In 2005, listeners of the BBC were asked to suggest a piece
of legislation that would improve their quality of life, with the
promise that it would be introduced to Parliament. The winning proposal, with 26,000 votes, was to allow homeowners to
use any means necessary to defend their home from intruders.
Stephen Pound, the MP who was supposed to propose the legislation, described it as "a ludicrous, brutal, unworkable,
blood-stained piece of legislation," and added, "the people
have spoken, the bastards!"

Of course, the legislation that Mr. Pound derided had once been a cornerstone of English common law: "The house of every man is to him his castle and fortresse, as well for his defence against injury and violence, as for his repose." In the centuries during which Britain maintained the right of self-defense, the nation was known for its low crime rate. Now, in the grip of more progressive attitudes, its rate of violent crime has surpassed that of the United States.

In 1811, when the public cheered John Purcell, it wasn't because he'd saved the rent receipts. It cheered him because he had stood up against an outrage—the violent invasion of his home—to which no one should have to submit.

NOTES

1. Raymond W. Thorp, *Bowie Knife* (Williamstown, NJ: Phillips Publications, 1991), p. 88.
2. "The Knight of the Knife," pp. 511–12.

Frank J. Reynolds
(1899–1969)

> *"He had a disdain for dan-*
> *ger and an outspoken hatred*
> *of all hoodlums, and his*
> *real exploits surpassed the*
> *legendary deeds of most*
> *famous Western lawmen."*
> —John Toland

Though police work sometimes requires the use of deadly force, it is considered a regrettable aspect of the job and one with the most serious repercussions. An officer who has killed as many as three times in the course of his career may find himself relegated to desk duty. No matter how justified each shooting may have been, politically sensitive departments are reluctant to keep such an officer on the beat once the press, pressure groups, and litigation-hungry lawyers start tossing around terms like "trigger happy" and "killer cop."

In compiling this book, I tried to identify the top police ace of the 20th century. Which police officer, in the proper perfor-mance of his duty, had accumulated the highest tally? In recent decades, such information is swept under the rug, but this was not always the case. In Chicago during the crime wave of the 1920s and 1930s, the public felt "there's nothing wrong with a little shooting as long as the right people get shot," as Dirty Harry put it. Officers who made a significant dent in the city's criminal population were praised and promoted, and news articles regularly updated their tally. Detective Chris Callahan and Lieut. Al Booth were both noted for having killed six outlaws. Capt. Frank Pape, dubbed the

·KIRCHNER·

Frank J. Reynolds.

Toughest Cop in America, killed nine. The most honored of Chicago cops, with a tally put officially at "over a dozen" and unofficially at 14 or 15, was Frank J. Reynolds. (The tally is not exact because Reynolds was often one of several officers shooting at a suspect.)

Reynolds was born July 24, 1899, the son of Chicago policeman Michael J. Reynolds.

Captain John Stege, under whom Reynolds worked during his early career, said, "I first remember Frank Reynolds when I was traveling post in the Woodlawn District years ago and he was a school kid. I boxed his ears or warmed the seat of his pants more than once for raising hell in the neighborhood."

Reynolds enlisted in the navy in World War I. He flew an observation plane from the naval base at Brest, France, and was later assigned as a gunner's mate, making 19 crossings of the U-boat infested Atlantic. On May 31, 1918, he was on the transport *U.S.S. President Lincoln,* heading back to the United States loaded with the wounded, when it was torpedoed some 800 miles from land. Reynolds was thrown into the water when the boilers burst. He and several others clung to a raft for 36 hours until they were rescued, by which time one of the men had died of exposure.

Reynolds joined the Chicago Police Department on May 8, 1924. Shortly afterward, Captain Stege, who was deputy chief of detectives at the time, had Reynolds transferred to the detective department.

Chicago in the 1920s was in the midst of a crime wave. The city had 98 officers killed in that 10-year period, almost four times as many as in the average decade. Of those, 13 were killed in 1924, and the same number the following year. In 1925, Chicago was America's murder capital, with 389 homicides. On October 25, 1925, Captain Stege declared war on crime. Every bad man left in the city was to be dealt one of three fates, he told his men: "You must send them to the penitentiary or gallows, you must drive them out of Chicago, or you must kill them. If he has a gun in his hand, kill him without any talk over it. And every time you catch one, don't handle him with gloves. Be tough and let him understand that if he doesn't skip out of our city he is going to lead a sorry existence."[1]

By 1926, Frank Reynolds had made the news for several arrests of armed robbers and killers. On October 31, 1927, his first shooting was reported when he and his partner, Patrick O'Day, confronted William McDermott, who was robbing a grocery store. As McDermott rushed at O'Day with a butcher knife, Reynolds and O'Day shot and killed him.[2]

On February 19, 1928, Reynolds' squad car was in pursuit of a stolen car. The car thief, later identified as Harry Davis, led them on a wild five-mile chase through the city at speeds up to 60 miles an hour. At last, losing control of his vehicle, Davis struck another vehicle and then plowed into a fence along the sidewalk. As Davis ran from the wreck, Reynolds and his squad brought him down with a volley. Mortally wounded, with four bullets in his body, Davis was taken to the hospital, where he confessed to having been involved in 25 robberies in the previous few months.[3]

On November 15, 1928, Reynolds made the front page under the headline "3 Robbers Kill Victim; Caught In 15 Minutes." Three holdup men held up a South Side drugstore. The owner made no resistance as they looted the till, but as they left, he got his pistol and followed them out onto the street. He fired at the robbers and missed; they returned fire and killed him. Reynolds and his squad were on the scene before the dying man was lifted into an ambulance. With information provided by witnesses, it was only a few minutes before the squad arrived at the apartment into which the killers had fled. Through the frosted glass panel of the apartment door, Reynolds demanded entrance. In response, one of the gunmen fired through the glass, the bullet missing Reynolds by inches and the flying shards cutting his face. Bullets flew back and forth until the robbers ran out of bullets, at which point they surrendered, "unhurt, and begging for mercy." Taken to the Wabash Avenue station, they confessed to a drugstore robbery the previous week in which they had killed a patron named Charles Metlock, who, like them, was African-American. As the newspaper account describes it, "The killing of Metlock was wanton, according to witnesses. The three youths met no resistance in the store, but Metlock, an elderly man who lived above the place, remonstrated with them for disgracing their race by robbing on Sunday. They shot him three times, looted his pockets, and fled."[4]

It is interesting to note the suspects' confession to the prior homicide. Many news accounts in this period mention confessions made by criminals within a few hours of their arrests. This was well before the advent of Miranda rights, and it was understood that the third degree to which suspects were subject while in police hands usually included a good working over.

Reynolds next made front-page news in what the newspapers dubbed the "Moorish Cult Battle" at the end of September 1929.

The Moorish Science Temple, a precursor to the Nation of Islam, was founded by Timothy Drew in South Carolina in 1923. In six years it had attracted nearly 15,000 members and had 21 temples nationwide, with headquarters in Chicago's South Side. Its top officials were earning $12,000 to $15,000 a month, leading to a power struggle after Drew's death in March 1929. After one official, Charles Kirkman, left to run a splinter group, he was kidnapped by the faction led by Ira Johnson, who called himself Ria Johnson El. Johnson ordered his band of followers to arm themselves to fight "our enemies, police, or anybody else who interferes."

Kirkman's wife called the police, and officers were dispatched to investigate. As they knocked at the door, they heard a man inside call out, "The law is here, get your guns."

Patrolman Stewart McCutcheon slipped in through a window and had just opened the back door for officers George Kleback and Jesse Hults when they came under heavy fire. In all, over 100 shots were exchanged in the fight. Hults, a father of three and a 21-year veteran of the force, was hit seven times and was mortally wounded. McCutcheon was shot through the leg, and a bullet clipped Kleback's ear. A radio call went out to Reynolds, who was attending an inquest. He immediately sped to the scene with his squad. Meanwhile, two of the gunmen, Johnson and John Stephenson, burst out of the front door, Johnson shooting and killing Officer William Gallagher, 40, father of three, who was guarding it.

When Reynolds arrived, he was told that the two killers were barricaded in an apartment in a nearby building. With a squad guarding the building's exits to prevent escape, Reynolds entered and found Stephenson hiding in the darkened apartment, a revolver in his hand. Reynolds ordered him to surrender. Stephenson's gun clicked twice as he pulled the trigger. Just as Reynolds fired in return, Stephenson dropped to the floor. As he arose and again tried to fire his gun, Reynolds shot him four times, killing him. Johnson was found in another apartment and surrendered without resistance.[5]

For his action, Reynolds was awarded the Lambert Tree award, presented annually by the city of Chicago to a member of the police or fire department for an outstanding act of heroism.

On February 14, 1930, the *Tribune* reported that Reynolds, while on patrol, saw suspicious activity in a parked cab. Reynolds and two of his men left the squad car and quietly approached. Reynolds saw the driver cringing over the steering wheel and a man in the backseat pressing a pistol into the back of his neck. Reynolds pulled open one of the rear doors and shouted, "Police officers!"

The robber, Theodore Murray, leapt out the opposite door and ran. Murray shot three times at Reynolds and his men before they returned fire and killed him.[6] Murray was identified as the culprit in eight recent armed robberies. The *New York Times* covered the story a few days later under the headline "Chicago Policeman Promoted for Killing Eight Bandits." After reporting that Reynolds was promoted to the rank of temporary police sergeant as a result of the shooting, it added, "Reynolds, who is 31 years old, has eight dead bandits officially to his credit, though his admiring colleagues say the number is in reality eleven. Many another gangster is carrying around wounds that bear Frank Reynolds's trademark."[7]

Less than ten days later, Reynolds had to use his gun again, this time when he was called to a rooming house where the landlord, Walter Collins, had threatened a visitor with a pistol. According to the news account, "As Sergt. Reynolds announced himself, Collins fired twice through the front door. Two detectives remained at the front door as the sergeant, Detective Ross and Detective John Enright went to the rear. Collins resumed firing from an upper rear window, hitting Ross, who was taken to Mercy Hospital.[8] Reynolds and Enright then forced the door, advanced up the stairs under Collins' sniping, and shot him."[9]

The following year, a lengthy article in the *Chicago Tribune*, headlined "70 Bandits Slain by Citizens and Police This Year," gave a progress report in the ongoing war on crime, crediting 39 kills to the police, five to private security guards, and 26 to private citizens. Frank Reynolds was mentioned as having killed one William Churchill after Churchill opened fire on him as he and three companions were being pursued.

In addition to his gunfights, Reynolds is regularly mentioned in news articles in connection with more routine arrests. He was regarded as a highly effective law enforcement officer. Despite his swashbuckling image, his colleagues described him as quiet and reserved, and "considerate in dealing with offenders who do not try to shoot it out with him."[10] When, after seven years on the South Side, he was transferred out of that area in 1931, 300 local businessmen signed a petition requesting that he be returned to the district, crediting him with holding down robberies and burglaries.

In 1933, the nation was consumed with the hunt for John Dillinger and his gang of bank robbers, who were often in the Chicago area. Besides Dillinger, the gang included Harry Pierpont, John Hamilton, Russell Clark, Charles Makley, and, sometimes, George "Baby Face" Nelson. On December 14, Sergt. William Shanley was fatally shot by Hamilton as he tried to arrest him. Shanley, who had been a recipient of a

Tribune hero award, was the fifteenth police officer to be killed in 1933, the year the city suffered its highest death toll ever. Two days later, Capt. John Stege assigned 40 "quick trigger men" to lead the manhunt. This elite group, called the Dillinger Squad, was divided into two shifts, with Frank Reynolds in charge of the night shift.

The Dillinger gang was heavily armed and proficient in the use of weapons. Edward Shouse, an escaped convict who had been with the gang for a time before his recapture, told authorities that gang members spoke of little else than killing policemen: "They are all kill crazy and that's why I left them. . . . If you policemen are married men with families I warn you to be careful about trying to take the other members of the gang. Every night they have a drill and each takes the position assigned to him in the event the police surprise them."

Shouse added that they wore bulletproof vests even when they slept, and jumped to their gun posts whenever the doorbell rang or there was a knock.[11]

On the night of December 21, 1933, the Dillinger Squad got a tip that the gang was holed up in a first-floor apartment at 1424 Farwell Avenue. Stege made his plans, and gathered 19 of his men. At 9 P.M. they surrounded the building. Briefing his squad leaders, Stege said, "To the best of our information, the men inside are members of the Dillinger crowd. They are good shots. But they must be taken."

Sergeant John Daly and two other officers, one of them armed with a submachine gun, were assigned to cover the rear door and windows. Others covered the front of the building.

> One of the policemen forced open the
> door to stairs that led to the apartment. This
> done, Sergt. Reynolds, Detective Jack Dawe,
> Capt. Stege and several other men crept up
> the stairs. Meanwhile, after a moment's wait,

one of the policemen left in the vestibule
pressed the call button of the apartment that
was to be raided. Cautiously, the door to the apartment was
opened. Someone peered out and asked gruffly,
"Who's there?"
Sergt. Reynolds leaped forward. "We're
police officers," he shouted. "Surrender."
Instead of surrendering, the man at the door
fired a shot at Reynolds. The sergeant was too
far to one side, however, to be hit by the bullet.
The gunman fired two more shots that missed
Detective Dawe by inches. He did not get a
chance to shoot any more. Reynolds forced his
way into the apartment, pushing the outlaw
back, and in the same movement lifted his gun
and dropped him with two shots to the head.[12]
Reynolds pushed on in, followed by Capt.
Stege, Dawe, and several other detectives. In
the living room, to the left, stood another hood-
lum, two guns in his hands. He blazed away
blindly at Reynolds, Capt. Stege, and the policemen who stormed in after them. His shots
went high. Reynolds disposed of him with one
quick shot in the chest. At the same time, Capt.
Stege and Dawe pumped more bullets into him.
There was one more suspect left. He backed
into the kitchenette, firing as he retreated. In a
group, Capt. Stege, Reynolds, and the others
swooped upon him shooting, just as Sergt.
Daly, breaking in through a rear door, cut off
his escape.
The man fell, wounded, his gun still in his
hand. With the last ounce of his strength he
raised and pointed it at Daly. Daly kicked the

gun to one side and fired a bullet into his head, killing him.

Forty-four shots were fired in all, according to Capt. Stege. The gunmen had fired twenty-four shots and the policemen twenty. The gunmen lay where they had fallen, all of them riddled with bullets.

The shooting brought hundreds of Rogers Park residents to the scene. Police immediately placed a guard around the apartment and refused admittance to the curious. At this time the police were confident that the dead men had been members of the Dillinger gang. While not committing himself on their identities, Capt. Stege said he was sure the men were Dillinger's companions.

When Deputy Blaul arrived he strongly supported this idea.

"This man's Dillinger," he said, gazing at the face of the dead gunman lying in the kitchenette. "The other two look like Jack Hamilton and Harry Pierpont."[13]

Reynolds wasn't convinced. "Those are Jews," he observed.

Three hours later he was proven correct when their fingerprints revealed that they were Louis Katzewitz, Charles Tattlebaum, and Sam Ginsburg. All had records for bank robbery, and Katzewitz and Tattlebaum were fugitives, having escaped from prison six months previously. At the morgue it was found that Ginsburg, the first man shot, was hit once in the head, twice in the left side, once in the left arm and once in the back. Tattlebaum, the next man to die, was shot once in the left chest, twice in the left arm and side, and twice in the left shoulder. Katzewitz was struck twice in the stomach, once

in the left side, once in the back, and once below the left ear.
Despite firing 24 times, the bandits did not hit any of the officers, which was a good thing for Reynolds as he would not
wear the cumbersome bulletproof vests that were available. "I
never liked the vests," he said. "If I am going to get it I'd
rather take it as I am."

At the coroner's inquest the following day, Reynolds gave
an account of the gunfight that on several significant points
contradicted the account published in the newspaper—a
reminder of how difficult it is to nail down the facts in such
incidents. According to Reynolds, he went to the front door
with Dawe, Daly, and seven others. He and his men listened at
the front door for five minutes, then pressed the bell and
plunged into the apartment as soon as the door was opened.

> I took a step into the front room and saw
> two men getting off a settee. They had guns in
> their hands. The smaller one fired three times
> point blank at me and I dropped on one knee.
> The other man rushed past me and grappled
> with Daly, who was the second policeman to
> enter the apartment. Daly killed his man and
> the body fell right beside me. I fired two shots
> at the little man, who then ran by me into the
> dinette. I fired twice again and he fell dead.
> Dawe had killed the third man by that time.[14]

Stege told the inquest that he had been with the squad at the
back door and had not been involved in the shooting at all.
"When we got to the level of the kitchen window we could see
clear through to the front room. We heard the men in front shout
that they were police officers and then the shooting began. By the
time we'd kicked in the back door all three men were dead."

The Dillinger Days, written in the early 1960s, gives a
third version of the shootout that contains additional detail,

and since author John Toland evidently interviewed Reynolds, it is worth including. According to Toland, the tip Stege had received included the information that the gang was waiting for a contact named "Mule." After Reynolds and two other officers positioned themselves outside the apartment door, a policeman at the building's entry door buzzed the apartment and identified himself as the Mule on the intercom. This sounds plausible and would be the kind of information the police might have withheld from the press at the time. After the door buzzer was activated, Reynolds knocked on the apartment door and heard someone inside say, "Okay, it's the Mule." Reynolds burst in, with his .38 revolver in hand. He put a bullet into one man on the settee, dropped to one knee as the man fired back, and, as the man scrambled to get behind the settee, put three more bullets into him, then turned on a second man who was getting up from a chair and shot him twice. At this point the other detectives had shot the third man, Katzewitz. As Katzewitz writhed on the floor trying to raise his gun, Reynolds dropped his empty revolver, drew his backup .38 Super automatic, and shot him in the head.[15]

The gang was identified as having been responsible for the submachine-gun killing of two police officers as well as two other homicides the previous July. In the apartment, the police found a repeating rifle; a shotgun; two snub-nosed revolvers; two bullet-proof vests; two Mauser pistols with extended magazines and shoulder stocks, capable of full-automatic fire; 1,000 rounds of ammunition; and six automatic pistols (identified as Lugers in the news reports, but later described by Reynolds as Colt .38 Supers, prized by gangsters for their ability to shoot through bulletproof vests and automobile bodies).

Captain Stege expressed disappointment that the gunmen slain had not been the suspects they were looking for, but observed that the raid was not without its useful purpose, saying, "John Dillinger and his gang can get an idea that we mean business from this."

After the raid, the State's Attorney recommended that the men involved be given a pay increase and added, "I shall request the civil service commission to give Sergt. Frank Reynolds the highest mark for efficiency in the examination for a lieutenancy."[16]

Reynolds was awarded the *Chicago Tribune*'s $100 hero award and the Lambert Tree Medal for the second time.

One wonders if Reynolds' willingness to be the first man to go into deadly situations may have stemmed not only from his courage, but also from the fact that at 34 he was still unmarried and childless. He may have felt that it was better that he take the risk rather than a man supporting a family. In those days, a policeman who was killed left his family destitute, as the Patrolman's Benevolent Association's insurance policy provided a mere pittance. (Reynolds would later marry, but never had children.)

Over the next six months, Reynolds led his squad on a number of well-publicized raids of gang hangouts in an unsuccessful search for Dillinger. During this time, the cocky outlaw liked to telephone Reynolds and taunt him.

"You'd better watch your ass. We'll get you," Dillinger threatened on one occasion.

"Any time, Johnny; you and me, alone," Reynolds answered.

On another call, Dillinger told Reynolds he was going to come to his home and kill him.

"Come on over. I can handle two like you without any help," Reynolds told him.

At the end of January 1934, Dillinger was captured in Tucson, Arizona, and flown to Chicago. Reynolds was among the reception committee at the airport, and Dillinger visibly paled when he came face to face with the burly cop with the cold blue eyes. Reynolds is said to be the only lawman Dillinger was afraid of; he described him as "my worst enemy."

Dillinger was brought to Indiana's Crown Point Jail in the backseat of a squad car, shackled between two officers.

Reynolds rode in the front passenger's seat, cradling a
Thompson. His orders, direct from Stege, were clear: "If any
effort is made to raid the caravan and release Dillinger, or if he
makes a break at escape, kill him at once."

Looking over his shoulder at Dillinger, Reynolds said,
"Just start something, Johnny."

For once, the wisecracking outlaw didn't have a comeback.

It was from the Crown Point Jail that Dillinger made his
famous escape with a pistol carved from a block of wood and
colored with shoeshine. But his days were numbered: on July
22, 1934, he was shot by FBI agents as he left Chicago's
Biograph Theater. As he lay in the Cook County morgue,
Reynolds was among those who came by for a look. As a
ghoulish gag, he marked his first face-to-face meeting with
Dillinger by shaking the dead man's hand.

Though Reynolds continued to be active in high profile
investigations, there are no further reports of him using his
pistol. However, on one occasion, in December 1942, his reputation apparently sufficed. Eddie Sturch, a minor Democratic
politician who fancied himself a tough guy, entered a tavern
and began terrorizing the place. Waving a pistol, he fired two
shots, ordered patrons to line up against a wall, and then
began smashing liquor bottles. Reynolds arrived at the scene
and walked into the tavern. When Sturch recognized him, he
instantly fell to his knees and begged for mercy.

Reynolds retired in July 1962. In a 38-year career, he had
risen from patrolman to captain, ending as commander of the
Deering district. Twice awarded the Lambert Tree Medal for
exceptional bravery, he had also won the *Tribune* hero award
three times and had 14 creditable mentions and 10 extra com-
pensations for outstanding work. He was given a testimonial
dinner attended by all the dignitaries of Chicago, including
the police superintendent, secretary of state, and Mayor
Richard J. Daley.

On November 29, 1969, Reynolds, who had never been

injured in over a dozen deadly encounters, died as a result of injuries suffered when he fell down the stairs in his home. He left a widow, Alvina.

NOTES

1. "Take Gunmen or Kill Them, Stege Orders," *Chicago Daily Tribune*, October 26, 1925, p. 1.
2. "Burglar Caught in Store, Killed; Policeman Shot," *Chicago Daily Tribune*, October 31, 1927, p. 3.
3. "Fleeing Robber Wrecks 2 Autos; Shot in Pursuit," *Chicago Daily Tribune*, February 20, 1928, p. 3.
4. "3 Robbers Kill Victim; Caught In 15 Minutes," *Chicago Tribune*, November 15, 1928, p. 1.
5. "Seize 60 After So. Side Cult Tragedy," *Chicago Daily Tribune*, September 26, 1929, p. 1.
6. "Two Bandits Slain in Crime War," *Chicago Daily Tribune*, February 14, 1930, p. 8.
7. "Chicago Policeman Promoted for Killing Eight Bandits," *New York Times*, February 19, 1930, p. 1. Reynolds won the civil service rating of sergeant on May 6, 1933.
8. Patrolman Orin Ross was wounded in the wrist. Ross had won a Tribune Award two years earlier in a shootout in which he killed an opponent in an alley.
9. "Gunman Slain, 2 Police Shot in Gun Battles," *Chicago Daily Tribune*, February 28, 1930, p. 2.
10. "Sergt. Reynolds Cuts Another Notch on Gun," *Chicago Daily Tribune*. December 24, 1933, p. 4.
11. "City to Shut Up Gang Bars," *Chicago Daily Tribune*, December 26, 1933, p. 1.
12. Actually, he fired one shot to the head, according to the autopsy report.
13. "Slay Three Gunmen in Trap," *Chicago Daily Tribune*, December 22, 1933, p. 1.
14. "Slain Gunmen Identified as Police Killers," *Chicago Daily Tribune*, December 23, 1933, p. 1.
15. John Toland, *The Dillinger Days* (New York: Random House, 1963), pp. 154–57.
16. "Stege's Squads Commended for Drive on Gangs," *Chicago Daily Tribune*, December 27, 1933, p. 4. Reynolds was promoted to lieutenant in October 1935.

Richard the Lionheart (1157–1199)

> *"Among our enemies he was a man of great activity and of high soul, strong-hearted, famous for his many wars and of dauntless courage in battle."*
>
> —Bohâdin, Muslim historian

Born September 8, 1157, the third son of King Henry II and Eleanor of Aquitaine, Richard I excelled at the military arts even as a boy. He grew to an adult height of six-feet-four, "his arms somewhat long and, for this reason, better fitted than those of most folk to draw or wield the sword."[1]

Invested with the duchy of Aquitaine and Poitiers while he was still in his teens, Richard honed his political and military skills exerting control over the unruly nobles in his kingdom. He besieged and conquered a number of castles, most remarkably the fortress at Taillebourg, which had long been considered impregnable. It was at this time that he was first called the *Coeur de Lion,* or the Lionheart.

With the death of his older brothers, Richard was crowned

Richard I. (Credit: Author's collection.)

King of England in September 1189. Though he remains one of that nation's best-known rulers, he spent less than a year of his life there, his possessions in France being of greater interest to him.

A century earlier, during the First Crusade, Crusaders recaptured Jerusalem from the Muslims and built a series of fortified cities along the coast. But in 1187, Saladin, Sultan of Egypt and Syria, recaptured Jerusalem and the Christian port city of Acre, causing great alarm in Christendom. Less than a year after his coronation, Richard left England to participate in the Third Crusade.

The Third Crusade brought together armies led by Richard I, Philip II of France, and Frederick Barbarossa. Frederick died while crossing a river in Turkey, thrown from his horse and drowning in water barely 3 feet deep. This calamity was regarded as a dire omen by many of his troops, who immediately returned home.

Traveling by ship, Richard took time to conquer Cyprus en route, delaying his arrival at Acre by two months. When he got there, on June 8, 1191, the Crusaders had had the city under siege for nearly two years. Richard put his expertise in this sort of warfare to good use. Using beams he had brought with him, he had a wooden tower built from which arrows could be fired into the city and set his engineers to work digging tunnels to undermine the walls. His ballistas and catapults were soon lobbing stones at the city. Richard had even thought to bring granite boulders from Sicily; they were much harder than the local sandstone and made far more effective missiles.

Shortly after his arrival, Richard had become ill, possibly with trench mouth or scurvy, and was forced to lie in bed while others performed feats of heroism. A knight named Alberic Clements declared, "Today I will either die or, with God's will, will enter Acre," and climbed a ladder to reach the top of the wall. As other knights tried to follow him, the ladder collapsed. Alone on top of the wall, surrounded by the Turks, Alberic fought until he at last succumbed to countless wounds.

Despite his weakness, Richard was determined to inspire his men by killing a few heathens. He had himself carried on silken cushions to a stout shed that had been constructed under the city's walls, from which crossbowmen launched bolts against the defenders. Being very skilled with the crossbow, Richard killed a number of the enemy from this firing point. One of the Turks put on the armor of the slain Alberic and taunted the Crusaders from a high point on the fortress wall. It must have been most gratifying to Richard to fire the bolt that killed him.

At last a tower wall collapsed, and the Crusaders launched an assault. The *Itinerarium*, the chronicle of the Crusade, reads: "The men-at-arms strove to get in; the Turks to hurl them back. Rolled together in a confused mass they fought at close quarters, hand against hand, and sword against sword. Here men struck, there they fell. Our men-at-arms were few, whereas the numbers of the Turks kept increasing."

At last the Muslims beat back the attack with Greek fire.

With several of their walls partially collapsed, and a large number of their warriors killed or wounded, the defenders of Acre called for a truce so that terms of a peace could be arranged. They were willing to leave the city if they were allowed to take with them their arms and belongings. The French agreed to this, but Richard refused. He at last consented to allow the inhabitants to leave if he could hold some 2,700 nobles as hostages. Saladin was slow to pay the ransom, however; so on August 22 Richard had the hostages marched to a plain between the two armies and, in sight of the Muslims, ordered them killed. This is regarded as a blot on his honor by modern historians, though it inspired one of his contemporaries to write, "For this the Creator be blessed!"

In the aftermath of the conquest of Acre, Richard seized the spoils for Philip and himself, while belittling the contribution of Crusaders from other European countries. When Leopold V, Duke of Austria, raised his banner alongside that of France and England, Richard had it torn down and thrown in the moat. This was an insult that Richard would live to regret.

While many Crusaders remained in Acre, Richard took an army of some 14,000 toward the city of Jaffa, 80 miles down the coast, which Saladin had captured in 1187. Richard arranged his army wisely: the baggage train moved in a column nearest the sea, the foot soldiers marched in a parallel column farther from the sea, and the knights rode between them. The army moved slowly, as Richard wanted no gaps in the columns. The unrelenting heat, quicksand bogs, stinging insects, and thorny brush made it a miserable journey. In addition, the Muslims kept up their raids, showering the Crusaders' rear guard with arrows. Says the *Itinerarium*, "So thickly fell the rain of darts and arrows that you could not find so much as four feet of earth all along the army's route entirely without them."

Nevertheless, the Crusaders maintained their discipline and trudged on. The crossbowmen wore thick padded garments that stopped the Turkish arrows and they returned fire effectively with their crossbows, even marching backward in order to cover the rear. On September 3, as the Crusaders approached the River of the Dead, the Muslims launched a concerted attack. In the thick of the fray, Richard was wounded in the side with a spear. According to the *Itinerarium,* "Yet did this light wound serve rather to excite him against the enemies, by making him more eager to avenge the pain he suffered. Wherefore he fought right fiercely throughout the whole day, vigorously driving back the Turks as they came on."[2]

Studying the route of the Crusaders, Saladin picked the area around the ruined Crusader fortress at Arsuf as being the most suitable for an ambush. The ground was good for cavalry, and the forested hills would conceal his men until they were practically on top of the Crusaders. At this time Saladin commanded an army of 20,000, most of them mounted.

On the morning of September 7, thousands of mounted warriors swept down from the wooded hills upon Richard's army, with the brunt of the attack falling on the rear of the column. The Crusaders were forced into an ever-tighter formation, their backs to the sea. Still, Richard refused requests to mount a charge and kept his army moving slowly toward Arsuf. His object was to hold his army together at all costs and let the Muslims wear themselves out in repeated charges.

The knights were well protected by their armor, but the rain of arrows was killing their horses. Finally, able to bear it no longer, two knights burst through the protective infantry line and charged. In the heat of the moment, the Hospitalers and Templars followed them, shouting their war cries, *"Adjuva nos, Deus!"* ("Help us, O God") and *"Sanctum Sepulcrum!"* ("the holy tomb"). Richard joined in the onslaught. The Muslims broke ranks and fled in confusion.

The chronicle gives this account:

> [Richard] bore on the Turks, thundering against them and mightily astonishing them by the deadly blows he dealt. To right and left they fell away before him. Oh! how many might there be seen rolled over on the earth, some groaning, others gasping out their last breath as they wallowed in their blood, and many too maimed and trodden underfoot by those who passed by. Everywhere there were horses riderless.
>
> King Richard, fierce and alone, pressed on the Turks, laying them low; none whom his sword might escape; for wherever he went he made a wide path for himself, brandishing his sword on every side. When he had crushed this hateful race by the constant blows of his

sword, which mowed them down as if they were a harvest for the sickle, the remainder, frightened at the sight of their dying friends, began to give him a wide berth; for by now the corpses of the Turks covered the face of the ground for half a mile. . . .

But still the Christians pounded away with their swords until the Turks grew faint with terror, though the issue is doubtful yet. Oh! how many banners and standards of many shapes, what countless pennons and flags might you see falling to earth; aye, and just as many good swords lying everywhere, lances of reed tipped with iron heads, Turkish bows and clubs bristling with sharp teeth. Twenty or more wagon loads of quarrels, darts, and other arrows and missiles might have been collected on the field.[3]

This, the Second Battle of Hattin as it is called, was more than a defeat for Saladin; it was a humiliation. Though superior in numbers, his troops had been routed by the English king. Three days later, Jaffa surrendered to the Crusaders. Saladin called together his emirs and told them, "We are a disgrace to our ancestors who wrought such violence upon the might of Christian insolence!"

Saladin's third and favorite son, Melek ez-Zaher, said, "With fearless hearts and zeal we attacked them, but they are armed with armor that no weapon can pierce, and so our blows fell harmless, as if against flint. Moreover, among their number is a leader superior to any man we have ever seen. He charges on his immense horse before the rest and slays our men by the score. No one can resist or escape this man they call Melek Ric. Such a King seems to be born to command the whole world."[4]

While the Crusader army rested at Jaffa, detachments sent out to scout or forage were frequently set upon by bands of enemy horsemen. Richard himself had a close call when he ventured out hunting and his party was attacked by a much larger force of Muslims. He was in imminent danger until one of his knights, William des Préaux, shouted that he was "Melek Ric" and claimed the Muslims had no right to take him captive. As they converged upon William, Richard was able to escape. William des Préaux languished in a Muslim prison until the end of the Crusade, when Richard was able to ransom him. His knights often admonished Richard for the unnecessary risks he took, but he answered, "No one can turn my nature, even with a pitchfork."

When the Muslims captured two knights who were scouting, Richard took off after them with a small retinue, hoping to rescue his men. Recognizing him by his banner, the Muslims cut off the prisoners' heads and took flight. "They were almost a hundred in number, of whom the king slew or captured seven as they made for the hills," says the chronicle.

Around Christmas 1191, the Crusaders moved to a camp at Beit Nuba, only 20 miles from Jerusalem. They seemed to be poised to retake the Holy City, but Richard held off, deciding against launching an attack in the winter months. Many of the Crusaders were dismayed at this decision, as the recapture of Jerusalem was their primary goal. Instead, Richard had them rebuild the Crusader fortress city of Ascalon, south of Jaffa, which Saladin had destroyed rather than let it fall into Richard's hands. Richard also besieged the fortress at Darum, the most southerly of the coastal fortresses which had been built after the First Crusade. Saladin had captured it and it was defended by a strong Muslim garrison. Richard's expertise at siege warfare won out, though, and in a mere three days, he destroyed the gate and main tower, forcing the Muslims to surrender.

In June 1192, the Crusader army set out for Jerusalem and, after several days' march, once again set up camp at Beit Nuba.

Muslim bands continued to raid the Crusaders. On one occasion Richard got word of a band of ambushers and went after them, an event described by the poet Ambroise:

> The king was then on Ramla plains,
> Fast riding through the fallow land
> Pursuing closely on a band
> Of Saracens, who 'fore him fled
> As one whom they most held in dread;
> For, since the time when God created
> The earth, no man exterminated
> So many Turks or wrought such woe
> Among them. Often he would go
> To fight the Saracens, and came
> Back with their heads, like so much game—
> Ten, twenty, thirty, would succumb
> Before him, grieving pagandom—
> And when he undertook to bring
> Back living captives, the brave king
> Would do so. No one man, in brief,
> Wrought them so much of death and grief.[5]

At this time, one of Richard's Arab spies came to him with news of great value: a huge caravan was heading through the Judean desert 30 miles to the south. It was an opportunity to deal Saladin a tremendous blow and be rewarded with ample plunder. After Richard's scouts verified the report, he led a large force into the desert. Two days later, at dawn, it fell on the caravan, and there followed an orgy of slaughter. According to the *Itinerarium*, the shaft of Richard's lance became so sodden with blood that it broke in his hand. "Then, without delay, he brandished his sword and thundered on," it continues, "threatening, overthrowing, taking prisoners, mowing down some, cutting off others, cleaving men from the top of the head to the teeth. No kind of armor was strong enough to withstand his blows. Then was the slaughter renewed, the heavens thundered, the air was bright with sparks struck from the swords. The ground reeked with blood, dismembered corpses were everywhere: lopped off arms, hands, feet, heads, and even eyes. Our men were hindered in walking over the plain by the corpses of the dead Turks, so thickly were they strewn about; and the bodies, which they had just dismembered, caused our men to stumble."[6]

Some 500 Muslims were killed, as well as the chamberlain Yusuf. Richard returned to Beit Nuba on June 24 with an astonishing haul, including 3,000 horses, 3,000 camels, and hundreds of mules loaded with spices, cloth, weapons, tents, grain, medicines, and money.

If Richard were going to recapture Jerusalem, this would seem to be the time. With the departure of King Philip the previous summer, the forces were unified under Richard's command. His men were primed and his siege engines assembled. Saladin had started to evacuate the city and had even poisoned the wells surrounding it as a last-ditch defense measure. But, although everything was in place, in the end Richard decided not to make the attack.

The Crusaders were utterly bewildered. This was the purpose for which they had left Europe, yet now their leader seemed to be growing faint of heart. More likely, though, was that Richard understood the practical problems. He could take the Holy City, but he could not hold it. It was too far from the coast, which would make it impossible to provision it, as caravans would be under constant attack by Muslim raiders. Moreover, once Jerusalem was captured, most of the Crusaders would consider their mission accomplished and want to return home. Who would remain to defend it? The Crusaders had barely enough troops to garrison the cities they had already captured.

On July 6, the Crusader force began leaving Beit Nuba.

The Muslims felt that the tide had turned in their favor. While Richard and the main body of the army headed toward

Richard at the Battle of Acre, by Doré. (Credit: Author's collection.)

Acre, Saladin attacked Jaffa, which he understood to be defended by only 5,000 sick, exhausted, and dispirited men. To his surprise, they put up a strong defense. Saladin thought he would take the city in a day, but five days later his army was still fighting to get inside the city though the breaches in its wall. The delay gave Richard time to get there.

On the morning of the sixth day, August 1, the red sail of the king's galley could be seen on the horizon, accompanied by 35 other vessels. As the fleet approached, a horde of Muslim soldiers waited on the beach. Richard surveyed the scene, unsure whether there were any defenders left to rescue in the city. Suddenly, a figure leapt from a tower to the beach, scrambled into the water, and swam to Richard's ship. As he was hauled aboard, he cried out, "Most noble king, the remnant of our people await your arrival."

"Good friend, how say you? Are some still alive?" responded the king.

"Aye, but hemmed in and at the last extremity in front of yonder tower."

"Please God, then, by whose guidance we have come, we will die with our brave brothers in arms and may a curse light upon him who hesitates," declared the king.

Richard was the first into battle. He removed the armor from his legs and waist and plunged into the hip-deep water, his sword in one hand and crossbow in the other. The Muslims drew back as the king advanced upon them, followed by his knights.

As the chronicle tells it,

> The king laid the enemy low everywhere with a crossbow he had in his hands . . . and carried on the pursuit till the whole shore was cleared. . . . The king was the first to enter the town by a certain stairway, which he had chanced to see in the houses of the Templars.

He entered alone and found three thousand
Turks plundering all the houses and carrying
off the spoil. Consider the courage of this invin-
cible king! For immediately on entering the city
he had his banners displayed on the highest
parts of the walls so that the besieged
Christians in the tower might see them. They,
on seeing it, took heart and snatching up their
arms came down from the tower to meet their
deliverer, who with unsheathed sword pressed
on, slaying and maiming his foes as they fled
from before his face . . . Indeed, the king pursued them beyond the city, thinking it well to
follow up his victory lest, perchance, anyone
should say he had spared the enemies of
Christ's cross when God had delivered them
into his hands. Truly, never did any man hold
half-heartedness in greater hatred. . . . Saladin
hearing of his arrival . . . fled like a hunted
hare or other timid animal; tearing up his tents
in haste, he put spurs to his horse and hurried
away lest king Richard should catch sight of
him. But the king and his comrades pressed on
the pursuit, slaying and laying low. The king's
crossbowmen too wrought such carnage among
the steeds of the fugitives that for more than
two miles the Turks fled away in the deadliest
terror. Then the fearless king gave orders to
pitch his tents in the very place whence Saladin
had a short time before torn up his.[7]

Saladin's army set out to counterattack. After marching
through the night, it came upon the 12 tents of the Crusaders
before dawn. Awakened by the neighing of their horses, the
Crusaders scrambled to put on armor and gather their

weapons. By the time that several thousand Muslim horsemen swept down on them, they had formed a defensive line.
The foot soldiers knelt shoulder to shoulder, each holding a
shield in front of him and a spear pointed outward, its butt
anchored in the ground. Behind this line were two-man teams
of crossbowmen, one man the shooter, the other the loader.
Though outnumbered four to one, the line of Crusaders halted the Muslim charge.

As the horsemen milled about, Richard—followed by 10
knights—burst through the line and attacked his enemies.

The chronicle says:

> Oh! how fiercely did the battle now rage!
> while the Turks rush on towards the royal ban-
> ner with its blazoned lion, more eager to slay the
> king than a thousand other warriors. Then in
> the stress of this conflict the king saw Ralph de
> Malo-Leone being carried off captive by the
> Turks: upon which, flying at full speed to his
> rescue, he compelled the Turks to let him go. . . .
> On that day might you have seen the king slay-
> ing innumerable Turks with his gleaming
> sword: here cleaving a man from the crown of
> his head to his teeth, there cutting off a head,
> an arm, or some other member. Indeed, so
> energetically did he exercise himself that the
> skin of his right hand was broken due to the
> vigor with which he wielded his sword.[8]

Saladin, watching from a hilltop, was so impressed by
Richard's valor that he sent two fine Arabian stallions as a gift
to him in the midst of the battle. Richard gratefully accepted
them, declaring, "In so urgent a moment I would accept many
such horses from even a fiercer foe."

Meanwhile, there arose a great cry from the city, where

Muslim horsemen had swept in through breaches in the wall.

> On hearing this, the king hurried up at the
> head of his crossbowmen, but with only two
> knights. In a certain street he met three Turkish
> horsemen most splendidly attired and, rushing
> on like a king, he slew them and thus became
> master of two horses. The other Turks whom
> he found offering resistance in the town he
> drove off with his sword till they were so fright-
> ened that they scattered, seeking for an exit in
> vain. Then the king ordered the breaches in the
> walls to be filled up and set guards to keep the
> city from attack. . . .
> Amongst many other illustrious deeds, with
> one blow of wonderful force, he slew a certain
> emir who surpassed his fellows in height and
> in the splendor of his apparel. This emir,
> vaunting much and reproaching his comrades
> with their cowardice and want of energy, had
> put spurs to his horse and galloped up to over-
> throw the king, who, receiving him with his
> sword, cut off his head, his shoulder, and his
> right arm. . . .
> The king's body was everywhere set thick
> with arrows, as a hedgehog is with bristles; so
> too his horse was covered with innumerable
> arrows that stuck to its harness.[9]

In this battle the Muslim side reportedly lost more than
700 men, while the losses of the Crusaders were two killed
and a small number wounded. This was the last battle of the
Third Crusade.

Saladin is said to have taunted his officers for their failure
to capture Melek Ric. One of them answered, "Know, O king,

for a surety that this Melek of whom you speak is not like other men. In all time no such soldier has been seen or heard of; no warrior so stout, so valiant, and so skilled. In every engagement he is first to attack and last in retreat. Truly we tried hard to capture him but all in vain, for no one can bear the brunt of his sword unharmed. His onset is terrible, it is death to encounter him, his deeds are more than human."

After the battle, Richard fell ill, as did many troops on both sides, perhaps as a result of the bodies left unburied around the city. Saladin sent messengers bearing fresh fruit and peace proposals. Richard gratefully accepted the former and haggled over the latter. At last, eager to get home and too dizzy to read the treaties he was signing, Richard agreed that Jaffa and Acre would remain in Crusader hands, along with several other coastal cities, while Ascalon would be destroyed.

To a bishop that served as an envoy between the rulers, Saladin made this observation about Richard:

> Brave and noble is the king,
> But with what rashness doth he fling
> Himself! Howe'er great prince I be,
> I should prefer to have in me
> Reason and measure and largesse
> Than courage carried to excess.[10]

Richard left the Holy Land in October 1192. Traveling through Austria, he was captured by Duke Leopold, whom he had so grievously insulted at Acre. Leopold turned him over to the Holy Roman Emperor, Henry IV, who held him for ransom. While Richard was in confinement, he learned of the death of his nemesis, Saladin, on March 3, 1193. Richard was released after a year, upon payment of a ransom so enormous that it left England destitute for years.

The last six years of Richard's life were spent at war in France, first with Philip, and then with his unruly barons. In

1199, he laid siege to the Viscount of Limoges' castle at Châlus, after he heard that he was holding on to a hoard of gold that had been uncovered by a peasant plowing the fields. As the king, Richard felt that the treasure was rightfully his. While waiting for his engineers to open a breach in the walls, Richard watched as a crossbowman stood on the parapet, holding a crossbow in one hand and a frying pan in the other. When he was fired upon, he would use the pan as a shield and respond with a bolt from his crossbow. Intrigued, Richard rode close to try to get a shot with his own weapon. He had not bothered to put on his armor. The crossbowman fired a bolt that hit Richard in the shoulder and penetrated deeply.

As his men took Châlus, Richard lay on his deathbed, his arm blackened with gangrene. He ordered that all the castle's defenders be hanged, but that the crossbowman be brought before him. "What harm have I done you that you should kill me?" Richard demanded of him.

"With your own hand you killed my father and my two brothers, and you intended to kill me," the young man answered defiantly. "Therefore, take any revenge on me that you want, for I will endure the greatest torments you can devise, so long as you have met your end."

Impressed by the warrior's spirit, Richard said, "I forgive you my death. Live on. By my bounty behold the light of day. Let the vanquished learn by my example."

He ordered that his assassin be given 100 silver shillings and set free.

Richard died on April 6, 1199.

NOTES

1.   *Crusade of Richard I*, p. 7.
2.   *Crusade of Richard I*, p. 145.
3.   *Crusade of Richard I,* pp. 157–58.
4.   *Chronicles of the Crusades*, p. 245.

5. *Richard Lion-Heart by Ambroise*, p. 340.
6. *Crusade of Richard I*, pp. 266–67.
7. *Crusade of Richard I*, pp. 291–92.
8. *Crusade of Richard I*, p. 308.
9. *Crusade of Richard I*, pp. 311–12.
10. *Richard Lion-Heart by Ambroise*, p. 442.

Manfred von Richthofen (1892–1918) and René Fonck (1894–1953)

> *"The crate does not matter as much as who sits in it."*
> —Manfred von Richthofen

As a boy, shortly after being given his first air rifle, Richthofen killed three ducks in his grandfather's pond. He pasted three of their feathers onto a piece of cardboard as a trophy, his first contribution to the collection of mounted heads of deer, elk, and wild boar that decorated the Richthofen manor. Later, he would cover the walls with trophies of a different sort—machine guns, flare pistols, and serial numbers painted on fabric, that he had taken from the wreckage of his opponents' planes.

Born on May 2, 1892, to a family of minor nobility, Manfred von Richthofen was put into the Cadet Corps at age 11. He had no particular interest in soldiering at the time, but, as he wrote, "My father wished it, and I was not consulted."

He graduated the Berlin War Academy in 1912, with a commission. Posted to a cavalry regiment on the Western Front, he earned an Iron Cross for his valor at the outset of World War I. However, once it settled into static trench warfare, he felt he was contributing nothing and grew bored. He put in a request to join the Flying Service and was transferred there at the end of May 1915.

Eager to get into the air as soon as possible, he decided to train as an observer. This got him an assignment on the Eastern Front, where he flew in a two-seat AEG G-type bombing aircraft. In addition to observing, Richthofen was bombardier and machine gunner. "I was much interested in bombing," he wrote. "It gave me a sinister pleasure to plaster our 'friends' down below. I often went out twice a day on such flights."

Richthofen occasionally got a chance to shoot at other planes, but found that they were not so easy to hit: "I had always believed that when I fired, the enemy would fall. But I soon learned that an airplane could endure a great deal. I finally became convinced that no matter how much I shot, it would never come down."

At last, on September 15, he had his first success, against a Farman biplane:

> When I had exhausted my magazine of 100
> bullets, I thought I could not trust my eyes
> when I suddenly noticed that my opponent was
> going down in curious spirals. I followed him
> with my eyes. . . . Our opponent fell and fell
> and dropped at last into a large crater. There he
> was, his machine standing on its head, the tail
> pointing towards the sky. According to the map
> he had fallen three miles behind the front. We
> had therefore brought him down on enemy
> ground. Otherwise I should have one more vic-
> tory to my credit. I was very proud of my suc-

Manfred von Richthofen. (Credit: National Archives.)

cess. After all, the chief thing is to bring a fellow down. It does not matter at all whether one is credited for it or not.[1]

While traveling by train, Richthofen had a chance meeting with Lt. Oswald Boelcke, a rising star in the Luftwaffe who had shot down four planes. Richthofen asked him, "Tell me honestly, how do you really do it?"

Boelcke laughed and answered, "Good heavens, it indeed is quite simple. I fly in as close as I can, take good aim, shoot, and he falls down."

Richthofen decided that he must learn to fly a Fokker if he wanted to hunt the enemy successfully. He attended the flying school at Doberitz, and by Christmas he had passed his pilot's examination. He returned to the Eastern Front, where he flew an Albatros two-seater. It did not have the offensive capability of the Fokker, but Richthofen had his mechanics fasten a machine gun to its upper wing so that it would fire over the propeller arc. With this jerry-rigged system he succeeded in shooting down a Nieuport scout on April 26, 1916. This kill also went unconfirmed.

Richthofen was flying bombing runs over Russia when Boelcke visited his airfield in August. After Max Imelmann's death in June 1916, Boelcke had become Germany's top ace and its most respected aviator. Now he was scouting promising pilots for a new fighter squadron, *Jasta 2*, and to Richthofen's delight, he was invited to join. "The thought of fighting again on the Western Front appealed to me," he wrote. "There is nothing finer for a young cavalry officer than flying off on a hunt."

Boelcke had developed eight rules for successful aerial combat, and he drummed them into his men.

Rule 1: Try to secure advantages before attacking. If possible, keep the sun behind you.

Rule 2: Always carry through an attack when you have started it.

Rule 3: Fire only at close range, and only when your opponent is properly in your sights.

Rule 4: Always keep your eye on your opponent, and never let yourself be deceived by ruses.

Rule 5: In any form of attack it is essential to assail your opponent from behind.

Rule 6: If your opponent dives on you, do not try to evade his onslaught, but fly to meet it.

Rule 7: When over the enemy's lines never forget your own line of retreat.

Rule 8: For the *Staffel* [fighter squadron]: Attack on principle in groups of four or six. When the fight breaks up into a series of single combats, take care that several do not go for one opponent.

On September 17, Richthofen was flying one of the new Albatros D.I fighters that had been delivered to *Jasta 2* just the night before. He got an English two-seater in his sights:

> I did not reflect very long, but took my aim and shot. He also fired, and both of us missed our aim. A struggle began and the great point for me was to get to the rear of the fellow, because I could only shoot forward with my gun. He was in a different situation, as his machine gun was movable and could fire in all directions. Apparently he was no beginner, for he knew exactly that his last hour had arrived at the moment when I got at the back of him. At that time I had not yet the conviction "He must fall!" which I have now on such occasions, but on the contrary, I was curious to see *if* he would fall. There is a great difference

between the two feelings. After one has shot down one's first, second or third opponent, then one begins to find out how the trick is done.

My Englishman twisted and turned, going crisscross. I did not give a moment's thought to the fact that there were other Englishmen in the enemy squadron who might come to the aid of their comrade. I was animated by a single thought: "The man in front of me must come down, whatever happens." At last a favorable moment arrived. My opponent had apparently lost sight of me. Instead of twisting and turning, he flew straight along. In a fraction of a second I was at his back with my excellent machine. I gave a short series of shots with my machine gun. I had gotten so close that I was afraid I might crash into the Englishman. Suddenly, I nearly yelled with joy, for the propeller of the enemy machine had stopped turning. I had shot his engine to pieces; the enemy was compelled to land, for it was impossible for him to reach his own lines. . . .

Both the pilot and observer were severely wounded. The observer died at once and the pilot while being transported to the nearest dressing station. I honored the fallen enemy by placing a headstone on his grave.[2]

After this kill, Richthofen wrote to a jeweler in Berlin and ordered a silver cup inscribed with "1, Vickers 2, 17.9.'16." The cup was to measure about 1 inch across and 2 inches tall. Why so small? Presumably, because Richthofen expected to collect a lot of them.

By October 28, Richthofen had six kills, and Boelcke had 40. That day, Boelcke led a patrol of five other planes, Richthofen at his right wing and Erwin Bohme at his left. As the planes dived to engage two de Havilland Scouts, the undercarriage of Bohme's Albatros scraped across Boelcke's upper wing, damaging it so badly that Boelcke lost control of his aircraft. The famed airman crashed and was killed. Richthofen wrote his mother, "It affected us all very deeply, as if a favorite brother had been taken from us." He added, "in six weeks, of our 12 pilots, we have had six killed and one wounded; two are washed up because of their nerves. Yesterday I shot down my seventh, after I had shortly before dispatched my sixth. My nerves have not yet suffered as a result of the others' bad luck."[3]

On November 16, with his 10th victory, Richthofen ordered a silver cup in the same style as the previous nine, but twice the size. From then on he would have every 10th cup made large to help him keep count.

Richthofen described a combat on November 23 with a jaunty nonchalance:

> One day I was blithely flying to give chase when I noticed three Englishmen who also had apparently gone a-hunting. I noticed that they were ogling me, and as I felt much inclination to have a fight I did not want to disappoint them. I was flying at a lower altitude. Consequently, I had to wait until one of my English friends tried to drop on me. After a short while, one of the three came sailing along and attempted to tackle me from the rear. After firing five shots he had to stop, for I had swerved in a sharp curve.[4]

Richthofen soon realized he was not dealing with a beginner. There followed three to five minutes of circling maneuvers as each tried to get behind the other. The diameter of these circles was about 250–300 feet and took them from an altitude of 10,000 feet down to less than a thousand. Meanwhile, the wind had blown them over the German lines. The pilots were so close that Richthofen could clearly see his opponent, who at one point gave him a cheery wave.

> My Englishman was a good sportsman, but by and by the thing became a little too hot for him. He had to decide whether he would land on German ground or whether he would fly back to the English lines. Of course, he tried the latter, after having endeavored in vain to escape me by loopings and such tricks. At that time his first bullets were flying around me, for hitherto neither of us had been able to do any shooting.
>
> When he had come down to about 300 feet he tried to escape by flying in a zigzag course during which, as is well known, it is difficult for an observer to shoot. That was my most favorable moment. I followed him at an altitude of from 250 feet to 150 feet, firing all the time. The Englishman could not help falling, but the jamming of my gun nearly robbed me of my success.
>
> My opponent fell, shot through the head, 150 feet behind our line. His machine gun was dug out of the ground and it ornaments the entrance of my dwelling.[5]

This victory was especially gratifying because of the stature of Richthofen's opponent, Maj. Lanoe Hawker, who had nine kills and held the Victoria Cross.

On January 4, 1917, with his 16th victory, Richthofen became Germany's foremost living ace. He was made *Rittmeister* of *Jagdstaffel 11* at Douai and awarded the *Order*

Pour le Mérite, the famed Blue Max. It was at this time that, as Richthofen wrote, "I came upon the idea of having my crate painted glaring red. The result was that absolutely everyone could not help noticing my red bird." He later said, "One cannot make oneself invisible in the air and so at least our people recognize me."

Jagdstaffel 11 had been created the previous September but had not yet scored a single victory. Richthofen corrected that shortly after his arrival, when on January 23, 1917, he shot down Lt. John Hay. Another British pilot reported seeing "a red machine," and the word soon spread. The legend of the Red Baron had begun. From a public-relations standpoint, it was pure genius, helping make Richthofen the best-known fighter pilot in history. He became Germany's number-one war hero, regularly profiled in newspapers and magazines. Photographs of him were widely sold, mostly to adoring young women.

In these days Richthofen could still speak of the exhilaration of combat, as he did on March 9, 1917:

> It tickles one's nerves to fly towards the enemy, especially when one can see him from a long distance and when several minutes must elapse before one can start fighting. . . . I like that feeling for it is a wonderful nerve stimulant. One observes the enemy from afar. One has recognized that his squadron is really an enemy formation. One counts the number of the hostile machines and considers whether the conditions are favorable or unfavorable.[6]

On a visit home, his mother asked him why he took such risks. He thought a moment and answered, "For the man in the trenches. I want to ease his hard lot in life by keeping the enemy flyers away from him."

René Fonck. (Credit: National Archives.)

Under Richthofen's leadership, Jagdstaffel 11 achieved great success. In emulation of its leader, all its pilots painted their planes red as well, though in different patterns so that they could tell each other apart. It picked up the nickname the Flying Circus. Among its new members was Manfred's younger brother Lothar.

Before dawn on April 2, Lothar and four other pilots suited up, to be ready for action at a moment's notice. Manfred was still asleep. When a call came that six Bristols were approaching, the pilots jumped in their planes and took off. Manfred's plane was on the field, ready for takeoff, but he was nowhere to be seen. The flight group took off, but after an hour returned to the base without having shot anything down. As Lothar landed, he noticed that his brother's plane was being worked on by mechanics. In the ready room he learned that Manfred had gotten up, put his flight suit on over his pajamas, taken off after the others, and returned in 20 minutes. During that time he had shot down an English plane. He was now back in his bed, asleep.

On April 11, Richthofen scored his 40th victory, equaling Boelcke's record.

On April 29, Richthofen's father came to the aerodrome to see Manfred and Lothar, who was already an ace himself. He arrived just as the morning patrol was landing. Lothar and Manfred were pleased to be able to report to him that each had just shot down an Englishman.

At midday, Richthofen flew again and shot down a second Englishman. This was his 50th victory, a long-sought goal. Still not done for the day, the brothers went on an evening patrol and encountered two English artillery spotters; each shot one down. After their flight group reformed and headed northward, it spotted an English squadron in the distance. At first the English seemed reluctant to engage. Richthofen wrote:

At last one of the men plucked up courage

and dropped down upon our rear machine. Naturally, battle was accepted although our position was unfavorable. If you wish to do business you must, after all, adapt yourself to the desires of your customers. Therefore we all turned round. The Englishman noticed what was going on and got away. The battle had begun.

Another Englishman tried a similar trick on me and I greeted him at once with quick fire from my two machine guns. He tried to escape me by dropping down. That was fatal to him. When he got beneath me I remained on top of him. Everything in the air that is beneath me, especially if it is a one-seater, a chaser, is lost, for it cannot shoot to the rear.

My opponent had a very good and very fast machine. However, he did not succeed in reaching the English lines. I began to fire at him when we were above Lens. I started shooting when I was much too far away. That was merely a trick of mine. I did not mean so much to hit him as to frighten him, and I succeeded in catching him. He began flying curves and this enabled me to draw near. I tried the same maneuver a second and a third time. Every time my foolish friend started making his curves I gradually edged quite close to him.

I approached him almost to touching distance. I aimed very carefully. I waited a moment and when I was at most at a distance of 50 yards from him I started with both the machine guns at the same time. I heard a slight hissing noise, a certain sign that the benzene tanks had been hit. Then I saw a bright flame and my lord disappeared below.[7]

Manfred von Richthofen had shot down four planes in one day, and Lothar had shot down two. Between them, they had eliminated a squadron. As for their father, "his joy was wonderful."

The following day, Manfred went off for a month's leave. On May 2, his 25th birthday, he had lunch with Kaiser Wilhelm. The following day he dined with Generalfeldmarschall von Hindenburg. During his time off he also dictated his memoirs, posed for more portrait photographs, greeted admirers, visited his family, and got in a bit of hunting.

On May 13, Lothar, who had been left in command of the Staffel, was shot down and would spend several months convalescing. When it came to injuries, Manfred had always been lucky. In August 1915, when still flying over the Eastern Front, he observed, "I have never really been wounded. At the critical moment I always bent my head or drew in my belly. . . . Once a shot went through both of my fur-lined boots; another time, through my scarf; and once, along my arm through the fur and leather of my jacket. But I was never touched."

On March 9, 1917, he had had a close call when his plane was hit and he was forced to crash-land. He refused to say he had been "shot down" as he had not lost control of the plane.

Nearly four months later, on July 6, Richthofen's good luck came to an end. He was pursuing an English two-seater whose observer was firing at him. "I calmly let him shoot," wrote Richthofen, "for even the best sharpshooter's marksmanship could not help at a distance of 300 meters. One just does not hit!"

Suddenly, he felt a sharp blow to the head. A bullet had fractured his skull, though it had not penetrated. Temporarily blinded and paralyzed, Richthofen plunged helplessly down thousands of meters, expecting at any moment that the wings would break off his plane. He recovered somewhat and shut off the ignition and his fuel. He stared toward the sun until he could at last see light, and gradually he was able to read his gauges, though it seemed as though he was looking at them through smoked glass. At an altitude of 800 meters, his vision cleared sufficiently to enable him to crash-land.

Richthofen was hospitalized for nearly three weeks. On July 25, he returned to Jagdgeschwader I, a fighter wing comprising four Jagdstaffeln, which were put under his command in June. He still suffered from throbbing headaches and nausea, possibly caused by bone fragments that had not been removed from his wound.

On August 16, he led the morning patrol and shot down a Nieuport. The effort exhausted him so much that, upon his return to the base, he spent the rest of the day in bed.

Richthofen was ordered to refrain from further combat unless it was absolutely necessary; the military worried that if he were to die in combat, it would greatly depress morale. Richthofen defined "absolutely necessary" as he saw fit and continued to fly regularly.

On August 28, the Jagdgeschwader took delivery of two new Fokker triplanes, the plane with which Richthofen is most closely identified. Richthofen took one, Werner Voss the other. Voss was an outstanding pilot who had recently gotten his 38th victory.

On the night of August 31/September 1, flying the triplane for the first time in combat, Richthofen shot down a British artillery-spotting aircraft. This was his 60th victory, and it was the last he was able to commemorate with a silver cup; due to wartime shortages, silver was no longer available in Germany.

His autobiography, *Der Rote Kampfflieger* (*The Red Battle-Flyer*), had come out, but Richthofen continued making notes for a future edition. In an undated entry titled "Thoughts in a Dugout," he describes lying awake on his cot at night, staring up at a lamp he had made from the engine of an airplane he shot down, with small lights mounted inside the cylinders. Grim thoughts ran through his mind.

"The battle now taking place on all Fronts

has become awfully serious; there is nothing left
of the 'lively, merry war,' as our deeds were called
in the beginning. Now we must fight off despair
and arm ourselves so that the enemy will not
penetrate our country. . . . When I read my book,
I smile at the insolence of it. I now no longer possess such an insolent spirit. It is not because I'm
afraid, though one day death may be hard on my
heels; no, it's not for that reason, although I
think enough about it. One of my superiors
advised me to give up flying, saying it will catch
up with me one day. But I would become miserable if now, honored with glory and decorations,
I became a pensioner of my own dignity in order
to preserve my precious life for the nation while
every poor fellow in the trenches endures his
duty exactly as I did mine."[8]

In early September, concerned about Richthofen's
health, the high command ordered him to take a recupera-
tive leave. When he visited home, his mother was shocked to
see that his head wound was not healing properly—his skull
was still exposed. He had severe headaches and was often in
a foul mood.

While Richthofen was away, his Fokker triplane was being
flown by Kurt Wolff, who was shot down and killed. Wolff had
been a rising ace with 33 kills. Less than two weeks later,
Richthofen's closest rival, Werner Voss, was killed after his
40th victory. On October 23, Richthofen was relieved to
return to the front, where he felt he belonged.

At the end of January 1918, he made his last trip home. As
his mother sorted through some photographs of him surrounded
by his fellow pilots, she pointed to one flyer and asked Manfred
how he was doing.

"He has fallen in combat," he responded.

She pointed to another, and he said, "Also dead." Then he told her, "Do not ask any more—they are all dead."

On March 13, Lothar was shot down and wounded for the second time. After recuperating, he returned to the front and was shot down again on August 13. Ultimately, he would survive the war with 40 victories.

On April 20, Richthofen got his 79th and 80th victories. "Three minutes after I had shot down the first one in flames, I attacked a second Camel from the same *Geschwader* [squadron]. The opponent went into a dive, pulled out and repeated this maneuver several times. As he did that, I came up to the closest fighting distance and fired about 50 rounds at him [until his machine] caught fire. The fuselage burned in the air, the rest of the airplane crashed northeast of Villers-Bretonneux."

As Richthofen headed back to the base, he flew low, waving at the infantrymen in the trenches and the columns of men marching on the roads. Recognizing his red Fokker, they waved back and threw their hats in the air. On his trip home in October, Richthofen had told his mother, "When I fly out over the fortified trenches and the soldiers shout joyfully at me and I look into their gray faces, worn from hunger, sleeplessness and battle—then I am glad, then something rejoices within me."

He was now the ace of aces among all pilots of the war. The German leadership again implored him to retire from combat, to no avail.

On April 21, 1918, Richthofen pursued a Sopwith Camel, so intent on making it his 81st victim that he flew two miles behind the British lines. RAF pilot Capt. Arthur Roy Brown dived on the red Fokker, firing his machine guns, even as antiaircraft gunners fired up at him from the trenches. The single .303 bullet that passed through Richthofen's heart was probably fired from the ground.

Richthofen managed to land his plane before he died.

The British buried him with full military honors. The *New York Times* wrote that the funeral "could have been marked by no greater solemnity if it had been the premier Allied pilot who had lost his life, instead of the intrepid German whom all honored." An army chaplain read the Church of England service, a rifle squad fired a 21-gun salute, and "Last Post" was played on the trumpet. The inscription on one of the floral wreaths read, "A valiant and worthy foe."[9]

The engine of Richthofen's plane was put on display in London's Imperial War Museum, where it remains today. The inveterate trophy hunter would have appreciated the irony.

• • •

Richthofen is the best known ace of World War I; indeed, he remains the best known ace of all time. Meanwhile, the second-highest ranking ace of the war, René Fonck, remains largely uncelebrated, despite the fact that he is the top Allied ace of both World Wars, with 75 kills and 52 probables. Considering that the Germans were slightly more liberal in their confirmation criteria, Fonck may even have surpassed von Richthofen's record.

An outstanding marksman, Fonck was known to take down opponents with as few as five rounds from his machine gun. He also mastered the difficult art of deflection shooting, which requires understanding the trajectories of bullets fired from a moving platform at a moving target. He wrote, "I had become a virtuoso, and having seriously practiced my art, I succeeded in hitting the enemy from every angle, from no matter what position I found myself in contact with him."

In the late summer of 1917, when Fonck had 13 victories to his credit, Georges Guynemer was France's reigning ace, with 53. Guynemer was an exalted national hero, whose personal charm and passionate fighting spirit endeared him to the public. He was the recipient not only of 26 citations for valor, but also of tens of thousands of adulatory letters from school-children. On September 11, he disappeared while on a solo patrol. The news of his death was withheld as long as possible for fear of its effect on morale. When it was announced, France reeled. A writer for *Le Temps* refused to accept it: "They say Guynemer is dead. Guynemer dead! Bah! Those who believe it don't know him." Churches were packed for special memorial masses. President Clemençeau eulogized him as "our pride and our protection. . . . He will remain the model hero, a living legend, the greatest in all history."

On September 30, Fonck was at 12,000 feet when he spotted a German Rumpler two-seater below him and dived at it. Its machine gunner fired three bursts at him but missed. Fonck held his fire until he positioned his Spad below and behind the Rumpler, and then, with one short burst of his twin Vickers, killed its pilot and gunner. The plane flipped over in the air, one wing tore off, and the bodies plummeted out. It was Fonck's 15th kill and would prove his most significant, for papers on the pilot's body identified him as Kurt Wissemann, credited by the Germans with Guynemer's death, which made Fonck Guynemer's symbolic avenger.

Fonck would soon surpass Guynemer's record. A 1918 news article described his best performance:

> Lieut. Rene Fonck, the young French "ace of aces" fought three distinct battles in the air when, on May 9, he brought down six German airplanes in one day. His record never has been equaled in aviation.
>
> All three engagements were fought within two hours. In all Fonck fired only 56 shots; an average of little more than 9 bullets for each enemy brought down; an extraordinary record in view of the fact that aviators often fire hundreds of rounds without crippling their opponent.

The first fight, in which Lieut. Fonck
brought down three German machines, lasted
only a minute and a half and the young
Frenchman fired only 23 shots.[10]

In July 1918, Fonck surpassed Guynemer's tally. On
August 14, he downed three German planes within 10 seconds. On September 26, in three separate engagements, Fonck
again downed six planes and was quick to insist he would
have gotten eight had his guns not jammed. On his best day,
Richthofen scored four. Three British aces also got six kills in
a day, but only Fonck managed to perform the feat twice. One
more such day and he would have beaten Richthofen's score.

Before Richthofen's death, Fonck told a reporter,
"Maneuvering your opponent is the chief thing. Directly I
engage an enemy I can judge what line to take. You can tell
from the outset just what quality of pilot is opposed to you, and
must act accordingly. I have never fought Richthofen, but I am
certain I should know in ten seconds that I was at grips with
him if we met, and he would know, too. The way a pilot handles his machine is an unfailing indication of his caliber."[11]

American ace Maj. Charles Biddle wrote:

Taking everything into consideration, Fonck
is, to my mind, in a class by himself as a fighting
pilot. There have been many other great pilots
just as brave, such as Guynemer and [Albert]
Ball, but none of them have combined with it
Fonck's marvelous skill. I know that up to the
time that I left Groupe 12 of the French
Aviation, Fonck had been hit only once, having
then gotten one bullet through a wing. I saw
Captain Deullin the other day and he told me
that he had maintained this record to the end,
throughout hundreds of fights. It is hard for one

not familiar with air fighting to realize what this means. Luck has, of course, had something to do with it, but I think the principal reason lies in Fonck's almost uncanny shooting ability, and his faculty of almost being able to smell a Hun, and thus always get the jump on him.[12]

Fonck was extremely serious about his training. Unlike France's third-ranked ace, Charles Nungesser, who drank, womanized, and rarely got more than two hours of sleep, Fonck was as abstemious as a monk. He wouldn't touch alcohol, would not fly without a good night's sleep, and had nothing to do with women. "Avoid all excess and train like a prizefighter," he advised other pilots.

Despite Fonck's success, he never displaced Guynemer in public esteem. It seems he had a rare gift for making himself unpopular. Lt. Claude Haegelen, one of the few who considered him a friend, expressed his mixed feelings: "He is not a tactful man. He is a tiresome braggart and even a boor, but in the air—and this is what really matters when we are struggling for national survival—this man Fonck is a slashing rapier, a steel blade tempered with unblemished courage and priceless skill. Up there he is transformed. If any of us is in difficulty with a Boche, or a whole flock of Boches, Fonck rushes to our aid. But afterward he cannot forget how he rescued you, nor let you forget. He can almost make you wish he hadn't helped you in the first place."[13]

A fighter pilot needs courage, aggressiveness, and skill, which Fonck had in excess; but to be a popular hero, one must also display modesty, grace, and generosity of spirit. Alas, those were not among Fonck's virtues.

Fonck made the headlines for a few weeks in 1926 when he was mounting an effort to claim the $25,000 Orteig Prize for a nonstop flight across the Atlantic. Fonck's overloaded three-engine Sikorsky could not get off the ground and crashed at the end of the runway, killing two crewmen. He further tarnished his reputation by blaming one of the dead men for the accident. Before Fonck could try again, Charles Lindbergh claimed the prize.

At the end of World War II, Fonck was accused of having collaborated with the Nazis but was never formally charged. He died in 1953.

NOTES

1. *Red Battle-Flyer*, pp. 78–79.
2. *Red Battle-Flyer*, pp. 111–13.
3. *Richthofen: Beyond the Legend*, p. 56.
4. *Red Battle-Flyer*, pp. 123–26.
5. *Red Battle-Flyer*, pp. 123–26.
6. *Red Battle-Flyer*, pp. 133–34.
7. *Red Battle-Flyer,* pp. 182–83.
8. *The Red Baron*, p. 119.
9. In 1925, Richthofen's body was returned to Germany.
10. "Brought Down Six Enemy Airplanes in One Day; Fonck's Record Unbeaten," *Olean Evening Herald*, June 19, 1918, p. 8.
11. "French 'Ace' Gives Our Fliers Advice," *New York Times*, April 13, 1918, p. 3.
12. Charles John Biddle, *The Way of the Eagle* (New York: Charles Scribner's Sons, 1919), p. 295.
13. Stephen Longstreet, *The Canvas Falcons* (New York: Barnes & Noble, 1995), p. 156.

Saburo Sakai
(1916–2000)

> *"I was blessed with the*
> *secrets of the art of escape,*
> *as well as the mysteries of*
> *shooting down an enemy."*
> —Saburo Sakai

Participating in roughly 200 dogfights and racking up 64 kills, Saburo Sakai was among Japan's top aces in World War II, and one of the few who survived to tell his story.

He was born on August 16, 1916, one of seven children in a samurai family. The samurai's aristocratic privileges had ended in the 19th century, and Sakai's family, like many others, had been reduced to scratching out a living like peasants. Sakai's earliest memory was of his mother tirelessly tilling the family's 1-acre plot, dressed in rags, a baby strapped to her back. When Saburo was 11, his father died, increasing the family's hardships. Still, his mother maintained her stern pride, and Saburo never heard her voice a complaint. When he would come home from school crying because he had been bullied by older boys, she offered no sympathy. "Shame on you" was her inevitable response. "Don't forget that you are the son of a samurai, that tears are not for you."

This advice served Sakai well when he enlisted in the Imperial Navy in May 1933. Discipline was harsh and recruits were beaten for the slightest infraction. If a recruit cried out in pain, or even emitted a groan, his entire barracks had to share his punishment. Seeking an escape from the ordeal, Sakai took the examination for flying school and was one of 70 accepted out of 1,500 applicants. There, cadets faced only one disciplinary threat: expulsion.

In addition to flight training, cadets had to master a variety of physical challenges. Every day, two of them would be chosen at random and ordered to fight. Whoever lost the bout had to face another classmate, and that loser had to face another, and so on even if one man had to fight the entire school. Injuries were common. To develop their neck muscles—crucial when performing aerobatics—cadets had to balance on their heads for at least 5 minutes. Cadets sharpened their observation by identifying objects, shapes, and aircraft types at the edge of their peripheral vision while reading a chart in front of them. They had to stare at the sky until they could pick out stars during daylight hours; their instructors warned them that an approaching enemy aircraft might be no more apparent. Once they had learned to discern a star, they practiced shifting their eyes away and then snapping them instantly back onto it. According to Sakai, this ability, along with his keen eyesight, saved him many times in aerial combat. He claimed he always spotted his enemy before his enemy spotted him.

In 1938, Sakai graduated first among the 25 students in his class. He would be the only one of them to survive the war.

He was stationed in China on October 3, 1939, when a formation of 12 Chinese bombers bombed his airfield, destroying most of the 200 planes there. Sakai ran from cover, found

Saburo Sakai at Hankow Air Base in 1939, the day before he attacked 12 Chinese bombers.

an undamaged Mitsubishi A5M4 Type 96 fighter, and gave chase. Alone against the bombers, he managed to shoot the engine on one, though he was wounded by the bomber's tail gun and collapsed immediately after landing. Sakai's daring exploit was heavily played up in the Japanese press.

Sakai flew his first A6M2 Zero early in 1941. Lightly armored, it was built for speed, climb rate, and maneuverability. Sakai appreciated the 360-degree visibility offered by its bubble canopy and its long range, which he demonstrated by flying 12 hours straight, at that time a record. "The Zero excited me as nothing else had ever done," he said. "Even on the ground it had the cleanest lines I had ever seen on an airplane. It was a dream to fly. . . . We could hardly wait to meet enemy planes in this remarkable new aircraft."

To maximize its performance, Sakai removed its heavy radio. As he observed, "There's nothing to talk about in a dogfight."

The Zero was armed with two fuselage-mounted 7.7mm machine guns and two 20mm automatic cannons in the wings; he recalibrated their convergence to be much closer in than the standard 200 meters.

Sakai was sent to the Tainan airbase on Formosa in the fall of 1941 in preparation for the Japanese attack on the Philippines. On December 8 his squadron attacked Clark Field, where he shot down a P-40, reportedly the first American plane lost over the Philippines. On December 10 he downed a B-17, the first Allied bomber to fall in the Pacific.

In mid-1942, Sakai was transferred to Rabaul, New Britain, and later to Lae, New Guinea. Conditions at the island bases were Spartan. Food was "the lowest level consumable by human beings," accommodations were primitive, there was no news or entertainment, and cigarettes were scarce. Still, morale was high, because there was plenty of fighting to be had, and as Sakai put it, "What were we fighter pilots for, but to engage enemy planes in combat?"

By early 1942 he had downed dozens of P-39s and P-40s.

He described his approach to an interviewer: "I strove to shoot down my enemy in the first dive or attack, tried not to open fire too soon, never followed an enemy into a dive, and tried to get behind my enemy and stay there." In dogfights, he used the Zero's superior maneuverability to evade opponents' attacks and to cut inside their loops until he had them in his sights. Still, it was not easy. As he described it, "Hitting a target with machine guns under these conditions was like trying to thread a needle while running. If it weren't so difficult, a pilot would never have enough lives to fight at all, let alone shoot down another plane."[1]

He had to estimate range and trajectories in his head. Subjected to as much as five g, his machine-gun fire dropped in a curve, a phenomenon he called "pissing bullets." Despite the difficulty, Sakai shot down as many as four opponents in a single battle.

He was also an excellent pilot. On May 17, he and two other top pilots, Hiroyoshi Nishizawa and Toshio Ota, put on an aerobatics display over the American airfield at Port Moresby. Flying wingtip to wingtip, they executed three perfect consecutive loops at an altitude of 700–800 meters. Rather than fire on them, the American troops cheered their audacity.

His flying ability enabled Sakai to score his 37th and 49th kills without firing a shot. The first of these followed a wild running duel with a P-39 at treetop level near Port Moresby on May 27. The pilot of the P-39 sought to shake him by banking and wheeling through valleys and mountain passes. Sakai never even got a chance to fire as he clung to his opponent's tail. Drenched in sweat, he concentrated solely on avoiding the trees and rock outcroppings sweeping by at several hundred miles per hour. After one tight turn, the pilot of the P-39 found himself facing a rock cliff. He jerked his Airacobra upward, but not fast enough. Sakai whipped his Zero up through the debris of the exploding P-39 and just cleared the cliff. His 49th kill came when, low on ammunition and wishing not to miss, he closed in on an opponent's tail until he was only 30 yards behind. Before Sakai could make his shot, the unnerved pilot bailed out.

By mid-1942, Sakai was Japan's leading ace.

The Japanese Empire seemed to be sweeping all opposition before it, but slowly, inexorably, America began to push back. The Japanese high command deceived its troops about the war's progress, but Sakai could see that there seemed to be no end to the resources America could bring to the fight.

When America made a beachhead on Guadalcanal, Sakai's squadron was ordered to counterattack, though Guadalcanal was 560 nautical miles from the Japanese base at Rabaul. The Zero was a good long-range fighter, but this was pushing it to its limit.

At 8:30 A.M. on August 8, 18 Zeros took off, escorting 27 "Betty" bombers. The day was clear. About 60 miles south of Rabaul, Sakai scanned the sea beneath him and was struck by a verdant, horseshoe-shaped atoll, identified on the map as Green Island. Before the day was over, the fact that he had noticed it would save his life.

As the Japanese neared their target, Sakai spotted yellow flashes in the sky over the island where Zeros were already dueling with carrier-launched Grumman Wildcats. The sea below was crisscrossed with hundreds of white lines, wakes left by the American fleet.

From 20,000 feet, the Japanese bombers dropped their loads against the American ships, failing to hit a single one, and then turned and headed back toward Rabaul. The Zeros escorted them beyond the American fighter patrols, then made their way back to Guadalcanal for aerial combat.

Though slower and less maneuverable than the Zero, the Wildcats had more firepower and used their numerical advantage skillfully. Groups of 6 or 12 would plunge from higher altitude against each three-plane Zero formation, fire their guns, then dive out of range while another group pressed the attack, a tactic dubbed "zoom and boom."

Sakai shot down a Wildcat that had engaged his wingman and, moments later, a Dauntless, his 59th and 60th kills. Well ahead of the rest of his group, Sakai spotted what appeared to be eight Wildcats in the distance. As he approached, their formation closed up, which made him think they had not spotted him. Attacking from behind and below, he figured he could take out at least two with his first pass. As he closed in to 60 yards, he suddenly realized that his targets were not Wildcats, but Grumman TBF-1 Avenger torpedo bombers, armed with rear-facing .50-caliber turret guns. Sakai had walked into their trap, and if he attempted to loop away, he would be totally exposed to their fire. There was nothing to do but continue his attack. As he pressed his firing button, every gun on the Avengers opened up in response. Two of the Avengers burst into flames under the hammering of his guns, but then "a violent explosion smashed at my body. I felt as though knives had been thrust savagely into my ears; the world burst into flaming red and I went blind."

Sakai blacked out. Seconds later he was brought back to consciousness by a cold wind blasting through his shattered cockpit. He felt as if he were lost in a murky haze, with waves of darkness passing over him. He blinked but could see nothing but red. He wondered if he was going to die. If dying was like this—a pleasant, overwhelming drowsiness without fear or pain—it was nothing to worry about, he thought. Visions swam before him. Suddenly, with astonishing clarity, he saw his mother's indomitable face. She cried, "Shame! Shame! Wake up, Saburo, wake up! You are acting like a sissy. You are no coward! Wake up!"

Sakai made an effort to assess his situation. He could smell no smoke, so his plane must not be on fire. It was plummeting earthward, but when he pulled his stick back, it leveled off. That much was good, but still he could not see. If he were blind, what chance would he have to get back to Rabaul? He tried to reach for the throttle, but he could not move his left hand. He tried to move his left foot against the rudder bar and found there was no sensation on his left side. He wept in despair. The tears washed enough blood from his vision that he was able to discern the post of his cockpit silhouetted against the sky, at least with his left eye. He began to make out the outlines of his instruments, but he could not read them. Looking out the side of the cockpit, he saw great black shapes sliding by below at tremendous speed: American ships, shooting at him! Only 300 feet over the water, his Zero rocked in the blast waves of bursting flak, but moments later it was out of range.

The thought of diving his plane into the sea appealed to him, but he felt a samurai should die fighting. Even if he were doomed, he must make the enemy kill him. Sakai knew the value of victories to a fighter pilot and he wanted his death to have meaning, even if it was only to raise the tally of an enemy. But where were the American fighters? He raved, "Here I am! Come on and fight!"

His thoughts wandering, Sakai pondered his luck at having survived so far, his plane still aloft and largely intact. He had a chance to live, and he must make the most of it. He raised his right hand to his head, searching for the source of the blood that covered his face. There were gashes and what felt like small pieces of metal in his face. His goggles were smashed. His right eye throbbed terribly, and when he moved his hand over it he could see nothing. On top of his leather flight helmet was a slit, which he gingerly probed with his fingers, afraid of what he might find. There was a depression, at the bottom of which he felt something hard. That must be his skull. Was it cracked? Might a bullet fragment have entered his brain? It was possible—he remembered once reading that the brain cannot feel pain. In any case, he had to stop the bleeding.

Every pilot carried four bandages for such emergencies, but it was almost impossible to apply them with one hand in an open cockpit. Each time he tried to tie a bandage to his head, it was ripped away by the 200-mph wind, until all were gone. He thought of his silk scarf. He pushed the end of it under his helmet and, while controlling the flight stick with his right knee, steadily worked it back until his wound was covered. Then he took his jackknife from his pocket, opened its blade with his teeth, and cut off the remainder. The bleeding was stanched.

The effort had been draining, and Sakai once again felt an overwhelming desire to sleep. Every 30 or 40 seconds, he slumped forward in his straps, only to jerk awake. Several times he found himself flying upside down. Once he awoke with the Zero skidding wildly to the right, its wings straight up and down.

He slapped his face furiously to keep himself conscious. He wondered how he could make it back to Rabaul. He knew he was heading north but was unable to spot any landmarks. The islands were like dots in the great ocean, and he suspected he had drifted off course. The compass appeared blurry, but he was able to get a reading by pressing his left eye up against it. He discovered that he was heading for the center of the Pacific. He took out his chart, scrubbed the blood from it with his sleeve, made a guess as to his position, and corrected his course.

Sakai passed out, again waking to find himself flying upside down, this time with the ocean racing by barely 100 feet below. With a struggle, he righted his plane and brought it back to 1,500 feet, when suddenly his engine went silent. The main fuel tank was empty. Now his will to live asserted itself against all fatigue. He pushed the stick forward to pick up speed and keep his propeller turning. The fuel-supply valve for his remaining tank was on the left side of the cockpit, but with a wrenching movement he managed to reach it with his right hand and open it. The fuel still would not flow through, as the lines had gone dry and the automatic pump had been sucking air. He desperately worked the emergency hand pump as his Zero glided toward the ocean. Finally, the engine roared back to life.

With only an hour of fuel left, he spotted a horseshoe-shaped island beneath him: Green Island. Now at least he knew where he was, but could he make it the 60 miles to Rabaul? More importantly, could he, half blind and half paralyzed, land his shot-up plane? It was all he could do to keep it on an even keel.

He saw two warships below him, Japanese cruisers on their way to Guadalcanal. He thought of crashing in the water near them, as they would stop and pick him up, but they were on their way to fight the Americans and he could not allow himself to hinder them.

Having returned to Rabaul two hours earlier, Sakai's fellow pilots had given him up for lost. When his battered Zero suddenly appeared, circling the airstrip, they ran from their barracks to watch, wondering if he could make it. He wondered that as well. He considered ditching in the water nearby, but the thought of his wounded head pitching forward upon impact was too painful to bear. As he circled the strip for the third time, his fuel tanks reading empty, he lowered his wheels and flaps and made an approach. Seeing that he was too far to the left and would hit the parked fighters, he brought himself around for another attempt. He touched down and taxied his plane to a halt near the command post. The pilots rushed over and pulled him from the cockpit. "I have to report. Let me go to the command post," he insisted. Barely conscious, he reported to his captain before allowing himself to be taken to the base hospital.

Sakai was sent back to Japan for eye surgery and recuperation. The operation had to be performed without anesthesia, and the surgeon warned him that he must keep his eyes open and immobile no matter how excruciating the pain or he would lose his sight. Never had his samurai stoicism been so severely tested.

Sakai gradually regained the use of his left side but remained blind in his right eye. He was put to work training pilots, most of whom would never have qualified in his day. The introduction in 1943 of such planes as the P-38 Lightning and the 4FU-Corsair gave America the edge in the air. By 1944, with the war going badly, Sakai's repeated requests to be allowed to return to combat were at last granted. Even with one eye, there was no question that he was a better pilot than those that were being tossed into the fray.

Sakai was stationed on Iwo Jima. On June 24, the air-raid siren sounded and he thundered into the sky in a group of 80 Zeros, facing the new Grumman F6F Hellcat. In the opening seconds of his first battle since being wounded, he cut inside a Hellcat's turn and fired a burst into its belly. Thick smoke poured from the plane, and it went into a wild, uncontrolled dive. Despite the victory, he realized the terrible liability of his blind eye. He had to turn his head frantically to scan the sky for opponents. Suddenly he saw six Hellcats on his tail. He reduced power, they overshot, and he got behind one, pumping cannon shells into its fuselage. Flames exploded through its cockpit, then it swerved off on one wing and plunged downward.

Sakai was in the midst of the greatest air battle he had ever seen, involving 200 planes on each side. He gaped as he saw a Hellcat pursued by a Zero, behind which was closing another Hellcat, which was tailed by another Zero, with another Hellcat behind it, and a Zero swooping in to bring up the rear. The column snaked along, each plane firing at the next, and within seconds they were all blown out of the sky like a string of firecrackers, with only the final Zero escaping.

Sakai headed for what he took to be a formation of 15 Zeros, but which turned out to be Hellcats. He cursed his faulty vision as they wheeled in pursuit of him, attacking in groups of four. Each time he rolled away from their streaming tracers, the next group moved in for the kill. Sakai could quickly size up the skill of enemy pilots and he knew these were green.

He turned away from their attacks with the same left roll every time, yet they never changed their tactics. Nevertheless, their Hellcats were far superior to the American planes he had fought two years before and only his well-honed skills were keeping him alive. Over and over he rolled, with his Zero hitting 350 mph, until he feared that his wings might shear off under the strain. Sweat poured into his eye but he had no time to wipe it. His left arm became numb with the exertion. His altimeter bottomed out. He had skidded and rolled through two and one-half miles of altitude since the beginning of the battle, nearly 15 minutes earlier. As the planes continued their firing passes, the .50-caliber slugs kicked up foam from the sea just beneath him. There was no more room to run—it was time to take the offensive. Sakai yanked back his stick and looped upward, firing on a Hellcat, but his arms were too weak to hold steady and the Hellcat rolled away. His unexpected move caused the other American planes to scatter, though, and Sakai seized the chance to fly into a large cloud and make a break for Iwo Jima.

Under a protective screen of antiaircraft fire, he landed his plane, to the cheers of his fellow pilots. Alone against 15 Hellcats, he had not only survived, but his plane had not been struck by a single bullet. It was a remarkable performance, but a bittersweet one for Sakai; once master of the skies, the Zero was now easy prey. Of the 80 that had gone up, only 40 returned. In the following days, every group of Zeros that set out returned with half its number, until after three battles only nine remained.

On July 4, Sakai received the most shocking assignment of his career: a group of bomb-laden Zeros and fully loaded Betty bombers were ordered to take part in a suicide mission, ramming American warships. The Zeros were not to engage enemy fighters. This was four months before Japan created its Kamikaze corps, and such an idea flew in the face of Sakai's Bushido ethic. He accepted the axiom, "A samurai lives in such a way that he will always be prepared to die," but there was a difference between dying and killing oneself. Nevertheless, he had no choice but to obey.

As the formation of bombers and fighters neared the American fleet, it was jumped by Hellcats. After watching seven of the eight Bettys explode in seconds and two Zeros plunge flaming into the sea, Sakai could no longer hold himself back. He turned into a diving Hellcat and fired his cannon into its belly. It flipped through the sky and then fell toward the ocean, trailing a plume of smoke. Then the Hellcats swarmed him. They were so eager for a kill that they got in each other's way, spending more time avoiding collisions than firing at him. One would make a firing pass only to have to break off to avoid the fire of another one heading in at a different angle. With his wingmen, Sakai fled into a thick cumulus cloud and passed through into a severe squall. Somewhere within it hid the American fleet. For 15 minutes he fought the turbulence and blinding rain, searching for a target. Daylight was fading, and his fuel was running low. Sakai glanced at his wingmen. In all his years of combat he had never lost a wingman, and he took more satisfaction from that fact than he did from all his victories. Now these men would smash themselves against the side of a ship if he led them there, or plunge into the sea beside him if their fuel ran out. Sakai could not stomach such a fate, for himself or his men. He turned back to Iwo Jima. His captain, who had sent the other men to useless deaths, did not fault him for his disobedience.

In the autumn of 1944, when it became clear that Iwo Jima could not be held, Sakai was evacuated along with the last of the fighter pilots. Japan's dreams of empire had been crushed, and its remaining hope was to defend the homeland.

On August 13, 1945, Sakai was among a group of officers secretly informed that Japan had decided to accept the American terms for surrender. He was devastated. He and another pilot resolved that they would fly one last, unautho-

rized mission against the bombers that battered their country nightly. After dark, when they got to the runway, they
discovered that others shared the same idea. Ten Zeros took
off as the bombers approached. With his weakened vision,
Sakai relied on his wingman to find a target. Following his
lead, he made several firing passes against a B-32. It began
dropping, and he saw it splash into the sea several miles off
Oshima Island. The kill went unrecorded, but it was Sakai's
fifth since he'd lost his right eye, and possibly the last
American plane downed in the war. Twelve hours later,
Japan surrendered.

Sakai had fought from the first day to the last. He had
been wounded four times, and out of 150 pilots who began in
his unit, he was one of only three to survive the war. His
score of 64 kills is based on his own reports, as the Japanese
did not keep official records of that sort, but it is accepted as
accurate. It included at least one of each type of plane the
United States flew.

For years after the war, the Japanese were reluctant to glori-
fy their heroes. However, interest in Sakai grew among fighter
buffs in the United States, especially after the publication in
1957 of his best-selling autobiography, *Samurai*. He traveled to
America a dozen times to take part in reunions and conven-
tions, and met and formed warm friendships with many of the
pilots he had fought against.

An interviewer asked if he had any ill feeling toward his
former enemies. "That would be self-defeating," said Sakai. "I
accepted the fact that my country was not in the right during
the war. It is not a matter of forgiveness; soldiers should never
have to forgive their enemy or themselves. If they did their job
the best they could, and lived by a code of honor, then they
understand that we pilots and soldiers do not make wars, but
we must try and end them."[2]

Sakai died on September 22, 2000, a day after he had
dined at the Atsugi Naval Air Station near Tokyo. He was

reaching across the table to shake hands with an American officer when he suffered a heart attack.

NOTES

1. *Japan at War*, pp.135–36.
2. "Japan's Legendary Zero Ace," p. 41.

Robert J. "R.J." Thomas (1945–)

"If you're going to be in that situation, it helps to have the best shooter in the United States Navy with you."
—L. Richard Barr,
Seawolf pilot

Born December 2, 1945, Robert J. "R.J." Thomas grew up on a cattle ranch that bordered the Los Padres Wilderness in the central California Sierra Madre Mountains. He said, "I always had a gun in my hands, and from the time I was about ten years old I spent all my free time hunting in the mountains. I hunted deer and lions, killed coyotes, and shot varmints at long range with rifles. I developed moving-target skills with a shotgun, hunting quail, ducks, and band-tailed pigeons."

Thomas was also a fisherman and free diver, and his ambition was to become a U.S. Navy frogman. "Being in the navy and having someone pay me to be a diver seemed like heaven—like underwater hunting," he said.

Thomas joined the Navy at 17 and was assigned to

Radarman "A" school and then served the required two years in the fleet before applying for Underwater Demolition Team Replacement (UDT/R) training. After being assigned to UDT 22 for a year and making a mandatory cruise, he decided to try out for the SEAL program, as he felt his shooting skills would serve him better as a SEAL than as a frogman. Describing himself as "a low-level competitive shooter," Thomas had already participated in matches and successfully competed against SEALs, which gave him credibility with that elite group. His application was accepted, and he immediately was assigned to the ordnance department.

In February 1969, Petty Officer Thomas of SEAL Team 2, Detachment ALFA, was sent to Vietnam. He said, "By virtue of the fact that I was the best shot in my platoon and I wanted the job, I was assigned as the platoon sniper. As a platoon ordnance petty officer, I shot all of the sniper rifles at Team Two and picked one that was a sub-MOA gun with selected lots of Lake City 7.62 MM National Match ammunition.[1] The rifle was a parkerized 700 Remington, in an oiled wood stock with a varmint-weight barrel. The scope was a 3-9 X Redfield Accurange with conventional crosshair reticle."

Thomas's platoon was stationed at Ha Tiên, a village on the Gulf of Siam along Vietnam's western border with Cambodia. Supporting the SEALs in the area was a detachment of Seawolves, the Navy's heavily armed UH-1 "Huey" helicopters. When they weren't operating, the SEALs and Seawolf crews relaxed in the ville. Pilot Lt. Richard Barr recalls one evening: "We're all just sitting around drinking beer and watching R.J. shoot. He had his sniper rifle and was dropping seagulls at 600 to 700 yards. You'd hear *Boom!* and we'd wait what seemed like two or three seconds and a seagull would fall off a piling. That was quite interesting."

On March 23, 1969, Barr piloted one of two Seawolves on a scouting/strike mission. Enemy activity had been spotted on Nuy Da Dung Mountain, which served as a sanctuary for a local warlord. As Thomas recalls, "Their typical tactic was to roll a 4.2-inch mortar out of a cave and shell nearby villages, particularly Ha Tiên, and then come down into the town and make their demands. So, the helicopter guys asked me if I wanted to jump in the helo with them and do a recon and see if I could determine which cave it was they were rolling this mortar out of."

It sounded to Thomas like this might develop into an ideal sniping opportunity, but for the recon he armed himself with a Stoner 63A machine gun and his SEAL Team issue Smith & Wesson Model 39 handgun.

As the Seawolves approached Nuy Da Dung on a rocket pass, they came under intense automatic weapons fire. The Americans didn't know that an NVA battalion had moved into the region and taken up positions on the mountain.

Barr, who was piloting the helicopter carrying Thomas, said, "We were able to make one 2.75-inch rocket run and we took a lot of automatic fire from the mountain. We came back around for another pass and shot some more rockets, at the same time we felt a real heavy hit. It knocked the helicopter on its side and took out the engine. I called on the radio to my wingman and said 'We're hit, we're going down.'"

Thomas said, "I was hanging out the side door on a gunner belt when we got hit. Several rounds came through the helo, fragmenting and hitting me in the chest and lodging between my ribs and over my kidney. We crashed; I'd estimate from around 300 feet. There was no opportunity to auto-rotate or employ emergency crash procedures."

The Seawolf hit the ground hard, shearing off the skids, and flipped over. The impact threw Thomas out the side door, breaking the gunner's belt and stripping his web gear and H-harness off him, including his sidearm. He landed on the hard clay of the dried-up rice paddy 30 or 40 feet from the crash. He had compression-fractured vertebrae and multiple impact wounds to his torso, knee, and hand, and his nose was nearly severed from his face. Although dazed, he was still conscious and ambulatory, and in better shape than the rest of the crew. He made his way back to the wrecked helicopter, which was now on fire. Barr was unconscious in his seat, suspended by his seat belt. Thomas released him and dragged him a safe distance from the flames. Barr's back, arm, and leg were broken, and one eye was hanging out of the socket.

The remaining Seawolf, piloted by LTJG Randy Miller, dropped off PO Dan Riordan to help Thomas. Miller then lifted off, staying out of range but providing what covering fire he could. Riordan and Thomas rescued a second unconscious crewmember from the wreckage, but the last two were consumed in the blaze before they could extract them. Both Thomas and Riordan were under increasing small-arms fire as NVA troops closed in.

The enemy fire was so intense that one observer said the paddy looked like a bare, dusty field that was being hit by a hard rain. Riordan was wounded in the leg. The NVA began moving toward the survivors to kill or capture them. There was no cover, but Thomas had one factor in his favor: he was surrounded by earthen dikes, at a distance of about 100 yards, and the only way to get at him was over the dike.[2]

As Thomas recalls, "My Stoner was bent into a crescent, an M-16 on the helo was broken off at the butt, and both of the machine guns were destroyed in the crash. The Model 39 went away with my web-gear, and the only thing I had left to shoot was Dick Barr's 1911A1."

Along with the .45, Barr had two extra fully loaded magazines in pouches and about 25 or 30 rounds in cartridge loops on the chest strap of his shoulder rig, providing a total of about 45 or 50 rounds.

"I got this old clunker gun out of Barr's shoulder holster and proceeded to try to defend our position. Reports have me throwing myself over Barr's body to protect him, but actually his helmet and unconscious body provided me a relatively

R.J. Thomas on patrol with the Stoner that was destroyed in the helicopter wreck described in this section. (Credit: U.S. Navy Special Warfare Archives.)

steady rest. He regained consciousness and asked if he could help. He loaded magazines for me as I was shooting, so I could concentrate on the job at hand. I was holding the pistol with both hands, resting my forearms on his helmet to give me a little elevation. It was a fairly stable position and I was able to hold on a man-sized target to 100 yards or so."

"In order to get into our rice paddy, the NVA had to come over the dike. They lined up behind the dike about 100 yards away. They'd stick their AKs up over it and spray us with full-auto fire, then they'd stick their heads up to see if they hit anything. When they'd stick their heads up, it was just like a turkey shoot. I'd shoot at them and every once in a while a round would go *thunk* and the head would disappear."

Barr said, "Petty Officer Thomas was laying across my shoulder with the .45, just aiming and shooting and killing an NVA with almost every round. He killed a number of them."

Thomas continued, "Finally one guy got brave and came over the dike and charged at us. I missed him the first shot, he was kind of zigging and zagging around, but I centered him with the second at about 50 meters. The rest of them lost interest in that approach and pretty much stayed behind the dike."

After nearly 40 minutes, Thomas was down to his last magazine and seriously pondering the possibility of capture when two Army Slicks came to the rescue.[3] One was crippled by the intense ground fire and returned to base, trailing fuel. The other, despite being hit 15 times with heavy machine gun fire and hundreds of AK rounds, was able to land and pick up the survivors. As he was loading Barr into the Slick, Thomas' injured back finally gave out, and he fell to the ground.

Barr recalled, "We all got in the helicopter except for R.J.—he was on the ground, laying on his back—and three NVA ran at the helicopter. The army pilot took his M-16 and stuck it out the side-door window and killed two of them. The third NVA ran right in front of the helicopter with an AK. He was about ready to blast us and the army pilot was trying to get his M-16 gun out the window and pointed in the right direction. Meanwhile, R.J., who was lying on the ground, rolls over with the .45 and—typical John Wayne–type move—

Blam! blows the guy away with one shot. Then he looked up, smiling, and said, 'Did you see that banana?' The army guy was just about dying, he was one second away from being shot, and R.J., with that big grin on his face, says, 'Did you see that banana?' I'll never forget that."

The pilot was severely wounded, making it necessary for the co-pilot to take control of the bird. As they lifted off, Thomas got behind the M60 door gun. As he put it, "I felt it was a terrific opportunity to have an advantage on these guys who had been trying to kill me for the last 40 minutes. I wanted to stick around and deal with them with the door gun. There was some discussion about whether we should stay and fight or go, between the O-6[4] and me (he kept trying to pull me off the M-60). Ultimately he prevailed, but I did get in a few licks on those NVA in that open paddy. It was like sluicing a covey of quail on the ground."

Jeff Cooper, the father of the modern technique of the pistol, wrote, "A pistol is a weapon of astonishing efficiency and versatility when skillfully used, but its skillful use is rare. This is odd, when you think of it, for while the pistol is commonplace throughout the 'civilized' world, only the merest handful of men—now or in the past—have ever approached the ability to make it do what it can. A really good man, wearing a really good sidearm, is a serious, almost insurmountable, problem for any person or group which contemplates his forcible coercion. He may be safely taken with poison gas, a tank, or a precision rifle—under certain circumstances—and that's about all."[5]

Cooper's claim may sound like hyperbole, but on March 23, 1969, a well-worn .45 in the hands of a really good man proved sufficient to hold off an enemy force armed with assault rifles for the better part of an hour. Thomas will not put a number on how many of the enemy he killed that day, saying it would be pure speculation. "Only two of them got close enough to me to ensure they were down for the final count," he said.[6]

R.J. Thomas training at Gunsite in 1978. Target shows results of three repetitions of the Mozambique Drill, a controlled pair to center of mass followed by a head shot. Jeff Cooper told Thomas, "If you're shooting that well, you should speed up," but Thomas noted that he was shooting faster than any of the Gunsite instructors. Thomas subscribes to Bill Jordan's maxim, "Speed is fine, but accuracy is final." (Credit: Courtesy R.J. Thomas.)

The pilot of the Army Slick subsequently wrote him up for the Medal of Honor and submitted the recommendation through the Army system. However, this would have made Thomas the first Medal of Honor holder in the Atlantic Fleet and therefore the senior award holder; he was forewarned that the Navy would not allow an enlisted man to hold that honor before an officer. The award was downgraded to a Navy Cross, but so strong were the feelings of the Army that the Medal of Honor recommendation was resubmitted, only to be shot down once more. In any case, the Navy Cross is high honor indeed, and Thomas was only the second member of SEAL Team Two to earn it. He was also presented with the Bronze Star with Combat V, Purple Heart, and Cross of Gallantry.

Thomas spent six weeks recuperating at the Yokosuka Naval Hospital in Japan, where he discovered that the most painful part of being shot down in a helicopter was the ensuing physical therapy. Hearing about a rifle competition at the nearby air base, he entered it, won, and became hooked on competition.

Thomas served a split tour in Vietnam, returning to Can Tho, RVN, and remaining with the 7th Platoon to turn over with the relieving platoon from SEAL Team Two.

Upon his return to CONUS (Continental United States), Thomas became the small-arms instructor for the SEAL Team Two Training Platoon. He subsequently tried out and qualified for the All Navy Rifle and Pistol Team. In his second year he qualified as a Distinguished Marksman with the rifle, one of the highest honors a military competitive shooter can attain, and as a Distinguished Pistol Shot several years later.

Eventually he became officer in charge of the Navy Rifle and Pistol Team and was the Navy's top shooter for several years. He instituted the Naval Special Warfare Sniper program, which he finds somewhat ironic, considering his own experience. "It's one of my eternal regrets that I never got to drop the hammer on that sniper rifle in a real-world situation. Here I am, the 'father of the sniper program in the SEAL teams,' and I never did the deed in reality. I whacked a few people with other guns, but never got to use the sniper rifle," he said.

Thomas was instrumental in the development of the SASR (Special Application Sniper Rifle) .50-caliber sniper rifle, the MK 13 .300 Win Mag sniper rifle, the SOCOM MK 23 Offensive handgun, and several other weapon-related projects.

Thomas was a SEAL for 32 years, retiring in 1995 with the rank of commander.

He now works as a small-arms consultant and developer

for the military and private industry, and has written regularly for Col. David Hackworth's Soldiers for the Truth (www.sftt.org). He continues to shoot competitively and remains an ardent hunter.

The success of Naval Special Warfare snipers, from Afghanistan to Iraq, is the legacy of which Thomas is most proud. He continues to support SOF (Special Operations Force) snipers through the SOPMOD (Special Operations Peculiar Modification) program development of the Precision Sniper Rifle and its associated sighting systems.

NOTES

1. MOA means "minute of angle," or 1 inch at 100 yards. A rifle that can put its shots within a group that size is considered highly accurate.
2. The dikes were about 20 to 30 inches high.
3. A Slick is a UH-1 Huey helicopter used for transport and armed only with an M60 door gun.
4. A U.S. Air Force colonel whom the Slick was transporting when it detoured to rescue the survivors of the downed Seawolf.
5. Jeff Cooper, "Jeff Cooper on Practical Pistol Shooting," *Guns & Ammo*, March 1963, p. 22.
6. A widely circulated account on the Internet states, "The downed helo's remaining crew were picked up and on their way out, they counted the dead VC; 37 in all. Their distances from the downed helo were from 3 to about 150 yards; all shot by the crewmember with his M1911 .45 ACP. About 80 rounds were fired by Petty Officer R.J. Thomas, a member of the USN Rifle and Pistol Team." Thomas dismisses this account as greatly exaggerated.

Tunnel Rats

"It's like crawling through hell. You're always scared."
—Tunnel rat
Douglas M. Jones

In 1948, during the French occupation, the Vietnamese living in the Cu Chi region began digging bomb shelters under their huts. When the communist Vietminh took control of this strategic area, they used conscripted labor to dig communication tunnels linking these bomb shelters. Neighboring villages were then connected in an underground network. By the time American troops were fighting in Vietnam, this network stretched from Saigon to the end of the Ho Chi Minh Trail at the Cambodian border, some 200 miles.

The Viet Cong may have had no air support, field communications, or medevac, but the tunnel system helped even up the odds. Through the tunnels they could move men and material undetected, shoot from well-camouflaged firing ports, or

Cpl. William G. Cox, USMC, emerging from a tunnel during Operation Bold Mariner in Vietnam (late January 1969), a Colt .45 in his left hand. Note his observance of Rule Three: his finger is off the trigger, a rare sight in Vietnam War photographs. (Credit: U.S. Marine Corps.)

pop out of trapdoors to attack U.S. troops and then disappear.

The tunnels were an engineering marvel. They often had as many as four different levels accessed through concealed trapdoors. They never went more than 10 yards without taking a turn of between 60 and 120 degrees, which diminished the effective range of firearms and explosives. They included underground rooms used as dining areas, dormitories, hospitals, small factories, and storage facilities for food and weapons. Air vents were created by attaching an open-topped cage to the ceiling, putting a burrowing animal in it, and letting it dig its way to the outside. Entrances were so well camouflaged that they often could not be detected by a man standing directly above them. The Vietminh—later called Vietcong, or VC—knew their way around the pitch-dark tunnels as well as you know how to navigate the inside of your home.

When American forces first became aware of the tunnels, they were content to try to blow them up or block the entrances. However, after one tunnel complex was found to contain VC documents of great intelligence value, it was decided that tunnels should be explored before they were demolished.

The men who performed this dangerous task came to be known as tunnel rats. They had to be slim, as the tunnels were scaled for the diminutive, rail-thin Vietnamese. They couldn't suffer from claustrophobia, or they would go mad in the close confines. They had to have courage, as they were venturing into Charlie's terrain, and he might be waiting around any corner. Finally, they had to be volunteers, as even a well-disciplined soldier could not be forced to explore the tunnels if he were not willing.

One Marine told a reporter, "I'm sure glad I got a big belly. That's one job I don't want anything to do with. It's like committing suicide. If there's anyone down there, that guy is in deep trouble."[1]

"If a guy gets hit, he's already buried," said another.

Tunnel rats often worked in two- or three-man teams. Basic tunnel-clearing equipment consisted of a flashlight, a knife, and a pistol. The flashlight was a mixed blessing, because it illuminated the tunnel only a few yards ahead while the enemy could see its reflected light from a considerable distance. The knife or bayonet was used to probe for booby traps. The pistol was often a .45 automatic, though many tunnel rats preferred smaller calibers, which were less devastating on the eardrums. Silenced .38-caliber revolvers were later issued, but many found these too unwieldy. When Capt. Herbert W. Thornton of the 1st Infantry Division organized the first dedicated tunnel rat teams, he armed them with .22-caliber pistols.

Tunnels were generally about 2 feet wide and about 2 1/2 to 5 feet high. They were often muddy and sometimes even partially flooded. Temperatures could be as high as 100 degrees. The air was fetid with body odor and the smell of excrement, and so stale that the rats often found themselves gasping for breath. In an underground firefight during Operation Piranha in September 1965, a Marine lieutenant died of asphyxiation as the rapid fire from his automatic rifle ate up the little bit of available oxygen.

Tunnels were infested with unpleasant forms of animal life: feral rodents, fire ants, scorpions, and enormous spiders. Then there were the booby traps. Trapdoors at entrances were often wired to grenades hung in nearby bushes or trees. Inside the tunnel, caches of rice or weapons would be similarly rigged. According to Captain Thornton, "If you found a Vietnamese body in the tunnel, nine times out of ten his group had rigged it as a booby trap—pulled the pin on a grenade and put it underneath the body. If you moved the body, you'd get blown up with him."

There were sections of floor that collapsed into pits filled with punji stakes, and poisonous snakes hung from the ceiling. The VC sometimes kept jars of excrement in the tunnels that they could smash on the floor behind them when they were pursued, forcing the tunnel rats to crawl across a hellish mixture of broken glass and sewage.

The VC usually preferred to evade the tunnel rats, but sometimes they would make a stand. They might ambush the tunnel rats as they turned a corner or approached a trap door. Trap doors that led upward were the most dangerous, as the VC could drop grenades through them. Sometimes, a tunnel rat would poke his head through a trapdoor only to have a sharpened iron bar plunged through his throat, killing him and preventing his buddies from dragging his body back down the tunnel.

Why would anyone volunteer for this job?

Partly, of course, out of a sense of duty. As Spec. 4 Walter Dula, put it, "If it's not you, it's gonna be your brother or your friend. You just gotta get the job done, I guess."[2]

There was another motive: curiosity. "You never know what you're going to find down there," said Pvt. Edward Garcia. Among the strangest things found underground by tunnel rats were two water buffalo, a hoard of gold bullion, and a complete M48 tank in a large underground chamber. (The captured tank had been driven into a pit, and then a roof had been built over it.)

There was also adventure and a kind of freedom. "Down there, you're your own boss," said Spec. 4 Edison Adkins. "It's the only place in the Army you don't get orders."[3]

Finally, there was the opportunity to hunt the enemy down and kill him where he lived. As SSgt. Pete Rejo put it, "I loved it. The enemy hit us, and then they went down the holes, and I knew we were going to get them down there. What other place were they going to go—deeper? I would have gone deeper too. I enjoyed it very much. I liked it a lot. In fact, when they told me they had a VC down there, I came unglued. I got over there about a hundred miles an hour. To me it was like going hunting."[4]

Despite the odds against them, the rats often prevailed in these subterranean encounters. In the following news account, Spec. 4 Jerry Rensel went against an AK-47 with his .45:

> "All I remember was hearing two loud shots and my glasses flying off my head," said Spec. 4 Jerry Rensel as he recounted his exploration of a Viet Cong tunnel.
>
> It all started when B Co., 4th Bn. (Mechanized), 23rd Inf., was on a search and destroy mission in the Xoi Moi area northwest of Saigon. Rensel, one of the company's "tunnel rats," was called on to explore a tunnel.
>
> Armed with a .45 caliber pistol and a flashlight, he lowered himself into the tunnel and found himself in a 3-by-5 foot room. After

checking for booby traps he eased the door open.
As it gave way, the hunter and the hunted were
face to face, only a few feet apart. The VC got off
two rounds from his AK-47 rifle. One shot hit
Rensel's glasses. All Rensel needed was one shot
from his pistol and he added one more VC to
his company's body count for the operation.[5]

Sgt. Craig L. Belden of Wichita, Kansas, had lettered in high
school gymnastics three years in a row. Weighing 180 pounds
and standing 6-foot-1, he was not a typical tunnel rat. While
exploring one tunnel, Belden came upon three Communist soldiers who fought to keep from being taken prisoner:

When the underground battle was over,
three Communists were dead. The sergeant was
not scratched.
Other times it was easier.
Once he captured eight enemy soldiers
who, he said, ". . . had had enough of the war.
They just wanted to surrender."
He captured over 20 armed Communists
during his eight months in the tunnels.[6]

Captain Thornton was once crawling through a tunnel
when he came head-to-head with a VC. Thornton put his .45
under the VC's nose and backed him up. When Thornton
finally got his man out of the tunnel, he found he had backed
out 54 of the enemy behind him, all of whom were then
taken prisoner.
During Operation Nevada in April 1966, Marine corporal
John Charles Johnson spent three days clearing a large tunnel
complex in the Chu Lai province as part of Operation Nevada.
Shortly after entering the village of Phu Qui on April 14,
his platoon found a tunnel entrance. At 5-foot-6 and 165

pounds, Johnson was one of the smallest men in the platoon
and the obvious choice to clear it. Did he volunteer? Well, as he
puts it, "When a Marine is asked to do something he doesn't
say no, he just goes ahead and does it. But even if they hadn't
come to me I would've probably done it anyway."

Another Marine, L/Cpl. Ronald Hannah, an African-
American friend of Johnson's, volunteered to go with him.
They were armed with a grenade and a .45 with two magazines. With the pistol in one hand and a flashlight in the
other, Johnson took the lead, crawling through the labyrinth.

In an interview with the author, Johnson described his
experience:

> I'll tell you, that first tunnel we went into, I
> made a right and a left and a right and a left, or
> something like that, and I didn't know how the
> hell to get out of there. You'd come to a section
> where there's three tunnels coming off the one
> you were in. There'd be a right, a left, and go
> straight. If you make too many turns down
> there, you just can't remember. I got lost. The
> second time we went down, I said, "We're just
> making right hand turns, and when we come
> out we're making left-hand turns."
>
> They built in dead-ends, and you would
> find sections of the tunnel that were not com-
> plete. They were so narrow that you couldn't
> get through them, even the smallest Marine
> couldn't get through them. There were sections
> where you'd come to water, and nobody's about
> to go under water in one of those tunnels. You
> couldn't even use your flashlight after that. We
> saw a trapdoor to a lower level, but we didn't
> go down there because of the orientation factor.
>
> I don't think anyone can realize how it

> affects you psychologically, being enclosed in a
> tunnel and knowing that they built these
> things. They know every square inch of this
> tunnel, and you don't know shit from wild
> honey. You've probably got, I'd say, about
> 75–80 percent of it against you. The rest is just
> gotta be luck.

Johnson and Hannah came under sporadic fire underground. They shot back and drove 17 or 18 of the VC to the
surface, where they were captured. They killed several of
the enemy, whose weapons they used to continue fighting.
However, they were not able to close with and destroy the
main body, so after three hours Johnson requested that tear
gas be pumped in. Donning gas masks, Johnson and
Hannah waited, but the gas failed to dislodge the enemy.
After bringing out caches of weapons, explosives, and medical supplies, they placed explosives in that part of the tunnel complex and blew it up. The following day the bodies of
six VC were unearthed.

A third Marine was added to Johnson's team, and they
spent a second day exploring other areas of the tunnel complex.
In one section they were confronted with an unfamiliar odor.

> I didn't recognize the scent at first but
> after looking to the right side of the tunnel
> wall I noticed a lot of loose soil. I scratched at
> the opening until a hand appeared. We had
> entered a section of the tunnel that the Viet
> Cong were using as a graveyard. What I had
> inhaled earlier was the decomposition of flesh,
> the decaying bodies that were loosely buried in
> the tunnel walls.

The Marines kept going:

Corporal John Charles Johnson, USMC. (Courtesy of John Charles Johnson.)

We were being so quiet and got so close to the enemy I could hear 'em talking. I just took off after them running as fast as I could on my elbows and knees, and unfortunately, when I got the flashlight in position and I looked up, I seen this board, and it was laying way in front of me. It was the board they used to crawl across this manhole. Unfortunately I didn't see it soon enough and I went straight down. They weren't wooden stakes; they were steel stakes in the bottom of that pit. It wasn't a serious wound. It went in, you pull it out, it bleeds, and then finally it'll clot.

Exiting the tunnel, the Marines found themselves about 1,000 yards from the point they had entered.

After getting a tetanus shot, Johnson was ready to return

to the tunnels a third day. He had been exploring for several hours when he poked his head around a sharp turn.

> There were many 90-degree turns down there. One of the main reasons they did that is we were throwing gas down there, and the gas wouldn't go round the 90-degree turns. They had thought about this before they built the tunnels. I turned around that corner, that 90-degree turn, and I was looking down the barrel of a machine gun. It looked Chinese to me; it had that ammunition canister on it. I said, "I'm in the wrong place."
> It's like my whole life went in front of me. I don't know how he missed me. He was firing down the tunnel.

Johnson pulled his head back. "Shit was flying every-where," he said. Dousing his light, he and his men crawled back to the last intersection and holed up in a side tunnel.

> I knew we weren't going to make it out of that tunnel alive, so I said the hell with it. A .45 auto was no match for that machine gun, especially in this environment, but I did have something that could match up. I had two grenades with me, one a fragmentation. I gave my flashlight and my .45 to the guy behind me and I told him, "Look, don't fire down the god-damned tunnel, it's going to take me quite a while to get back down there."
> It's pitch black. You couldn't see your hand right in front of your face. I just felt my way down that tunnel until I came to that 90-degree turn. I waited and listened as I heard the VC

talking. There were three or four of them. I put the grenade inside my utility jacket while I pulled the pin so you couldn't hear the spoon pop. You've got plenty of time with those things, they say three seconds but you've got more like four or five seconds before it goes off. I threw it around the corner and I heard it clink—it hit something metal—and then I put my fingers in my ears and opened my mouth.

After that I went back and got the other two guys. I didn't want to go around that turn without a .45, you know. We waited 15 minutes then crawled up to that 90-degree turn. I rolled the flashlight out into that turn. Then I looked. They'd apparently carried the bodies off, but there was plenty of blood there. It was all over the base and sides of the tunnel.

We still heard an occasional voice coming from down the tunnel, but we didn't come under fire again. We found an exit and returned to the village we had come from.

The following day Johnson supervised the placement of explosives to blow the tunnel. The detonation set off a secondary explosion of an estimated 800 pounds of NVA/VC explosives stored underground. Half the village dropped into the resulting crater.

For his valor, Johnson was awarded the Bronze Star with V device (the "V" indicates that the medal is for valor).

He is now retired and lives in Las Vegas, Nevada.

NOTES

1. Joseph Galloway, "Little Guys Get Dirtiest Job of War, *Washington Post*, April 3, 1966, p. E1.

2. Bernard Weintraub, "U.S. Volunteer 'Tunnel Rats' Search Vietcong's Underground Hide-outs," *New York Times*, November 9, 1967, p. 5.

3. "U.S. Volunteer 'Tunnel Rats,'" p. 5.

4. *Tunnels of Cu Chi*, p. 245.

5. "Tunnel Rat Outguns Hidden VC," *Pacific Stars and Stripes*, August 6, 1967, p. 41.

6. "Kansas Soldier Tells of Life in Viet Tunnels," *Great Bend Daily Tribune*, September 5, 1967, p. 2.

Adelbert F. Waldron III (1933–1995)

"Bert was a wonderful soldier; he loved his country, he would have died for this country, but he had a lot of problems as a human being."
—Betty Waldron

When I began looking into subjects for this collection, one that came to mind immediately was Adelbert F. Waldron III. During his eight months in Vietnam he racked up the highest number of confirmed kills of any American sniper, and yet very little has been written about him. He seemed to have fallen entirely out of sight by the time of his death in 1995. All that is available over the Internet is a few rehashed stories, a number of people asking, "Why is so little information available about Adelbert Waldron?" and occasional answers to that question, some of it speculative and some of it apparently informed. The gist of the latter is that if you knew Waldron, you'd understand why no one wants to talk about him.

To someone who has an interest in history, this answer is not satisfactory. With two Distinguished Service Crosses (DSCs), one Silver Star, and three Bronze Stars, Waldron was one of the most highly decorated soldiers of the Vietnam War. If he had character flaws, so be it; but that does not make him any less worthy of interest.

I got an idea of Waldron's early life from wedding announcements, birth announcements, and obituaries, which are searchable through online newspaper archives. Adelbert Francis Waldron III was born in Phoenix, Arizona, on March 14, 1933, to Adelbert F. Waldron Jr. and Virginia Forderkonz Waldron. Both were from the Baldwinsville, New York, area and moved back there after his birth. Adelbert Jr. is described as having held several jobs: he worked for the William J. Burns Detective agency in Syracuse and the Dell Fish Company, and later operated a parking lot.

Bert, as Adelbert Waldron III was called, had no siblings. His parents divorced when he was young. His father remarried and moved back to Phoenix, Arizona, where he remained until his death in 1966 at age 56. His mother remained in Baldwinsville and married an Army veteran of World War II named Ernest Searle. Ernest worked as a mason, while Virginia held a job as a buyer for Sears Roebuck for 25 years. Virginia died in 1979, at age 64.

I spoke with Betty Waldron, who was married to Bert for 11 years (from 1969 to 1981), and she told me that he said very little about his past. "Bert was raised by a single mom and later a stepfather he despised," she said. "He always told me how lonely he was as a child. He was so unhappy in his home life that he spent all his time hunting in the woods around Baldwinsville. I'm sure that's when he learned his marksmanship. He could mimic wild animal sounds perfectly."

Waldron enlisted in the navy on January 25, 1953, from Syracuse, New York, but records of his assignments are unavailable. He was discharged July 27, 1965, and lived for a time in Virginia. At some point in the 1960s he was married and fathered three children.

On May 7, 1968, Waldron enlisted in the Army in
Richmond, Virginia, and on May 14 he began his infantry training at Fort Benning, Georgia. After his arrival in Vietnam on
November 4, 1968, Waldron entered a sniper-training program
run by Major Willis L. Powell. Volunteers were interviewed and
selected at the company or battalion level for participation in
the 18-day program. Graduation required a high level of skill,
and only about half the entrants made it through. Powell recalls
that Waldron was not the "honor graduate" or even one of the
outstanding marksmen in this elite group. However, within
months of completing the program, he distinguished himself as
a highly effective sniper, using an accurized M14 rifle known as
the M21. The model with which he got most of his kills was fitted with the Starlight scope, a night-vision device. Powell recalls
that at this time his snipers were getting about 85 percent of
their kills at night with this scope. The M21 was often fitted
with a suppressor developed by Sionics, a company owned by
Mitch WerBell.

Waldron soon earned a Bronze Star with the "V" device (V
for valor). His citation reads:

> Sergeant Waldron distinguished himself by
> valorous actions on 19 January 1969 while
> serving as a Sniper with Company B, 3d
> Battalion, 60th Infantry, on a reconnaissance in
> force mission in Kien Hoa Province. After the
> hours of darkness, Sergeant Waldron coura-
> geously left the confines of the company's
> defensive position, moving through the inse-
> cure area to set up in a position along a rice
> paddy dike. Disregarding his own safety,
> Sergeant Waldron mortally wounded enemy
> soldiers that night as he maneuvered through
> the area using his night vision equipment.

A few days later, Waldron was awarded the Silver Star. The citation reads:

> Specialist Four Waldron distinguished him-self by exceptionally valorous actions on 22 January 1969 while serving as a Sniper with Company D, 3d Battalion, 60th Infantry, on a reconnaissance mission in Kien Hoa Province. After setting up in a night position, Specialist Waldron spotted enemy movement to his front. Disregarding his own safety, Specialist Waldron courageously engaged the enemy for over three hours before his position was detected and he was forced to withdraw from the area. As a result of his heroic acts, eleven enemy were mortally wounded.

On January 29, Waldron was promoted to sergeant first class.

Waldron earned his first DSC, the military's second high-est award, for actions performed between January 16 and February 4. Army policy was to award a medal when the sniper reached a set number of confirmed kills; 50 kills auto-matically qualified a sniper for a DSC.

The citation for this award was missing from Waldron's file, but we can get a good idea of the actions for which it was given by examining the after-action reports of that period. Here are some examples:

> Sergeant Waldron and his partner occupied a night ambush position with Company B, 3rd Battalion, 60th Infantry on 30 January 1969, northeast of Ben Tre (XS 528351). The area selected for the ambush was an intersection of two dikes surrounding a large rice paddy. The fact that the rice had recently been cut provid-

ed the snipers with good fields of fire and
enabled them to use a prone position.

Just before dark, two or three individuals
were sighted moving toward a nearby village.
Curfew was not in effect at that time and therefore the individuals were not fired upon. At
approximately 2000 hours, one Viet Cong was
observed moving near a tree line forward of the
snipers' position and a request for artillery fire
was called in. The request was denied since the
area was considered populated. Sergeant
Waldron observed the Viet Cong again and
engaged him, resulting in one Viet Cong killed.

The next contact took place at 2040 hours,
when 16 Viet Cong were observed moving in a
line across the edge of the rice paddy. Sergeant
Waldron took the first VC under fire, resulting
in one Viet Cong killed. The remainder of the
group immediately hit the ground. Five minutes later, the group got up and resumed moving, apparently not sure of what had happened.
Sergeant Waldron engaged and killed one more
Viet Cong, causing the remaining Viet Cong to
panic and start running toward the ambush
position. They apparently thought the fire was
coming from the wood line. Sergeant Waldron
subsequently engaged and killed five more Viet
Cong, bringing to eight the total number of Viet
Cong killed during the night. Eight rounds
were fired in obtaining these kills at an average
of 500 meters.

Sergeant Waldron and his partner occupied
a night ambush with Company D, 3rd
Battalion, 60th Infantry on 3 February 1969,

approximately three kilometers south of Ben Tre (XS 518281). The area selected for the ambush was in a large rice paddy bordered by a wooded area. At 2109 hours, five Viet Cong moved from the wood line to the edge of the rice paddy and the first Viet Cong in the group was taken under fire by Sergeant Waldron. The first shot missed the target, necessitating that Sergeant Waldron readjust his starlight scope. The missed target prompted his partner to comment, "You missed that one, didn't you?"

After necessary adjustments were made, Sergeant Waldron again engaged the first Viet Cong in the group, resulting in one Viet Cong killed. Immediately the other Viet Cong formed a huddle around the fallen body, apparently not quite sure of what had taken place. Sergeant Waldron continued engaging the Viet Cong one by one until a total of five Viet Cong were killed. The next contact took place at 2225 hours, when one Viet Cong returned across the rice paddy, apparently looking for equipment and weapons near the bodies of the fallen Viet Cong. Sergeant Waldron took him under fire, resulting in one Viet Cong killed, bringing to six the number of Viet Cong killed during the night.

Sergeant Waldron and his partner occupied a night ambush position with Company D, 3/60th Infantry on 4 February 1969, approximately three kilometers south of Ben Tre (XS527283). The area selected for the ambush was at the end of a large rice paddy adjacent to a wooded area. Company D, 3/60th Infantry

had conducted a MEDCAP [Medical Civic
Action Project] and ICAP [Intelligence Civic
Action Project] in a nearby hamlet during the
day, hoping to gain information on Viet Cong
movements in the area. At approximately 2105
hours, five Viet Cong moved from the wooded
area toward Sergeant Waldron's position and he
took the first one in the group under fire, resulting in one Viet Cong killed. The remaining Viet
Cong immediately dropped to the ground and
did not move for several minutes. A short time
later, four Viet Cong stood up and began moving again, apparently not aware of the fact that
they were being fired upon from the rice paddy.
Sergeant Waldron took the four Viet Cong
under fire, resulting in four Viet Cong killed.
The next contact took place at 2345 hours,
when four Viet Cong moved into the rice paddy
from the left of Sergeant Waldron's ambush
position. The Viet Cong were taken under fire
by Sergeant Waldron, resulting in four Viet
Cong killed. A total of nine enemy soldiers were
killed during the night at an average range of
400 meters. Sergeant Waldron used a starlight
scope and noise suppressor on his match-grade
M-14 rifle in obtaining these kills.

The citation for Waldron's second DSC reads:

> For extraordinary heroism in connection
> with military operations involving conflict with
> an armed hostile force in the Republic of
> Vietnam: Sergeant Waldron distinguished him-
> self by exceptionally valorous actions from 5
> February to 29 March 1969 while serving as an

After the ceremony in which he received his second Distinguished Service Cross, S. Sgt. Bert Waldron shows it to his wife and stepchildren. The caption to this newspaper photograph notes, "Waldron holds two Purple Hearts, two Silver Stars and two Air Medals in addition to the two DSCs." In fact, Waldron held no Purple Hearts or Air Medals, and one Silver Star, not two. (On another occasion he claimed to have four Silver Stars.) This compulsion to exaggerate when the truth would seem to suffice was one of the odd aspects of Waldron's personality. (Courtesy of Betty Waldron.)

expert rifleman on eighteen separate sniper missions in Kien Hoa Province. On 14 February while his squad was conducting a night patrol near Ap Phu Thuan, Sergeant Waldron, observing a militarily superior hostile force maneuvering to assault a friendly unit, moved rapidly from one position to another to deceive the enemy as to the actual strength of his squad and killed several Viet Cong. As a

direct result of his determination, the enemy
was routed and their assault prevented. On 26
February near Phu Tuc, he located a Viet Cong
team preparing to launch a rocket on a Mobile
Riverine Force. He adroitly shot and killed the
soldiers. At Ap Luong Long Noi on 8 March,
his company was attacked by a Viet Cong force.
Sergeant Waldron killed many of the communists and forced them to withdraw. Despite
adverse weather conditions, poor illumination
and the pressure of arduous missions night
after night, he repeatedly located and engaged
many hostile elements, killing a number of the
enemy. Sergeant Waldron's extraordinary heroism and devotion to duty were in keeping with
the highest traditions of the military service
and reflect great credit upon himself, his unit,
and the United States Army.

Lieutenant General Julian J. Ewell, commander of the 9th
Infantry Division, was largely instrumental in developing the
Army's sniping program. He wrote, "Our most successful
sniper was Sergeant Adelbert F. Waldron, III, who had 109
confirmed kills to his credit. One afternoon he was riding
along the Mekong River on a Tango boat when an enemy
sniper on shore pecked away at the boat. While everyone else
on board strained to find the antagonist, who was firing from
the shoreline over 900 meters away, Sergeant Waldron took up
his sniper rifle and picked off the Viet Cong out of the top of a
coconut tree with one shot (this from a moving platform).
Such was the capability of our best sniper."[1]

Another time, also from shipboard, Waldron broke up an
enemy rocket and mortar attack at Dong Tam, firing five shots
to account for three of the enemy. The others withdrew.

According to Waldron, he picked up the code name

"Daniel Boone" for his field craft and marksmanship. He said the Vietcong knew him by reputation, and as a result posters appeared around Dong Tam offering a $50,000 reward "for the sniper known as Daniel Boone." Out of concern for his safety, the Army sent Waldron Stateside on July 21, 1969, returning him to the USAMTU (United States Army Marksmanship Training Unit) at Fort Benning, Georgia.

While stationed at Fort Benning, Waldron was a frequent visitor to Military Armament Company (MAC) in Powder Springs, Georgia, owned by the colorful and controversial Mitchell Livingston WerBell III. They had been introduced by Col. Robert F. Bayard, commanding officer of the USAMTU until he retired from the Army and went into business with WerBell.

A veteran of the Office of Strategic Services (OSS), WerBell was a soldier of fortune, military adviser, weapons developer, international arms dealer, and passionate anticommunist who was described in FBI documents as "unscrupulous" and "a promoter of grandiose schemes." Over the years he was indicted several times, on such charges as planning a takeover of Haiti for use as an anti-Castro base, possession of 3,400 improperly registered machine guns, and conspiracy to smuggle marijuana; he was acquitted in each case. He operated out of a 66-acre estate in Powder Springs, Georgia, he called "The Farm," after the CIA's training facility.

A week before Veteran's Day, 1969, Waldron went on a blind date with Betty, the daughter of a MAC employee, and they married five weeks later. She had a 4-year-old daughter and a 6-year-old son from a previous marriage.

After being discharged from the Army on March 16, 1970, Waldron went to work for MAC. The company produced the MAC-10 and MAC-11 submachine guns designed by Gordon Ingram, as well as a line of 007-type devices such as a decorative brass cannon desk accessory that fired real bullets. It also

Bert Waldron aims a G3 rifle while working for Mitch WerBell. The pin on his beret is that of the French Foreign Legion 2nd Paratroopers. The pin was popular during the 1970s as a mercenary emblem. (Courtesy of Waldron family.)

manufactured high-quality "silencers," or suppressors, used by law enforcement and the military, under the company name Sionics (Studies in Operational Negation of Insurgency and Counter-Subversion).

Waldron served WerBell as a technical adviser, demonstrator, and bodyguard. In 1970, he was identified as a counter-sniping expert in a wire-service story:

> The former soldier says he is convinced that the countersniper concept, which is just emerging as a law enforcement tool, is a vitally important method of controlling sniping in riot situations.
>
> He says it is important to remove a sniper quickly, with a minimum of shooting. "I think the Army has proved the validity of the sniper program," Waldron said in an interview. "In most cases, it is only one, or a very few, who are causing the problem. The former system of riot control, of turning out every available man for a massive confrontation causes unnecessary injury to too many people.
>
> "In each case where there has been shooting at policemen, firemen, or others in emergency situations, the number of persons doing the shooting has been few. Control them and you control the gunfire hazard."
>
> Or as Waldron says, "We must fight fire with fire."[2]

Betty said, "Bert was at MAC for two or three years, and kept in contact with Mitchell the whole time we were married. I'm sure he was still in touch with him after he left here. There was a connection there that I never really understood."

MAC went bankrupt in 1975, after which WerBell started a company called Cobray International. Advertising itself as a counterterrorism school, it catered to the burgeoning survivalist movement, teaching basic combat skills to civilians. It also provided security for the fringe political figure Lyndon LaRouche. Waldron taught rifle marksmanship at Cobray.

WerBell offhandedly told reporters that Waldron had 113 kills, and that number has appeared in a number of books and articles. However, within the sniper community, there is skepticism even about the official figure of 109. It does seem strange that Waldron claimed only 10 probables ("blood trails"), as it is very difficult to confirm kills in a combat situation. Mawhinney had over twice as many probables as kills, while Hathcock had more than three times as many. One officer who served with Waldron suspected that kills obtained by Waldron's security element were added to his total.

In the late 1970s, Waldron got involved with an anti-

At WerBell's estate, Waldron fires a Remington 700 modified by MAC for use as a sniper rifle, with a thumb-hole stock and a MAC suppressor. (Credit: Courtesy J. David Truby.)

terrorism school being set up in Florida and financed by Ferdinand Marcos of the Philippines. He disappeared for months. "It was all shrouded in mystery," said Betty. Eventually the deal fell through and Waldron returned, but at that point Betty described the marriage as effectively over. The couple was divorced in 1981.

In 1983, Waldron went to work for the MARS Center for Counter-Terrorist Training, also known as the Starlight Training Center, in Idyllwild, California. The operation was founded by Mike Hargis and Col. Lewis L. Millett, who brought in Waldron to instruct in rifle and pistol marksmanship. Millett must have had great confidence in Waldron; in a demonstration for a reporter, he stood beside a silhouette target and pointed out hits as Waldron shot at it from 300 meters, defying 25 mile-per-hour crosswinds. All shots were centered on the silhouette, ranging from the base of its throat to its heart.

Ray Pezolt, a private investigator who worked for Hargis, heard stories of Waldron's exploits and initially was skeptical. In an interview with the author, he said:

> When I first met him, I pegged him as another BS story, another wannabe. I thought, if this guy's so good, how come I never heard about him? Show me something where this guy's really a hot dog. Well, as time went on the evidence was starting to mount that he *was* a hot dog. The guy could shoot. Whether he did everything he said he did, he *could* do everything he said he did. One day, he had this book and it had all these certificates in it—DSC, Silver Star—and I'm looking through it and thinking, "This guy *did* it." It wasn't like he was carrying it around saying, "Hey, look at me." He didn't have a press agent, didn't adver-

tise it, and didn't talk about it, although I guess
he would occasionally leak it to people.
We weren't good buddies, he was a guy I
really didn't want to mess with. I thought he
was a crackpot, a dangerous crackpot. You
looked in his eyes and there was nothing there.
Late in 1983, he left Starlight, telling us he
was going to train the FBI countersnipers for
the '84 Olympics in LA. I thought that was
pretty cool. Well, a week or two later an FBI
agent shows up to meet with Mike [Hargis],
and I was there. The FBI agent says, "We're
looking for Bert Waldron."
Mike says, "Why call me? He's working for
you guys."
The FBI agent gets this perplexed look on
his face and says, "He's not working for us,
we're trying to find him. We want to identify
where he is before the Olympics."
I never found out what that was all about,
but you don't send out field agents for no reason.

There is little further information available about Waldron
until his death on October 18, 1995, from a heart attack. His
death certificate indicates that he was separated from his third
wife and was working as an apartment manager in Long Beach,
California. The autopsy report shows that he had suffered from
dilated cardiomyopathy (enlargement of the heart), emphysema,
hardening of the arteries, and diabetes. His remains went
unclaimed until November 30. He was cremated and his ashes
interred at Riverside National Cemetery on December 12.

When I began researching Waldron, I wrote to the
National Personnel Records Division for his military records.
In other cases when I have done this, I received an envelope in
the mail a few months later containing the open elements of a

veteran's file, such as a record of his assignments and his medal citations. This time, I got a telephone call from an officer working at the records center. He was curious about the reason for my interest in Waldron's file and noted that it had been the subject of several prior Freedom of Information Act searches. He said the file was very unusual; for example, the absence of the citation for the first DSC struck him as so odd that he checked a backup file in another wing of the building, and it was missing from that as well. The officer was not authorized to release those elements of the file that were confidential, but I got the feeling he was bursting to tell me something. He kept muttering about "discrepancies" and alluded to AWOL charges and disciplinary proceedings. Finally he said, "Mr. Kirchner, speaking to you in an unofficial capacity, all I can say is that I recommend you resubmit your request though your congressional representative and hire an attorney. I believe you would find the results very . . . enlightening."

I did resubmit the request as he suggested, but I was never granted full access to the file. Nevertheless, by talking to people who knew Waldron during and after the war, things came into focus. It is not my intention to harp on the negative, but in order to understand Waldron it is necessary to know about his dark side, primarily his lifelong pattern of compulsive lying.

I spoke with an officer who served with Waldron in Vietnam, and who asked to remain anonymous. He scoffs at his claim that a $50,000 reward was put on his head. He knew of a high-ranking American officer on whom the VC did put a bounty, and it was 10,000 *piasters*, the equivalent of about $100. Furthermore, he told me that Waldron was not sent home early—far from it. He returned Stateside on an R&R basis before his tour was completed and did not return; he was, in fact, AWOL. "He flamed out in Vietnam," as this source put it.

Lt. Col. Frank B. Conway (ret.), who was head of the Advanced Marksmanship Training Unit during the Vietnam

War, said, "After his return to the States, he passed out the word that he was getting the Medal of Honor and was inviting people to the ceremony! He later got out of that by saying no definite date had been set."

Conway also recalled Waldron showing off an M21 rifle that he said he had been awarded for his performance as a sniper. It later turned out that Waldron had borrowed the rifle from the Rock Island Armory, claiming he needed it for a program he was teaching and ignored repeated requests that he return it. The matter was finally brought to the attention of his commanding officer.

Waldron's military career was cut short due to a pattern of erratic and unacceptable behavior. To spare itself the embarrassment of court-martialing such a highly decorated veteran, the Army encouraged him to accept an honorable discharge and leave.

Mitchell WerBell IV wrote, "There is no written history of Bert partly because no one could get to the real truth of his background or family. There were so many lies—death of parents in an auto wreck, a home in Williamsburg, etc., etc. He was a habitual fabricator of stories that simply were not true. It was near impossible to separate truth from fiction, and that is how he operated, I suppose, until he passed away. However, his exploits in Vietnam were absolutely true. He never got the recognition that Hathcock received, partly due to his own character."

Don Thomas, who worked with Waldron at MAC, wrote, "As MAC started to fall apart and eventually ended up in bankruptcy, Bert was laid off along with the rest of us. He was selling cars for a while, and then bounced around the country from one job to another, borrowing money from anyone who would lend it to him. He seemed never able to adjust to civilian jobs and life. He was highly prone to exaggerate his accomplishments and awards in the military."

"Bert was an enigma, even to me, after 11 years of marriage," Betty said. "There are probably a lot of things you'll never know and never find out. I think a normal person who killed as many people as he did would find it hard to live with, and I don't think it was hard for him. He was not proud of it, but it didn't bother him. I know it was in combat, but it's got to take a toll on you. He talked about it one time with me, in the eleven years of our marriage. Other than that he never talked about it. His behavior may have been a manifestation of all the things that were going through his mind, I don't know."

Betty's attitude toward Bert was sympathetic and forgiving, which I felt spoke well not only for her, but for him. She described him as a good stepfather to her children, participating in their school and sports activities. "My son, particularly, cared a lot about him," she said. "Bert was the team father for his Little League football team. He built him a racing bike and bought him a miniature motorcycle. They rode together frequently. He never took him shooting, which I thought was very strange. Never introduced him to guns. He tried to teach me how to shoot, but he never, ever, did that with my son."

"Because of all his problems we had a very tumultuous lifestyle and there was always a problem with money. Looking back on it, after all the anger, I realize he really tried, but he just couldn't quite pull it together. He tried very hard. He could go in and learn things so quickly; he was very bright. It was amazing to me that he was so smart and could do anything, but he couldn't seem to hold it together. He was a wonderful soldier, he did a lot of heroic things, but he had some flaws as we all do. Who is perfect? Nobody but Jesus."

NOTES

1. Lt. Gen. Julian J. Ewell, "Sharpening the Combat Edge: The Use of Analysis to Reinforce Combat Judgment," Department of the Army, Washington, D.C., 1995, p. 123. In an interview, Waldron said the Navy duty officer said the distance was "nearly 900 yards."
2. "Former Army Sniper Now Civilian Police Sharpshooter," p. 41.

Samuel Woodfill
(1883–1951)

Born in Jefferson County, Indiana, on January 6, 1883, Samuel Woodfill grew up on a steady diet of war stories told by his father, John Samuel Woodfill. A veteran of the Mexican War and the Civil War, John was 60 years old when his son was born. He was regarded as an expert marksman in his backwoods community and consistently took the prize in local shooting contests. When Sam was seven years old, his father taught him to shoot his squirrel rifle. With its 42-inch octagonal barrel, the muzzleloader was a foot longer than the boy, and so heavy he had to rest it on the windowsill. "I pulled the trigger and I got a bull's-eye, and you bet I was the happiest boy in the countryside that day," he recalled.

By age 10, Woodfill was big enough to carry the gun and

regularly sneaked out of the house with it to go squirrel hunting. He had to stand on a fence rail to pour the charge down its
barrel, and rest it on a log to aim it, but by the time he went
home he had his game bag filled. He'd quietly slip the rifle back
into its place and tell his mother he'd been given the squirrels
by a neighbor. Eventually, she caught him and told his father
what he had done. Sam was less concerned about getting a lick-
ing than about not being allowed to shoot anymore, so when
his father confronted him he launched into what he called "a
regular Patrick Henry speech," demonstrating how well he
could handle the rifle and telling how many squirrels he'd
bagged. His father was impressed, and from then on Sam was
allowed to take out the rifle whenever he wanted.

Fourteen years old when his father died, Sam had to drop
out of school to go to work. He used some of his earnings to
buy himself a Winchester rifle and soon achieved local
renown as a crack shot. He was the man to beat in turkey
shoots and other competitions, and eventually had to accept a
handicap of 10 to 15 yards.

Woodfill tried to join the Army during the Spanish-
American War, but he was not old enough. By the time he
turned 18, the Army was glad to get him, as it needed troops
to fight the Philippine insurrection.

In his first time on the Army range, shooting at 600 yards,
he made a bull's-eye with his first shot; unfortunately, the
bull's-eye was on the target of the man next to him. Despite
this initial mistake, Woodfill earned high score of the day with
his next 10 shots, shooting eight bull's-eyes and two just outside. He would eventually earn an expert badge.

While in the Philippines, Woodfill was stationed in
Manila and did not see much combat. He returned home in
1904, but found that "the army fever was in my blood." He
reenlisted in the Third Infantry, which was about to be shifted to Alaska. There he was stationed at Fort Egbert, the
northernmost American military post at the time, and he took

on the duty of providing meat for the camp. This, to him, was paradise. He would head out for a week at a time in search of caribou, moose, and bear, with a trapdoor Springfield or a bolt-action .30-40 Krag-Jorgensen, which he loaded with expanding bullets he had specially ordered from Chicago. On one occasion, while hunting caribou with the Krag, he made several extremely long shots. As Woodfill told his biographer, Lowell Thomas:

> At an elevation of 45 degrees, it was claimed that our rifles would carry three miles. Now was the chance to try mine out. I ran the sight up to 1200 yards, lay down on the snow, jammed my elbows into the crust, put my bandolier in front of me and let fly with my first shot. The caribou just turned and looked. I raised my sight several hundred yards and fired again. The caribou took up a trot for a little way, then slowed down again. I raised the sight for the third time and fired. This time I saw the bullet strike just in front of them. At last I had the range. My sight was at 1800 yards! I pulled the trigger once more and brought one of them down. They were loping now, but that didn't make so much difference so long as I had the range. I fired two more times. Both bullets missed by a few yards. The third bullet brought down another of the herd. Slipping in a new clip of bullets, I began again. After dropping a third, the others disappeared over the crest. . . . [Jack] Hardy got there about this time. He had seen the herd before I had but never thought they were close enough to hit. Then to his amazement, he had seen them drop one after another in front of his eyes.

"Ye bloody blighter," he exclaimed, "ye
were shootin' 'em at better'n a mile."[1]

On another occasion it was his quick reflexes that saved
him. He had been hunting bear and had gotten two, the first
with a single shot and the second with two. He was heading
back to camp, his rifle slung on his back, when he heard a
rustling in the brush behind him.

> I wheeled like a shot. There 30 feet back
> was an enormous brown fellow, crashin'
> through the bushes at me. Mebbe you think I
> didn't tear the rifle off my head with record
> speed! I turned the safety lock, but there wasn't
> time to even raise the rifle to my shoulder. I
> pulled the trigger while it was still under my
> arm—with that bear not over six feet away,
> already with all fours off the ground, makin'
> his final spring. He looked as big as an elephant
> and twice as ornery. You bet I was excited. But
> not enough to spoil my shootin'. I guess I'm
> lucky in just never getting so nervous as that,
> no matter how tight a jam I'm in.[2]

The bullet broke the bear's spine. The bear jackknifed
and hit the ground two feet in front of Woodfill. It roared,
thrashed, hurled itself about, and then died. A second shot
was not needed.

Woodfill served eight years in Alaska, until Fort Egbert
was closed. His experience hunting big game would later be of
great value to him. "Whatever natural instincts I had for
trekking and stalking, keeping cover and creeping up for a
shot, were developed considerably," he recalled. "Whatever
may have been my qualifications as a soldier, more than anything else I was just a woodsman and a hunter."[3]

When Woodfill went home for a visit, his family was impressed by how much he had grown. He stood 5 feet, 10 3/4 inches, weighed 180 pounds, and measured 42 inches around the chest. During this stay he met Lorena Wiltshire, whom he described as "the first real flame I ever had." The two fell in love and became engaged to marry.

After the Villa raids, Woodfill was posted to the Mexican border with the Ninth Infantry. He continued to hunt and target practice at every opportunity. In a regimental shoot he got the best score in his company and the third best in his regiment.

The United States declared war on Germany in April 1917. Woodfill remarked to a buddy, "I've been practicing shooting all my life, and now it looks as though I'll have plenty of chance to try out my marksmanship on the sort of targets that soldiers are supposed to be ready for."

"Hell's bells," his friend replied, "just what good is your damn rifle going to be in this man's war? It looks to me as though the whole stunt in France is machine guns, poison gas, and artillery. From what I hear, your rifle will be as out of date as a bow and arrow, and I wouldn't be surprised if you went through the war without even seeing anything to shoot at."

"Buddy," said Woodfill, "the rifle is one weapon that's never going to be out of date. Where there's a war there's going to be rifle shooting."

Before the American Expeditionary Force (AEF) could be sent to Europe, vast numbers of green troops had to be enlisted and trained, and experienced noncoms like Sergeant Woodfill were temporarily made officers. He was appointed acting captain in command of Company M of the 60th Infantry, Fifth Division.

On December 26, 1917, he and Lorena were married. The couple had postponed their wedding for four years until they had saved enough for a down payment on a farm.

Woodfill shipped out in April 1918. Within a few weeks of his arrival in France, he experienced the full range of trench warfare, from shelling to poison gas to machine-gun fire and aerial bombardment. He escaped injury from enemy action, but he broke his right shoulder while practicing hand-to-hand combat with one of his recruits and was sent to the hospital at Bruyères for treatment. While convalescing, he was out walking with a friend when an old French farmer called them into his house. The farmer gingerly lifted a loaded .45 automatic from a drawer. It had been left behind by American troops camped there a while back, and the farmer wanted nothing to do with it. Woodfill and his friend had a shooting contest with it to settle its ownership, with each firing three shots at a target. As Woodfill's right arm was in a sling, he had to shoot left-handed. However, having trained himself to shoot with either hand, he won the contest.[4] Woodfill was glad to get the automatic, as

Woodfill when he held the temporary rank of captain. (Credit: National Archives.)

he had loaned out the Colt Frontier Model .45 he had
brought from home.

Woodfill returned to his company in August. He was part
of the last great drive of the war, the Meuse-Argonne offensive, which began on September 26 and lasted until November
11, when the armistice was signed. It involved approximately
1 million American and 300,000 French troops. Woodfill's was
one of nine divisions participating.

On October 11, Woodfill's company was crossing a clearing
south of the village of Cunel when it came under machine-gun
fire. Woodfill threw himself into a partially dug trench, which
was only 14 inches deep. His pack, sticking up well above it,
betrayed his position to a German gunner.

> Plunk! a bullet sunk into my pack. Then
> two more ripped through it. Then a hail of
> them sprayed the ground hardly two feet from
> my head, kicking dirt all over me. My thoughts
> were a bit disconnected, but I kept wondering
> why that gunner was picking on me. . . . Then
> several more machine guns joined the party.
> The Boches were sweeping the entire field
> now. . . . All I could do was lay still and hug
> the bottom of my little trench. . . . The way the
> bullets were plowing up the ground all around
> me and zipping through my pack I figured the
> jig was up.[5]

Woodfill itched to take on the gunners with his rifle, but
he couldn't risk raising his head to take a look. Then the
shelling started, with 77mm rounds landing all around.
Convinced he would be killed, he took out the wedding photo
he carried of Lorena and scrawled her a farewell note on its
back, concluding with, "I will prepair a place and be waiting at
the Golden Gait of Heaven for the arrival of my Darling

Blossom." However, it was not his time; the shooting and shelling stopped as the Germans were pushed back.

The following day Woodfill would exact a terrible toll on the German machine gunners, but to him it was not vengeance, just his job. "Personally, I never had much luck at working up any spirit of hatred against the lads we were fighting," he later wrote. "Maybe I'd had too many German friends in my time. . . . But we were having a war, and a stiffer one than men were ever mixed up in. And our business in France was to kill the other fellow before he could plug us."

Shortly after daybreak, the Third Battalion was ordered to make a combat reconnaissance of the Bois de Pultière to locate the German defensive line. "In other words, over the top and fight," as Woodfill put it.

A low fog and bushes helped cover them as they advanced in long skirmish lines, 16 paces apart, rifles at the ready, bayonets fixed. As they emerged into a clearing, German machine gunners opened fire from entrenched positions well hidden by the woods in front of them. Half a dozen of Woodfill's men were hit. Then the shelling began. Any attempt to advance further would sacrifice the entire company.

Woodfill knew he had to locate and destroy the machine gun nests largely by himself, as most of his troops were green. He cached his pack and, armed with his Springfield, his .45 automatic and extra ammunition in bandoliers, he dashed forward across the clearing, diving into the first available shell hole as bullets struck all around him. From this position, he identified three sources of fire: one gun was to his right in an abandoned stable, another was somewhere in front of him, and one was in a church tower in the village 200 to 300 yards to his left.

Woodfill could not see the gunner in the church tower, but there was a small window at the top from which he must be shooting. Woodfill fired five rounds into it, and the firing stopped. He had either killed the gunner or driven him from his position. He reloaded his magazine.

He then studied the stable. A board had been removed at the end of a gable, making a firing position. Again, though Woodfill could not see the gunner, he fired at the hole and silenced him.

The machine-gun nest to his front was out of his line of sight, so he advanced about 150 yards, making his way from shell hole to shell hole. He soon found himself short of breath, his eyes and throat burning, and realized he had inhaled mustard gas, which had collected in the craters. He had a gas mask with him but couldn't wear it without impairing his shooting ability.

He reached a small knoll. From behind it, he listened intently to fix the position of the third machine gun. Once he had done so, he crawled around its flank until, peering over the top of a small gravel heap, he could see the machine gun nest in a clump of brush about 40 feet ahead of him. He set his rifle down on the gravel heap along with an extra clip of ammunition and his .45. Slowly, he slid his rifle over the heap, nestled its butt into his shoulder, and raised himself up on his elbows. He could see the machine gun's muzzle flash, but it took him a moment to discern the outline of a well-camouflaged helmet behind it. He sighted at the face beneath it and squeezed off a shot. The firing ceased.

The gun was set up in front of a trench, and a second gunner shoved the body of the first out of the way and replaced him. Woodfill fired again, killing him. Two more times a gunner took up the position, and Woodfill killed each in turn. "The third and fourth ones must have known what to expect," he observed. "That was nerve—to take their places knowing they would be picked off."

A fifth man began to crawl away. Woodfill could see him clearly through the foliage, and he killed him with the last round in his magazine. Another German jumped up and ran from the machine-gun nest. Woodfill drew his .45 automatic and killed him with a single shot.

Woodfill reloaded his rifle and ran to the machine-gun

nest. Beside the gun was a pile of dead Germans, the tops of their heads blown off. Woodfill signaled his scattered troops to advance.

As he moved forward, he nearly stumbled across what appeared to be a dead German officer sprawled on the ground.

> I started to swerve around him when he sprang to his feet, grabbed my rifle and threw it into the air. If his Luger had been in his hand instead of in its holster he could have got me. I snatched my pistol from my belt and fired; got him in the body and he doubled up with a grunt and dropped.[6]

Woodfill pocketed the Luger and tore the *Oberleutnant*'s insignia from his shoulder as a souvenir.

Crawling, crouching, and running from one point of cover to another, Woodfill kept moving ahead until he identified another machine gun nest about 200 feet ahead of him. He crept to its flank, and when he had gotten himself into a good firing position, he again killed five gunners in succession. He approached the nest, verified that the gunners were dead, and put a round through the jacket of the water-cooled gun to disable it. He continued to push ahead and was passing a patch of thick brush when he nearly collided with three Germans who were carrying belts of machine-gun ammunition. As he covered them with his rifle, they threw their hands in the air and shouted, "*Kamerad* [Comrade]!"

Woodfill disarmed them and motioned them back to his rear, where his men would take them prisoner.

Woodfill located another machine gun, set up in front of a trench. He again crawled through mud and thick underbrush to a good firing position, and again took out five gunners. He stood up and ran toward the gun. As another machine gun to his right began firing on him, Woodfill jumped into the trench, almost landing on top of a German who was on his way to man the gun.

As Woodfill said:

> He was just crawlin' along the trench up to the machine gun. The quarters were too close for me to use my rifle, and I had my automatic ready. As he raised his Luger I fired. I beat him to it by a split second, and he doubled up and rolled to the ground.
>
> Another German came rushin' from behind me around a turn in the trench, rifle in hand. I pulled the trigger. My automatic jammed. My eye fell on a long-handled pick-mattock stuck into the side of the trench. I grabbed it, and as the second German tried to level his rifle I crashed the pick down on his head with both hands. He fell like an ox.
>
> I wheeled just in time to miss a bullet in the back from the first German. Wounded in the stomach he still had enough strength to regain his Luger and aim. Another blow of the pick, and I finished him off and bounded out of that trench.[7]

Seeing Germans retreating through the woods on all sides of him, Woodfill began picking them off. Soon he was joined by one of his men. The two of them continued to snipe at the Germans, who were unable to pinpoint their location because of the heavy fire from all sides. As other Americans filtered up and joined them, Woodfill sent a runner back to the battalion commander, Major Davis, for orders. Davis told him to pull back, as he was far ahead of the Allied lines with no supporting troops on either side.

When Woodfill returned, Davis asked him what he'd been doing to the Germans.

Woodfill photographed with his medals. (Credit: National Archives.)

"I got a few," Woodfill admitted.

"Yeah, I know you did," responded Davis.

That was Woodfill's last full day in combat. The mustard gas combined with his exposure to the relentless rain had worn him down to the point that he had to be hospitalized. By the time he returned to the front, the war was over. It was some time after the armistice that Woodfill asked his commanding officer, Capt. Roy Woodruff, for permission to go to Bordeaux for a few days. When he came back, he did not say anything about the purpose of his journey. Later, Captain Woodruff learned that Woodfill had received the Medal of Honor at Bordeaux from Pershing himself.

Woodfill returned to the United States and was mustered out of the service. Having no affinity for civilian life, in 1919 he reenlisted at his old rank of sergeant, planning to serve long enough to qualify for a pension.

He remained in obscurity until 1921, when a ceremony was planned to dedicate the Tomb of the Unknown Soldier. It was decided that three members of the AEF should serve among the pallbearers, and a committee reviewed the records of 3,000 men who had been decorated. From them it selected 100 to present to General Pershing for his consideration. When he came across Woodfill's name, he exclaimed, "Why, I've already selected that man as the most outstanding soldier of the AEF!"

The others chosen were Sgt. Alvin York and Col. Charles Whittlesey, commander of the "Lost Battalion."

Woodfill traveled to Washington with his wife, where he was honored at a banquet by the House and Senate, photographed with the president and secretary of war, and met Marshall Foch. He was thunderously applauded at every public event he attended and received wide press coverage. The *New York Times* wrote:

> The man whose deeds of valor have been
> buried in the records of the War Department

for three years is extremely modest, and it is difficult to get him to talk. In fact, when he reached Washington, it was evident that he would rather face German machine guns than newspapermen. When asked about the exploits for which he has been decorated by his own and foreign governments, he shifted from one foot to the other, mumbled something about wishing he could have done more than he did, and then abruptly ceased speaking.

However, because he is a soldier and because the War Department practically ordered him to tell something about himself, the Sergeant, a strapping fellow with a magnificent physique, tried hard to overcome his taciturnity. The truth is that Sergeant Woodfill considers that what he did was only the duty of a professional soldier. For if Woodfill is anything he is a professional soldier—in almost every mental and physical aspect, the epitome of what the average American would like his country's soldiers to be.[8]

Woodfill retired from the service in 1923. There was a bill introduced to retire him at the rank of captain, rather than sergeant, to increase his pension. "I would like the rank," Woodfill admitted. "I could get along all right by myself, but it takes some money to have American standards of living and I want them for my wife." However, the bill was voted down out of concern that it seemed to put a monetary value on heroism.

With a monthly pension of $138, Woodfill struggled. In the early 1920s, he was unable to pay his mortgage and in danger of losing his farm. After this was reported in the press, a public subscription bailed him out. He worked as a night watchman and, later, for the state government. He maintained his skills as a marksman and competed at Camp Perry in the interwar years. At the outbreak of World War II, both Woodfill and Alvin York were recalled to active duty, mostly as a publicity stunt. York failed the physical examination, but the 59-year-old Woodfill passed and returned with the rank of major. He spent a year touring bases around the country, lecturing recruits on the importance of physical toughness, mental conditioning, and familiarity with and confidence in their weapons. He opened with the words, "War is legalized killing. To win the war you must kill the enemy."

He left the service the following year when he reached the mandatory retirement age, but he put on his uniform again in 1948 to serve as a pallbearer at General Pershing's funeral.

Woodfill died on August 10, 1951, and was interred with full military honors at Arlington National Cemetery, less than 30 yards from Pershing's grave.

NOTES

1. *Woodfill of the Regulars*, p. 158.
2. *Woodfill of the Regulars*, p. 191.
3. *Woodfill of the Regulars*, pp. 197–98.
4. Woodfill trained himself to shoot ambidextrously so that he could avoid being taken prisoner if he was wounded in his right arm, according to "'To Win the War You Must Kill the Enemy,' Major Woodfill," *Abilene Reporter-News,* January 3, 1943, p. 3.
5. *Woodfill of the Regulars*, pp. 267–68.
6. *Woodfill of the Regulars*, p. 284.
7. *Woodfill of the Regulars*, p. 288.
8. "Woodfill, Rifleman," *New York Times*, November 6, 1921, p. 83.

Vassili Zaitsev
(1915–1991)

"The sniper must identify his target, immediately size it up, and then destroy it with a single shot."

—Vassili Zaitsev

Born on March 23, 1915, in Russia's Ural Mountains, Vassili Zaitsev was taught to hunt as a small child. When he turned 12, his grandfather presented him with a single-shot 20-gauge shotgun. Zaitsev was so short that when the gun was slung over his shoulder its butt rested on the floor, but he now considered himself a man, as boys did not have real guns. In the following years, he killed hundreds of animals, from squirrels to wolves, for meat and their pelts.

In 1937, Zaitsev was drafted and assigned to the naval fleet in Vladivostok, where his mathematical abilities earned him a position as a bookkeeper. After the German invasion, Zaitsev was eager to get into combat, but with his short stature and bookishness, his superiors had trouble seeing him as a fighting man. A year into the conflict, his request for combat duty was finally accepted, and, along with a group of other sailors, he was put on a train headed west.

After weeks of travel, the soldiers reached the outskirts of Stalingrad. The battle had been going on for a month, and the city was largely reduced to rubble. To Zaitsev, seeing it from a distance, it looked like a huge volcano spewing fire and smoke. Over it, like a swarm of wasps, were German planes dropping bombs. Zaitsev's unit made the perilous trip across the Volga on the night of September 22, 1942, without incident.

As the sun rose, Zaitsev's unit came under mortar fire. He huddled in a crater listening to the cries and groans of the wounded. Volleys of Katyusha rockets soon blasted the German positions, the dismembered limbs of the mortar crews flying into the air. An officer ordered a charge toward several huge petrol tanks beside which German machine gunners had dug in. When the assault was pinned down, Zaitsev was ordered to circle around and take out a machine-gun nest with grenades. He did so, and the Russians resumed their attack. A German artillery strike sent burning fuel spewing from the storage tanks. As their uniforms caught fire, some of the soldiers tore them off but continued to advance. "An attack of naked, burning men—what the Germans thought about us I can only guess," Zaitsev wrote.

The Germans fell back, and the Russians fought their way into the sprawling Metalworking Factory, where fighting was hand-to-hand. Suddenly a big German was on top of Zaitsev, hitting him with the butt of his rifle. As the blow glanced off his helmet, Zaitsev slipped behind the German and locked his arm around his neck, choking him as he thrashed around desperately. "Finally the Kraut stopped struggling and I smelled something foul. He had shit himself at the moment of death."

Exploring the extensive passages and air ducts under the ruined factory, Zaitsev and another soldier came to a loose vent through which they could see a roomful of German

Vassili Zaitsev. (Credit: National Archives.)

troops. There were more than 60 of them, eating their lunch and looking relaxed and "arrogant." Zaitsev sent his companion back to organize an attack. It opened with 30 or more grenades being tossed through vents and doorways. As the room erupted in explosions, two Germans took cover near Zaitsev. He pushed aside the vent and rolled a grenade toward them. "They glanced in my direction and our eyes met . . . they didn't look so arrogant anymore," he wrote.

Streams of fire from PPSh 41 submachine guns tore up and down the room, and within a minute no German was left alive. After the Russians mopped up that section of the factory, they transported their wounded back to the Volga.

So ended Zaitsev's first day in Stalingrad. At the outset of the siege, the average life expectancy for a Russian soldier was 24 hours. From that day on, as far as Zaitsev was concerned, he was living on borrowed time.

Combat continued with the same desperate intensity in the following days. Control of the Metalworking Factory could change hands several times a day. Fighting was often room-to-room, the enemies so close they could hear each other talking, even breathing.

Zaitsev provides vivid images of Stalingrad: trees along the streets burned to charcoal posts; trolley cars scattered like broken toys, their tracks curling into the air; soldiers with heat-cracked lips and hair fused together; human remains ground into the earth under the treads of tanks; a thin young girl in a torn blue dress and red boots leading a line of wounded soldiers toward an aid station.

On October 5, Zaitsev and several of his comrades were huddled in a bomb crater as a machine gun opened up on them at a distance of 600 yards. One of the men had a trench periscope and with it Zaitsev was able to see the gun's position. He quickly rose up and, almost without aiming, shot and killed the gunner. Within seconds two more gunners appeared, and Zaitsev killed them both as well.

The regimental commander, Major Metelev, witnessed Zaitsev's marksmanship and ordered that he be issued a sniper rifle. The Soviet sniper rifle was the same Mosin-Nagant 1891/30 bolt-action rifle issued to troops, but handpicked for accuracy and fitted with a 3.5-power telescopic sight.[1] It fired the 7.62x54 cartridge, ballistically equivalent to the .30-06 used by the U.S. Army. Metelev told Zaitsev to keep track of the Germans he killed. "You've already got three," he said, "start your tally with them."

Zaitsev wrote, "I liked being a sniper and having the discretion to pick my prey. With each shot, it seemed as if I could hear the bullet smashing through my enemy's skull, even if my target was 600 yards away. Sometimes a Nazi would look in my direction, without having the slightest idea that he was living out his final seconds."

A few days later, the building Zaitsev was in came under

intense machine-gun fire. The bullets coming through the windows and doors forced all activity to a standstill. Judging the machine-gun nest to be about 550 yards away, Zaitsev adjusted his scope for the distance and checked the wind by looking at the columns of smoke rising from various points on the battlefield. He squeezed off a round that killed the machine gunner, then quickly killed two ammo carriers who were not quick enough to take cover. With the enemy gun silenced, the Russian signalmen, messengers, and ammo carriers who had been hunkered down were able to return to their activities. It was after this incident that the high command began to realize the vital role a sniper could play. Zaitsev was soon ordered to recruit and train other marksmen to form a sniper group. "And thus began our sniper's training school," he wrote. "I, the professor, had in reality been the school's first student. Up to now my only teacher had been my own mistakes."

Starting with five or six apprentices, Zaitsev would eventually train 30 snipers.

Zaitsev taught his students that the sniper had to learn to camouflage himself completely, keep a low profile, and remain completely silent and immobile for long periods. He taught them to select several landmarks and make an exact determination of their distances to help them estimate range. He taught them to map every detail of a landscape in their heads, because small, seemingly insignificant changes in it could reveal enemy activity. He taught them to prepare multiple firing positions and never take more than two or three shots from one without moving. He taught them to make realistic dummies and use them to draw enemy fire. He taught them to cultivate friendships with the regular troops around them and to pump them for information. He taught them to beware of tunnel vision, because focusing on one target might cause them to lose sight of what was going on elsewhere on the battlefield.

The snipers shot at most targets of opportunity but they concentrated on machine gunners, artillery spotters, officers, and—

most important—enemy snipers. It took a sniper to find a sniper. Only a sniper could spot the telltale signs of a hiding place while ignoring decoys set up to confuse him. Only a sniper could figure out where an opponent might be hiding by the trajectory of the shots he had fired. Only a sniper had the patience to wait as long as it took to identify an opposing sniper, and the ability to kill him at the instant of opportunity.

Zaitsev coached one student as he sighted in on a German digging a trench. Zaitsev told him not to fire until the soldier turned to face him, explaining, "Think of this as a game of billiards—you're always trying to set up your next shot. If you shoot him now, while he's turned away from you, both he and his shovel will fall into the ditch. But if you get him when he's facing toward you, his shovel stays up on the near side of the embankment. That way, when the next guy grabs the shovel, you can get him too."

According to Zaitsev, the real trick of sniping was not to shoot an enemy in the head, but to make him raise his head in the first place.

Soviet propagandists soon began publicizing Zaitsev's exploits. In mid-October he was awarded a medal for valor by Gen. Vassili Chuikov, commander of the army, who told him, "Our resolve to fight amid the ruins of Stalingrad under the policy 'Not a Step Back' is fulfilling the mandate of the people. How could we ever look our countrymen in the eyes if we retreat?"

Zaitsev answered, "We have nowhere to retreat. For us there is no land beyond the Volga."

The general was quite taken with Zaitsev's turn of phrase, and it became a rallying cry for the Soviet forces.

Zaitsev fought his first sniper duel after one of his close friends, Sasha Gryazev, was killed in a trench on Mamayev Hill, after falling for a sniper's ruse. When several German troops briefly revealed their position, Gryazev rose to throw a grenade at them. The instant he exposed his upper body to make the throw, he was shot and killed.

Thirsty for vengeance, Zaitsev spent the entire day studying the German area through a trench periscope. As the setting sun illuminated the hillside on which the Germans were dug in, Zaitsev looked at a pile of German artillery shell casings. With his habitual attention to detail, he counted them. There were 23. Then he did a double take as he noticed that one of the shells had no bottom. As if to confirm his suspicion, he saw a tiny flash of light from inside the casing, followed by a bullet hitting the embankment behind him.

As dawn broke the next morning, Zaitsev was in position opposite the pile of shell casings, along with a student, Nikolai Kulikov. Using an artillery periscope with excellent optics, he counted the pile again. This time there were 22 casings; the one he was looking for was not there. Patiently and methodically, he scanned the hillside. Near the summit was a small depression, and in it lay the artillery shell with the missing bottom. In its dark interior, Zaitsev was fairly sure he could make out the scope of a rifle.

Zaitsev instructed Kulikov to put a helmet on a stick and raise it a few inches above the trench. The German took the bait and fired a round through the helmet. Watching through his telescopic sight, Zaitsev saw him reach forward to pick up his empty shell, standard procedure after making a kill. As he did so. he raised his head slightly, and Zaitsev put a bullet into it.

Mamayev Hill, where this incident took place, was the most dangerous battleground in Stalingrad. Over 100 meters high, it commanded an excellent view of the city. The Germans held its summit, but the Russians had managed to hang on in their trenches on its southern slope, where they were exposed to fire from both directions.

One night Zaitsev and Kulikov set themselves up near a small reservoir at the bottom of a ravine, where the Germans from a nearby bunker came to get water. In the morning a soldier appeared, carrying a bucket, and looked around. After five minutes, two more soldiers appeared with buckets. As they filled them and made their way back to their positions, Zaitsev forbade Kulikov to shoot, telling him, "Strong is the fighter who is able to master himself."

Zaitsev had decided that he would not shoot that day, but just observe. Kulikov could hardly contain himself as several Nazi officers appeared and began washing themselves, but Zaitsev insisted they hold off; the officers were mere lieutenants, and he was looking for bigger fish. That night he brought in two more pairs of snipers and positioned them to completely cover the bathing area and nearby bunker.

In the morning, Zaitsev saw an officer's cap appear over a trench near the bunker. He recognized this as bait and did not rise to it. At lunchtime, a German soldier went to the reservoir to fill a bucket. Again, Zaitsev ordered his snipers to let him go undisturbed. Ten minutes later, a colonel appeared, followed by a German sniper carrying a hunting rifle with a large scope. Two other officers followed, a colonel and a major, the latter wearing a Knight's Cross with Oak Leaf clusters. Zaitsev nodded to Nikolai, who signaled the other teams. Six shots rang out, and all four Germans dropped with headshots. Ten or 15 minutes later, the Germans responded with a massive artillery barrage, followed by waves of dive-bombers. "You know you must have taken out some serious Nazi brass for them to call in the Luftwaffe," wrote Zaitsev.

The bombardment blew away wooden panels that had been camouflaging nearby German artillery emplacements. "Their gun crews were swarming over the artillery pieces like rats," wrote Zaitsev.

The Russian snipers picked off the officers and then finished off most of the crews as they froze in confusion. Because of the noise of the ongoing barrage, the Germans had no idea where the shots were coming from.

Afterward, Zaitsev asked, "Now do you understand why we needed to be patient?"

One night, as the snipers sheltered in their bunker during

a hard rain, two of them picked up their submachine guns and began to load their pockets with grenades. When Zaitsev asked them what they were doing, they told him that for several days they had been carrying out a surveillance of a bunker on the German side of Mamayev Hill. They had learned the approaches and knew the positions and rotations of the sentries, and had been holding off raiding it until there was a heavy rain to cover their movements. Zaitsev liked the plan and invited another sniper, Stepan Kryakhov, to join him in helping carry it out. After arming themselves with grenades, submachine guns, and knives, they carefully made their way through the darkness.

A sentry stood at the entrance of the German bunker, holding a lady's parasol over his head to shelter himself from the rain. One of the snipers crawled up behind him and killed him with his knife.

As two men stayed outside as lookouts, Zaitsev and Kryakhov entered the bunker. Inside, under a dim electric bulb, they could see rows of soldiers sleeping on cots, their uniforms hung above them. The Russians raised their PPSh-41s and opened fire, raking up and down the rows of cots. They spared one German, whom they took prisoner. Upon returning to his bunker, Zaitsev described the mission to his comrades. He later observed, "It was a hard story to tell. Something didn't sit right with me about what we had just done."

Several days later, Zaitsev and an old friend from his village, Pyotr Ivanovich Tyurin, were in a bunker on Mamayev Hill when a mortar round exploded just outside, collapsing the entrance and burying them in dirt. As they began to dig their way out, they heard footsteps above them. They didn't know whether they were from their own troops or Germans, as the Germans were usually quick to follow up a bombardment with an infantry assault. They continued to dig quietly until they had created a small opening. Through it Zaitsev could see the broad back of a German soldier, as well as an unmanned MG-34 belt-fed machine gun nearby. He aimed his submachine gun at the soldier, but when he pulled the trigger, nothing happened—the breech was jammed with sand. Zaitsev then pulled the pin from a grenade, placed it beside the German's feet, and ducked back in his hole. After the explosion, Zaitsev and Tyurin dug themselves out. Beside the bunker were two dead Germans. The Russians picked up their Schmeissers and began shooting at Germans who were all around them, obscured in the haze and smoke. Seeing an officer about 50 feet away, holding a pistol and gesturing to his men, Zaitsev retrieved his rifle and shot him. Meanwhile, Tyurin, having exhausted the ammunition for the Schmeisser, began firing at the backs of the enemy with the MG-34. When the Germans figured out where the firing was coming from, they launched another mortar barrage, which knocked Zaitsev unconscious. When he came to, he and Tyurin were surrounded by Russian troops, who congratulated them on having beaten back the German attack.

The fictionalized accounts of Zaitsev's experiences in *War of the Rats* and *Enemy at the Gates* (both the book and movie) make much of Zaitsev's duel with a German master-sniper, Maj. Erwin König, also known as Heinz Thorvald, head of the Wehrmacht's sniper school near Berlin. There is no evidence that such a man existed, nor is there any documentation for this duel either in German or Soviet records. Moreover, in an account of his experiences that Zaitsev gave the Soviet press in 1944, he describes the particulars of the duel but does not mention the "master sniper." In his autobiography, *Notes of a Sniper*, Zaitsev identifies his opponent as König, but rather than being the focal point of the book, it is one incident among many.

According to Zaitsev, under interrogation a captured German soldier revealed that König had been flown in for the express purpose of taking out the Russian "main rabbit." Zaitsev means rabbit in Russian, but this may have been an expression, like "head honcho," or else the Germans may have learned of him from the Soviet press.

The German major soon made his presence known. In a single day, he wounded one of Zaitsev's most experienced snipers and put a round through the telescopic sight of another. Before dawn the following day, Zaitsev and Kulikov set up an observation post in the area where their friends had been hit. They studied the opposing front all day, but saw nothing unusual until late afternoon, when they spotted a helmet bobbing along above the German trench. They knew from its slightly unnatural movement that it was a decoy being moved by König's assistant in an attempt to get them to shoot and reveal their position.

On the third day of their stakeout, a political officer named Danilov accompanied Zaitsev and Kulikov to their position. Danilov thought he spotted König's position, and in his excitement he exposed himself for a half-second over the top of the trench, long enough for the German to shoot and wound him. Maddeningly, Zaitsev still could not spot König's location; he only knew, from the quickness of the shot, that he must be directly in front of them. There was a bombed-out tank on the left and an abandoned pillbox on the right, but neither was a good sniper's roost. Between them, beside a small pile of broken bricks, lay a sheet of iron. It had been there since Zaitsev had started his surveillance, but it suddenly caught his attention. "What if König had dug a foxhole under that sheet of iron?" he wondered. It would make an ideal blind.

To check his hunch, Zaitsev put a mitten on a narrow plank and raised it above the trench. A shot rang out, and a bullet passed through it. Zaitsev carefully lowered the plank so that it remained at the same angle. The hole through the board was flat and round, with a 90-degree angle of entry. As he expected, König's position was right in front of him.

Zaitsev and Kulikov spent a bitter-cold night in the trench. The howling of the wind was interrupted by eruptions of artillery and mortar fire, as well as a nighttime bombing attack.

They decided to remain inactive through the morning hours, as the sun was shining toward their position and might reflect off their scopes. Later in the afternoon, the situation was reversed. Zaitsev thought he saw a glimmer under the bottom edge of the sheet of iron. Was it a reflection off a random shard of glass or a riflescope?

Kulikov took off his helmet and slowly raised it, a ruse that only an experienced sniper could pull off convincingly. The German fired. Loudly crying out, Kulikov threw himself up and back. At this, König briefly stuck his head up from behind the sheet of iron. Zaitsev fired, and the master sniper dropped his rifle and slumped down. Kulikov laughed hysterically with the release of tension, but Zaitsev suddenly shouted at him: "Run!"

The two men ran, as German artillery pounded the position they had occupied moments before. As darkness fell, the Russians attacked the German lines. Under cover of the assault, Zaitsev and Kulikov dragged König out from under the sheet of iron and took his documents, which they delivered along with his rifle to the division commander, Colonel Batyuk.

Batyuk immediately gave them another assignment. Intelligence had learned of an assault planned for the following day. Before it began, the top German officers would emerge from their command posts for a final look at the battle zone. Batyuk wanted Zaitsev's group to be waiting, to "greet each with the recommended apportionment of lead," as Zaitsev put it. For this plan to succeed, the officers had to be killed simultaneously, or as nearly so as possible. This would be a group hunt, an "assault of concentrated sniper fire," as Zaitsev called it. The technique had been successfully employed on several occasions previously.

The 13 snipers in Zaitsev's group spread themselves out, sighting in on all the known observation and command posts, some far behind the enemy lines. Shortly after dawn, before the assault began, the snipers spotted German officers peering though binoculars, some even wearing *jäger* hats with cockades. They were well lit in the morning light. Zaitsev quickly went through two five-round clips of ammunition, as did Kulikov. The other snipers were equally active, and the German officers were annihilated. "But," as Zaitsev wrote, "the German attack began, nevertheless. A fascist officer in a far-off command post that our bullets couldn't reach was driving the enemy soldiers to their doom."

Soviet artillery, machine guns, and riflemen had zeroed in on the paths of advance and mowed the troops down.

Zaitsev wrote, "Goaded by some foolish heroic impulse, I tried to capture some prisoners. I guess this impulse came from that same hellish fever of battle that sometimes eclipses clear thinking." As he ran out to a German position, a mortar round exploded about 30 meters from him.

When Zaitsev came to, he was in a hospital bed, his head swathed in bandages. He had lost his sight. He was operated on, and on February 10, 1943, his bandages were removed and he could see once again. Just eight days earlier the German Sixth Army had surrendered, ending the 199-day Battle of Stalingrad.

It was a catastrophic loss for Hitler. Of the estimated 850,000 casualties the Germans had suffered, Zaitsev is officially credited with 242, including 11 enemy snipers. Most authorities believe his actual tally was higher, perhaps as many as 400. It was a matter of honor to Zaitsev that he never recorded a shot as a kill unless he was certain that his target was dead. He wrote, "Observers would sometimes inflate my kills, because they would simply count how many shots I had fired. To them, three shots meant three kills. . . . But whether or not my bullets actually penetrated their intended targets— only I knew this."

Zaitsev was transported to Moscow for further treatment and recuperation. He was awarded the Order of Lenin as well as several other decorations, and made a Hero of the Soviet

Union. He returned to the front and finished the war with the rank of captain.

Zaitsev died on December 15, 1991, at the age of 76. His battered Mosin-Nagant rifle is on permanent display in the Volgograd State Panoramic Museum.[2]

NOTES

1. Mosin-Nagant sniper rifles were picked out of normal production after they displayed unusually good accuracy when test-fired. The triggers were rough and the telescopic sight, mounted several inches above the receiver, made it impossible to get the "cheek weld" that good marksmen rely on. Nevertheless, the Russians were able to do good work with them, proving once again that it is the man and not the weapon that wins the fight. In addition to the Mosin Nagant, Zaitsev also mentions using a scope-sighted Tokarev SVT-40 semiautomatic rifle, which used 10-round detachable magazines.
2. The name Stalingrad was changed to Volgograd in 1961 during the de-Stalinization period.

Bibliography

Hank Adams
Background on Adams was gathered from newspaper and
magazine articles, as well as an interview with Adams'
daughter, Leilani Maguire, and files released by the Federal
Bureau of Investigation under the Freedom of Information
Act.
Alexander, Joseph. *Edson's Raiders: The 1st Marine Raider
Battalion in World War II*. Annapolis, MD: Naval Institute
Press, 2001.

Chevalier Bayard
Powell, George H. *Duelling Stories of the Sixteenth Century:
From the French of Brantôme*. London: A. H. Bullen, 1906.

Simms, William Gilmore. *The Life of the Chevalier Bayard*. New York: Harper & Brothers Publishers, 1847.

Walford, E. *The Story of the Chevalier Bayard*. London: Sampson, Low, Son, and Marston, 1869.

Tsukahara Bokuden

Hurst, G. Cameron. *Armed Martial Arts of Japan: Swordsmanship and Archery.* New Haven: Yale University Press, 1998.

Sugawara, Makoto. *Lives of Master Swordsmen*. The East Publications, Tokyo, 1986.

Tokeshi, Jinichi. *Kendo: Elements, Rules, and Philosophy*. Honolulu: University of Hawaii Press, 2003.

"Mad" Jack Churchill

Featherstone, Donald. *The Bowmen of England*. London: Jarrolds, 1967.

"History of No. 2 Commando," Commando Veterans Association site. http://www.commandoveterans.org/history_2cdo_d.html.

King-Clark, Rex. *Jack Churchill: Unlimited Boldness*. Knutsfor, Cheshire, UK; Fleur-de-Lys Publishing, 1997.

Messenger, Charles. *The Commandos 1940-1946*. London: W. Kimber, 1985.

St. George Saunders, Hilary. *The Green Beret: The Story of the Commandos 1940-1945*. London: Michael Joseph Ltd., 1949.

Cassius Marcellus Clay

Carlée, Roberta Baughman. *The Last Gladiator: Cassius M. Clay*. Berea, KY: Kentucke [sic] Imprints, 1979.

Clay, Cassius Marcellus. *The Life of Cassius Marcellus Clay: Memoirs, Writings, and Speeches*. Cincinnati: J.F. Brennan & Co., 1886.

"His Life a Stormy One: Cassius Clay Talks of His Numerous Fights." *Chicago Daily*, December 27, 1897, p. 10.

Smiley, David M. *The Lion of White Hall: The Life of Cassius M. Clay*. Gloucester, MA: Peter Smith, 1969.

John Dean "Jeff" Cooper

Burroughs, Ben. *Quoting Cooper: The Wisdom of a Warrior*. (Self-published, n.d.)

Cooper, Jeff. "Combat Shooting to Combat Crime." *Guns & Ammo*, April 1970, pp. 32-75.

Cooper, Jeff. *Cooper on Handguns*. Los Angeles: Peterson Publishing Company, 1974.

Cooper, Jeff. *Principles of Personal Defense*. Tempe, AZ: Wisdom Publishing Co., 2002.

Lake, Peter A. "Shooting to Kill." *Esquire*, February 1981, pp. 70-75.

Wisdom, Lindy Cooper. *Jeff Cooper: The Soul and the Spirit*. Tempe, AZ: Wisdom Publishing Co., 1996.

David

Grunfeld, Foster. "The Unsung Sling," *MHQ: The Quarterly Journal of Military History*, Autumn 1996, pp. 50–55.

Korfmann, Manfred. "The Sling As a Weapon." *Scientific American*, October 1973, pp. 34-42.

Kotker, Norman. "King David's Wars." *MHQ: The Quarterly Journal of Military History*, Winter 1989, pp. 80-90.

McKenzie, Steven L. *King David: A Biography*. New York: Oxford University Press, 2000.

Jonathan R. Davis

Boessenecker, John. *Gold Dust and Gunsmoke: Tales of Gold Rush Outlaws, Gunfighters, Lawmen and Vigilantes*. New York: John Wiley & Sons, 1999.

"Desperate Fight: Three Miners Attacked by 11 Robbers." *Mountain Democrat*, December 30, 1854, p. 1.

Kenelm Digby

Bligh, E. W. *Sir Kenelm Digby and his Venetia*. London: S. Low, Marston & Co. Ltd., 1932.

Digby, H. M. *Sir Kenelm Digby and George Digby, Earl of Bristol*. London: Digby, Long & Co., 1912.

Digby, Sir Kenelm. *Private Memoirs of Sir Kenelm Digby*. London: Saunders & Otley, 1827.

Longueville, Thomas. *The Life of Sir Kenelm Digby*. London: Longmans, Green, and Co., 1896.

Petersson, R.T. *Sir Kenelm Digby: The Ornament of England*. Cambridge: Harvard University Press, 1956.

Herman H. Hanneken

Franck, Harry A. *Roaming Through the West Indies*. New York: The Century Co, 1920.

"Marine Rival of Funston in Haiti Exploit." *Chicago Daily Tribune*, February 29, 1920, pp. 1, 6.

Oral History Transcript of Brigadier General Herman H. Hanneken. Benis M. Frank, interviewer. History and Museums Division of the US Marine Corps, 1982.

John Wesley Hardin

Hardin, John Wesley. *The Letters of John Wesley Hardin*. Transcribed and compiled by Roy and Jo Ann Stamps. Austin, Texas: Eakin Press, 2001.

Hardin, John Wesley. *The Life of John Wesley Hardin*. Seguin, Texas: Smith & Moore, 1896.

Marohn, Richard C. *The Last Gunfighter: John Wesley Hardin*. College Station, Texas: Creative Publishing Company, 1995.

Metz, Leon. *John Wesley Hardin: Dark Angel of Texas*. El Paso, Texas: Mangan Books, 1996.

Joseph E. Harrison

Weiss, Mike. "The Fat Man," *California Magazine,* February 1984, pp. 123–27, 152, 154.

Kitty Hesselberger and Dorothy Raynes-Simson

Majdalany, Fred. *State of Emergency: The Full Story of the Mau Mau.* Boston, Houghton Mifflin: 1963.

"Martial Law Demand by Kenya Settlers." *The Daily Telegraph,* January 5, 1953, pp. 1, 10.

Ruark, Robert C. *Robert Ruark's Africa.* Traverse City, Michigan: Countrysport Press, 1991.

"Women Fight Intruders." *The Times* [London], January 5, 1953, p. 6.

Ito Ittosai Kagehisa and Ono Tadaaki

Hurst, G. Cameron. *Armed Martial Arts of Japan: Swordsmanship and Archery.* New Haven: Yale University Press, 1998.

Sugawara, Makoto. *Lives of Master Swordsmen.* The East Publications, Tokyo, 1986.

Lozen

Ball, Eve. *In the Days of Victorio: Recollections of a Warm Springs Apache.* Tucson: University of Arizona Press, 1994.

Roberts, David. *Once They Moved Like the Wind: Cochise, Geronimo, and the Apache Wars.* New York: Simon & Schuster, 1994.

Chuck Mawhinney

Roberts, Craig, and Charles W. Sasser. *Crosshairs on the Kill Zone.* New York: Pocket Books, 2004.

Senich, Peter R. "The Shooter: Scout-Sniper Chuck Mawhinney." *Precision Shooting,* December 1996, pp. 10-20.

"Snipers," *In Their Own Words: Vietnam.* (Recorded interview.) First Person Productions, 2002.

"Top Marine Corps Sniper." Interview by Marc Honorof. *Vietnam Magazine*, April 2003, pp.18-25.

Ward, Joseph T. *Dear Mom, A Sniper's Vietnam.* New York: Ballantine Books, 1991.

"Paddy" Blair Mayne

Bradford, Roy, and Martin Dillon. *Rogue Warrior of the SAS: Lt-Col "Paddy" Blair Mayne.* London: Arrow Books, 1989.

James, Malcolm. *Born of the Desert: With the SAS in North Africa.* London: Greenhill Books, 1991.

Ross, Hamish. *Paddy Mayne.* Gloucestershire, UK: Sutton Publishing, 2006.

Vick, Alan. *Snakes in the Eagle's Nest: A History of Ground Attacks on Air Bases.* Santa Monica: RAND, 1995.

Lewis L. Millett

DeLong, Kent. *War Heroes.* Westport, CT: Praeger, 1993.

Glenn, John M. "Lewis L. Millett: Cold Steel in Korea." *Military History*, February 2002. Available on-line at http://www.historynet.com.

Jacobs, Bruce. *Heroes of the Army.* New York: W. W. Norton & Company, Inc., 1956.

Marshall, S. L. A. *Battle At Best.* New York: William Morrow and Company, 1963.

Murphy, Edward F. *Korean War Heroes.* Novato, California: Presidio Press, 1992.

Jeff Milton

Haley, J. Evetts. *Jeff Milton: A Good Man With a Gun.* Norman, OK: University of Oklahoma Press, 1982.

Moros

Bullard, Major R.L. "Among the Savage Moros." *The Metropolitan Magazine*, June 1906, pp. 263-79.

Bullard, Major Robert L. "The Caliber of the Revolver." *Journal of the U.S. Military Service Institution*, 1905, pp. 300–304.

Cato, Robert. *Moro Swords*. Singapore: Graham Bash, 1996.

Feuer, A.B. *America at War: The Philippines, 1898–1913*. Westport, CT: Praeger, 2002.

Marshall, Captain F. C. "The Revolver and Its Holster." *Cavalry Journal*, 1903, pp. 136–38.

Roth, Russell. *Muddy Glory: America's "Indian Wars" in the Philippines, 1899-1935*. West Hanover, MA: Christopher Publishing House, 1981.

Scott, Hugh Lenox. *Some Memories of a Soldier*. New York: The Century Co., 1928.

Rich Owen

"Convicts Slain in Prison Break in M'Alester, Okl." *Nebraska State Journal*, November 38, 1936, p. 1.

"How an Executioner Feels About His Job." *Waterloo Sunday Courier*, July 24, 1938, p. 6.

Parnell, Percy. *The Joint*. San Antonio: The Naylor Company, 1976.

Parr, Ray. "Afraid of Death? Now Rich Owen Has the Answer." *Daily Oklahoman*, February 27, 1948.

Frank Pape

Adamson, Charles F. *The Toughest Cop in America*. 1st Books Library, 2001.

Keegan, Anne. "Toughest Cop In Town." *Chicago Tribune*, February 9, 1994, p. 1.

Slocum, William J. "The Scourge of Chicago's Hoodlums." *Coronet*, April 1949, pp. 42-46.

George S. Patton
Blumenson, Martin. *Patton: The Man Behind the Legend*. New York: William Morrow and Company, 1985.
D'Este, Carlo. *Patton: A Genius for War*. New York: HarperPerennial, 1995.

Elser, Frank B. "Cardenas's Family Saw Him Die at Bay." *New York Times*, May 23, 1916, p. 5.

John Purcell
"History of the Munster Circuit." *Dublin University Magazine*, Vol. 88, August 1876, pp. 192–95.
Kelly, Martin. "The Knight of the Knife." *Chambers's Journal*, July 11, 1903, pp. 511–12.
Steyn, Mark. "An Englishman's Home is his Dungeon." *Telegraph*, December 7, 2004, online edition.

Frank J. Reynolds
Articles from the *Chicago Tribune*, as noted.
Toland, John. *The Dillinger Days*. New York: Random House, 1963.

Richard the Lionheart
Ambroise. *The Crusade of Richard Lion-Heart*. Translated from the Old French by Merton Jerome Hubert. New York: Columbia University Press, 1941.
Archer, T.A. *The Crusade of Richard I, 1189-92, selected and arranged by T.A. Archer, B.A.* New York: G.P. Putnam's Sons, 1889.
Reston, Jr., James. *Warriors of God: Richard the Lionheart and Saladin in the Third Crusade*. New York: Doubleday, 2001.

Manfred von Richthofen and René Fonck
Fonck, Captain René. *Ace of Aces*. Garden City, New York: Doubleday & Company, Inc., 1967.

Kilduff, Peter. *Richthofen: Beyond the Legend of the Red Baron.* New York: John Wiley & Sons, Inc., 1993.

Norman, Aaron. *The Great Air War.* New York: The Macmillan Company, 1968.

Richthofen, Manfred von. *The Red Battle-Flyer.* New York: R. M. McBride & Company, 1918.

Richthofen, Manfred von. *The Red Baron,* translated by Peter Kilduff. Garden City, NY: Doubleday & Company, 1969.

Simmons, Shane. "Red Baron: World War I Ace Fighter Pilot Manfred von Richthofen," *Aviation History Magazine,* http://www.historynet.com.

Wohl, Robert. "The War Lover," *Military History Quarterly,* 14 (Autumn 2001), pp. 86-97.

Saburo Sakai

Cook, Haruko Taya. *Japan at War: An Oral History.* New York: New Press, 1992.

Heaton, Colin D., and Jeffrey L. Ethell. "Interview: Japan's Legendary Zero Ace." *Military History Magazine,* December 2002, pp. 35–41.

Sakai, Saburo, with Martin Caidin and Fred Saito. *Samurai.* New York: E. P. Dutton and Company, Inc., 1957.

R.J. Thomas

Interviews with R.J. Thomas, Richard Barr.

Rutledge, Bill. "Seawolf Detachment Three." http://www.seawolf.us/stories/det3battles.asp.

"Vietnam: The Soldiers' Story." *From the River to the Sea.* TLC Video, ABC News Production, 2000.

Tunnel Rats

"Headfirst into Underground Battle." Interview by Beth Levine. *Military History,* February 1987, pp. 42–48.

Interview with John Charles Johnson.

Mangold, Tom, and John Penycate. *The Tunnels of Cu Chi: The Untold Story of Vietnam.* New York: Random House, 1985.

Adelbert F. Waldron III
Interviews, military records, newspaper and magazine articles as noted.
Truby, J. David. *Silencers, Snipers, and Assassins: An Overview of Whispering Death.* Boulder: Paladin Press, 1972.

Sam Woodfill
Blumenson, Martin, and James L. Stokesbury. *Masters of the Art of Command.* Boston: Houghton Mifflin, 1990.
Thomas, Lowell. *Woodfill of the Regulars.* Garden City, NY: Doubleday, Doran & Company, 1929.

Vassili Zaitsev
Zaitsev, Vassili. *Notes of a Sniper.* Las Vegas: 2826 Press, 2003.

About the Author

Born in 1952, Paul Kirchner has worked most of his life as a freelance writer and illustrator. He is the author of three other Paladin books: *The Deadliest Men, Dueling with the Sword and Pistol,* and *Jim Cirillo's Tales of the Stakeout Squad.* He is also known for having illustrated Jeff Cooper's books.